PUBLIC SPEAKING
IN THE
RESHAPING OF GREAT BRITAIN

Winston Churchill addressing the Congress of Europe in May 1948. *(Photo courtesy of Black Star.)*

PUBLIC SPEAKING
IN THE
RESHAPING OF GREAT BRITAIN

Robert T. Oliver

DELAWARE

NEWARK: UNIVERSITY OF DELAWARE PRESS
LONDON AND TORONTO: ASSOCIATED UNIVERSITY PRESSES

Associated University Presses
440 Forsgate Drive
Cranbury, NJ 08512

Associated University Presses
25 Sicilian Avenue
London WC1A 2QH, England

Associated University Presses
2133 Royal Windsor Drive
Unit 1
Mississauga, Ontario
Canada L5J 1K5

The paper used in this publication meets the requirements
of the American National Standard for Permanence of Paper
for Printed Library Materials Z39.48-1984.

Library of Congress Cataloging-in-Publication Data

Oliver, Robert Tarbell, 1909–
   Public speaking in the reshaping of Great Britain.

   Bibliography: p.
   Includes index.
   1. Oratory—Great Britain—History—19th
century.   2. Oratory—Great Britain—History—
20th century.   3. Great Britain—Civilization—
19th century.   4. Great Britain—Civilization—
20th century.   I. Title.
PN4055.G7043   1987   808.5'1'0941   86-40355
ISBN 0-87413-315-7 (alk. paper)

Printed in the United States of America

Men are never so likely to settle a question rightly as when they discuss it freely.
                    —Thomas Babington Macaulay

How badly off are we for leaders who can challenge, inspire, or direct our thoughts, emotions, and behavior today? Has this always been so?
                    —Lord George-Brown

The leader is a stimulus but he is also a response.
                    —Paul Pigors

CONTENTS

PREFACE

Historians, as E. H. Carr reminds us, seek to serve as "guardians of mankind's collective memory"; but every historical writing is necessarily selective and interpretative. What a particular history is like depends not only on its subject matter but also upon its exemplification of one or the other of the two major historiographic convictions: the one, that people are shaped by circumstances, the other that circumstances are shaped by people. Obviously, both are partly true, but it makes a basic difference which view predominates.

One school of historians holds that "the engine of history" proceeds with only minimal human guidance. As the French historian Fernand Braudel, author of the three-volume *Civilization and Capitalism*, puts it: "Men are unable to make history. They can only watch it happen, like a television program." In similar fashion, the distinguished British historian Arnold Toynbee posits the course of history as a pattern of inviolable challenge-and-response cycles.

This book belongs in the other category, which holds that individuals do indeed make a difference. The kind of difference that is represented in this narrative is that of effectively persuasive public speaking. My theme is that society is knit together and directed in the choices it makes largely by communication, and that eloquent leadership is a factor of consequence in social development.

In order to assess the influence of public speaking, it has to be viewed in the broad historical setting. Public speaking occurs in context, and the context must be the set of circumstances that make the speaking significant.

The judgment of what effects flow from public speeches is exceedingly uncertain. Votes, for example, are not changed by one or by many speeches but by an interwoven complexity of factors (persuasion among them) that are virtually all-inclusive. This difficulty, however, is not unique to a history of public speaking. It applies with equal stringency to histories of military, political, economic, or demographic trends. Speeches are by no means the determinants of events. But because they are not everything does not mean that they are nothing. Along the broad spectrum of history-shaping factors, public speaking must be included. Persuasive eloquence, like party loyalty, class consciousness, religious faith, and natural resources (along with much else) has a shaping role that requires consideration.

What prominent speakers talk about, to what audiences, in what manner, and

9

from what points of view, in successive eras, are factors that not only illuminate the nature of historic trends but that also help to guide them. These are factors that define the province of a history of public speaking.

Much of the basic work of outlining and of evaluating British history has been done and redone by multiple general and specialized historians. My minimal footnote references are merely indicative of my dependence on them. No writer would any more undertake to write an "original" inquiry in the history of Great Britain than a traveller would traverse the British Isles without using available road maps and without proceeding along existing highways and byways. This does not preclude originality. No two travellers see precisely the same scenes or react to them in the same way. In this book, recent British history is interpreted in terms of my theme: namely, that persuasive leadership makes a difference.

My most personal appreciation is extended to Dr. Carroll C. Arnold of Pennsylvania State University and to Dr. J. Vernon Jensen of the University of Minnesota, who have been generously helpful in their criticism of draft chapters. My son, Dr. Dennis M. Oliver, Minister of the Morningside-High Park Presbyterian Church in Toronto, has helpfully criticized my interpretation of religious trends and of preachers. A longtime friend, Dr. Katharine Stokes, has thoughtfully read the manuscript. My sister, Leah Sherman, has been consistently helpfully encouraging. My wife Margaret has been patiently understanding, faithfully encouraging, and helpfully cautionary in her observation of the work in progress. All those others (teachers, colleagues, family members, friends, librarians) who have helped in many ways, especially in aiding the development of such understandings and of such critical faculties as I have, I thank collectively and gratefully. I want also to express my special pleasure in working with Ms. Beth Gianfagna, managing editor, and Ms. Cynthia Perwin Halpern, copy editor, with appreciation for their gracious helpfulness.

All of these are absolved of responsibility for what I have written, which, inevitably devolves from my own judgment. Finally, I am also thankful for the continuance of health and for the leisure provided by retirement, which together have enabled me to complete a task that I began with ardor more than fifty years ago.

PUBLIC SPEAKING
IN THE
RESHAPING OF GREAT BRITAIN

INTRODUCTION
RHETORIC, SCIENCE, RELIGION, AND DEMOCRACY

The concept of an old England of monarchal and aristocratic supremacy over voiceless, voteless, and mindless lower classes is more myth than reality. In virtually every century the poor had their spokesmen and their champions. The kings and the nobles had to justify what they took and to defend their means of taking it. In the seventeenth century a king was beheaded and the Roundheads briefly routed the Cavaliers. In the eighteenth century the aristocracy crowded the monarchy from the center of government and the established bishops were challenged by outcast preachers to share their role as spiritual guides. Parliament whittled away at the authority of the crown and, within Parliament, the Commons gained influence at the expense of the Lords. In the law, in learning, and in literature the masses gradually and surely won a wider range of opportunities to express and to develop themselves. So far back as English, Scottish, and Irish history may be traced, it was neither stagnant nor rigid. Even so, the dividing line between the upper and the lower classes remained the evident social reality. How this pattern was shaped and reshaped while the nation of Great Britain evolved has been narrated many times from the perspectives of military power, of constitutional evolution, and of economic developments. In a prior volume, *The Influence of Rhetoric in the Shaping of Great Britain: From the Roman Invasion to the Early Nineteenth Century*, I have viewed this same historical process in terms of the influence exerted by persuasive leadership and by the unifying and directive influence of rhetorical communication.

Through all the centuries of English history, effective leadership depended not only upon military might, or ownership of property, or monopoly control of religion, but also upon the courageous presentation of new ideas and upon skill in persuasive discourse. In this second volume, the history of this rhetorical influence in the island nation is brought up to the present time.

"Challenge to Established Beliefs"

The advent of modernization in Great Britain required significant changes in the nature of political, social, and religious leadership. Rhetoric—the process of interpreting meanings and of shaping behavior and attitudes—continued its role

13

of guiding society. But the means by which it functioned had to change. Communication took on a new tone. Along with pointing the way, as leaders prior to 1800 had done, the new aspirants for power were required to deal with their listeners in the spirit of talking it out. Equality rather than hierarchy became the basic premise from which argument, persuasion, and discussion commenced.

Leadership became less directive and more representational. Public speakers felt sharper need to discern public opinion and to heed it. Speakers gradually evolved into spokesmen. This was the new factor that transformed the modes of communication. It is this distinction that marked the generations living between the 1770s and the 1880s as a veritable continental divide in the history of Great Britain.

In the early years of the nineteenth century, "democracy" was a term of reproach. It aroused dread and dislike, much as "communism" does in more recent times. In the course of a mere two or three lifetimes, the many meanings implied by the term "democratic" were transformed. In this process, the nature of society was transformed as well. As Woodrow Wilson pointed out, labels are important precisely because "men are governed by the winning tag." Tags that trigger strong emotional reactions may be either denunciatory or favorable. During the span of two or three generations, "democracy" shifted from the one to the other.

Democracy stresses equality not only of rights and of justice and of opportunities but also equality of judgment and of will. The guiding truths that come to be considered inalienable were no longer the divine right of kings and the inherited superiority of the aristocrats, but the intuitive understanding by the masses of what is good and proper for them and therefore right for the nation. The new premise governed what speakers could and must say and how they must say it. It also shaped the reactions of listeners.

Basic to the understanding of social processes is the cardinal fact that "what is" often is subordinate to "what is believed." What individuals, and what the mass public, perceive is to a high degree determined by their prior conceptions. Reality, in pragmatic social terms, is what the culture of the society portrays it as being. The influence of the physical universe is filtered into our minds by the symbols that represent it. In a real sense, we dwell in a linguistic universe, a world of labels. The labels that shape understandings, and feelings, and attitudes—and, therefore, actions—are largely the products of slow growth as centuries of traditions shape a society's culture. But there is constant need for the interpretation of meanings, for the definition of problems, and for the consideration of solutions. To satisfy this is the function of leaders. It is by this means that societies change.

Among all the generative factors that stirred the depths of English society in the nineteenth century and changed its nature, science was the most potent. One generative form of science was technology, which swept the nation into the

Industrial Revolution. Another of its forms was ideational, the unveiling of new knowledge, which resulted in a no-less-shattering Intellectual Revolution. Within the span of a few years, England burst forth from an agrarian into a factory economy. Not only were families and communities disrupted, but so, too, were old customs and old certainties. New problems had to be dealt with. New ways of living and of thinking were explored. Alternative solutions had to be searched out and their relative merits debated.

The challenge to established beliefs came from new understandings concerning the nature of divine superintendence over the universe. This involved a new view of the nature of man and of the proper structure of society. Both politics and religion—which is to say, how people live together and what they as individuals live for—had to be reexamined and reassessed. Leadership was burdened with the demand that it find new answers for new questions. It had first to define problems and then to propose suitable solutions for them. The challenge was enormous in its weight and in its complexity. By contrast, the role of leadership in earlier times had been relatively simplistic. As traditional modes lost influence, ingenuity had to devise new guidelines.

And it had to do so in new terms. The public that leaders had to persuade was less acquiescent than it had been through prior centuries. The masses demanded and won the right of participation in the making of policies. Democracy became the generator of a wide range of nearly unprecedented systems of thought, of feelings, and of consequent social, ideational, religious and political change.

This is what launched Great Britain into the modern era. In historic terms, the transformation was rapid, even though its roots had been nurtured through preceding generations. The Tudor period was marked by a tremendous outreaching of human interests and imagination; the seventeenth century by liberating political, philosophical, scientific, and religious innovations; the eighteenth by a sharpening struggle between reaction and reform. New ideas were debated well before the nineteenth century undertook the tasks of broadening the electorate, curbing both royal and aristocratic prerogatives, and redefining the meaning of religion. But after the victory at Waterloo permitted a shift of interest from international to domestic concerns, the English engaged in active discussions of the essential differences between human rights and property rights. The distinction between humanism and supernaturalism became another central concern. Meantime, suppressed political problems, such as the rights of the Irish, of the factory workers, and of women, came to the fore. The eighteenth-century ideal of empire also had to be reshaped.

"An Explosive Growth of Debate"

Such changes demanded and induced an explosive growth of debate and discussion. Under the impact of new egalitarian convictions, the very nature of rhetorical leadership was revised. Earlier leaders had tended to be orators, who set forth their proposals and contended among themselves for their adoption. As the public power base expanded to include first the middle classes and then all adults, leaders changed from orators to discussants.

Naturally, this change was less than sudden and less than complete. The old view of the "leader" as "one who knows" has never wholly disappeared. Noticeably, oratory revived for a brief period in the persons of Randolph Churchill and David Lloyd George, then even more strikingly in the wartime speaking of Winston Churchill. In a sense these three were throwbacks to the eighteenth century, partly because of their temperaments, partly because of the roles they were called upon to play. But such exceptions enforce rather than vitiate the rule. Exceptions are in fact exceptional. As the following chapters will show, leadership from time to time and in various ways and degrees continued to exemplify oratorical tendencies. But this ceased to be the norm.

As the generative ideal of society changed from one of stability to one of progress, the rhetorical role of leaders had to be revised. The vast diversity of new ideas demanding consideration had to be talked out. Speakers gradually evolved toward being spokesmen for groups whose support established their leadership status. Participation in decision making became widespread. Leaders could no longer primarily "tell" the people; they had also to "ask" them. The transformation swept through every aspect of society: the workplace, the centers of intellectual study, government, religion, domestic affairs, colonial relationships, and, eventually, into the age-old disparate roles of men and women. These were fundamental changes to which the new rhetoric had to adapt.

The classical Aristotelian model of speaker-listener relations had to be converted into a new model of retroactive and responsive communication. Public speaking tended to assume the qualities of coordinate discussion.

The need for leadership remained no less acute than it had been before. But it had to take new forms. The basic rhetorical principle continued as Aristotle stated it in his *Rhetoric:* "So let Rhetoric be defined as the faculty of discovering in the particular case what are the available means of persuasion." It is always true that problems have to be defined and available solutions have to be proposed and evaluated. But how this rhetorical process proceeds depends upon the cultural format of society. And the culture of Great Britain, like that of other nations, has become much less provincial, much less static, and much more open to questioning than before the industrial and intellectual revolutions opened the floodgates to change.

As the nineteenth century opened, dissatisfactions in society were both general and virulent. New yearnings, new questionings, and new demands were insistent and widespread. During the preceding two or three generations, conservatism had been jarred from dominance to defensiveness. But workable solutions for the urgently felt problems were far from being self-evident. New knowledge and new ideas splintered long-accepted certainties. But what should take their place?

Democracy became an inevitability. But its meanings had to be clarified and its forms and methods had to be developed. Leadership did not and could not operate as an impersonal, inarticulate force. Its importance was never doubted, but its nature was not always clear. As James MacGregor Burns wrote in his 1978 book *Leadership*, this function "is one of the most observed and least understood phenomena on earth."

Across the broad spectrum of social affairs from politics to religion and in the relationships of groups and of individuals, in the following chapters this puzzling phenomenon of leadership is considered in its rhetorical mode.

"Wandering between Two Worlds"

The changing intellectual values and moral standards, which guided what was discussable, are clearly evident in the literature of the era. The novels of Henry Fielding and Samuel Richardson dealt with moral quandaries into which individuals drifted and from which they should and could extricate themselves. A hundred years later, the novels of Dickens and Thomas Hardy centered around the plight of characters who were beset by social conditions that they were unable to control. Alexander Pope, in his "Essay on Man," asserted a view that was typical in pre-modern times:

> How few of all the ills that humankind endure
> Are those that kings or laws can cause or cure.

A mere generation later, Oliver Goldsmith was asserting, in "The Traveller," that "Laws grind the poor, and rich men rule the law." In "The Deserted Village" he added that

> Ill fares the land, to gathering ills a prey,
> Where wealth accumulates and men decay.

Conservatism, however, was not easily dislodged from the generality of minds. A generation after Goldsmith, its essence was well pictured by William Wilberforce in his 1797 book, *A Practical View of Christianity*, which so well represented general feelings that in six months it went through five English printings, while being simultaneously translated into French, Italian, Dutch, and German. Wilberforce's social sympathy was extensive and sensitive, as was illustrated especially by his leadership of the movement to abolish the slave trade. But not even he could shake off the oldtime assumptions. "The more lowly path of the poor," he wrote, "has been allotted to them by the hand of God." Instead of seeking to improve their condition, "it is their part faithfully to discharge its duties and contentedly to bear its inconveniences." In return for this submissiveness, divine mercy and justice decreed that "if their superiors enjoy more abundant comforts, they are also exposed to many temptations from which the inferior classes are happily exempt." The problem of poverty was to be left alone; it was what God had ordained.

A mere short generation later, in December 1831, in the House of Commons, Thomas Babington Macaulay described with dismay the turmoil of class strife that was disrupting English society: "a narrow oligarchy above—an infuriated multitude below; on the one side the vices engendered by power—on the other the vices engendered by distress; the one party adverse to improvement—the other party blindly clamouring for destruction."

Modernism wrenched society out of the course it had pursued for centuries to set it upon a new course that had yet to be explored. It was this recognition and this exploration that demanded rhetorical examination.

Scientific curiosity took giant leaps, nudged into activity by such innovative inquiries as Sir Charles Lyell's *Principles of Geology*—which vastly extended the acknowledged age of the universe; and by Charles Darwin's *The Origin of Species*—which demolished the view of the sudden creation of life forms. The common-sense observation that "Facts are facts and that's the end of it," was challenged by a new uncertainty as to what facts were relevant and what they might mean. What are the "natural laws" became a question to be debated, with the scientists well aware that the so-called "laws" are largely a set of bold conjectures.[1] What to believe became subject to skeptical reevaluation.

So shaken was religious orthodoxy that Thomas Huxley invented the term agnosticism, to make questioning as acceptable as faith. Leigh Hunt, in "Abou Ben Adhem," boldly pronounced that to love one's fellow men is more consequential for salvation than to love God. Algernon Charles Swinburne, in "The Garden of Proserpone," took a further step toward atheism:

> We thank with brief thanksgiving
>   Whatever gods may be
> That no life lives forever;
> That dead men rise up never;
> That even the weariest river
>   Winds somewhere safe to sea.

The uncertainty that challenged traditional beliefs was acknowledged even by the eminently respectable Matthew Arnold, a leading spokesman for established intellectualism. In his "Stanzas on the Grande Chartreuse" he mused that his generation was

> Wandering between two worlds, one dead,
> The other powerless to be born.

Then, in his "Dover Beach," he spelled out the consequences of this, much in the vein of Hunt and Swinburne:

> The Sea of Faith
> Was once, too, at the full, and round earth's shore
> Lay like the folds of a bright girdle furled,
> But now I only hear
> Its melancholy, long, withdrawing roar. . . .
>
> Ah, love, let us be true
> To one another! For the world, which seems
> To lie before us like a land of dreams,
> So various, so beautiful, so new,
> Hath really neither joy, nor love, nor light,
> Nor certitude, nor peace, nor help for pain;
> And we are here as on a darkling plain
> Swept with confused alarm of struggle and flight,
> Where ignorant armies clash by night.

Pessimism, hovering close to despair, was widespread during much of the century. But there were also influential prophets of reform, such as the poets Byron and Shelley; and celebrants of simple joys, such as Wordsworth, and Browning, and Tennyson; and defenders of the old faith, such as Francis Thompson and Cardinal Newman. Many of the literati shared the puzzlement expressed by William Blake, when, contemplating the fierceness of the tiger, he somberly inquired: "Did He who made the lamb make thee?" Many more shared the malaise of John Keats, as expressed in his "On Seeing the Elgin Marbles," when he wrote:

> My spirit is too weak—mortality
> Weighs heavily on me like unwilling sleep,
> And each imagined pinnacle and steep
> Of godlike hardship tells me I must die
> Like a sick eagle looking at the sky.

But there also were others who welcomed the new challenges, as did Tennyson in his poem "Ulysses," when the aged wanderer assured his fellows that " 'Tis not too late to seek a newer world,"

> for my purpose holds
> To sail beyond the sunset, and the baths
> Of all the western stars, until I die. . . .
> Made weak by time and fate, but strong in will
> To strive, to seek, to find, and not to yield.

As the nineteenth and then the twentieth centuries unfolded, literature— which aims to be timeless—produced many more moving descriptions of the nature of man and of basic human problems, often accompanied by suggestions for fundamental improvements. One of them, which struck so popular a note as to make it often quoted, was William Ernest Henley's "Invictus," which found cause for hope even in the midst of despair:

> Out of the night that covers me,
> Black as the Pit from pole to pole,
> I thank whatever gods may be
> For my unconquerable soul.

The rhetoric represented in public speaking by aspiring leaders had a different, a more timely and pragmatic, task to perform: namely, to search out and to advocate available solutions suitable for dealing with imminent and urgent problems. Democracy became the regnant political philosophy, with meanings that leaders had to explore and to explain.

"They Must First Agree on Principles"

Both democracy and rhetoric are processes with meanings that are continuously in need of adjustment. Both are distorted by internal contradictions. Democracy finds its justification in the value of individuals; yet, contrarily, its methodology is to subject these values to majority controls. Rhetoric aims to depict what is true; but it does so in terms of the purpose or preconceptions of the speaker as they are adjusted to the emotions, convictions, and readiness to respond of the listeners. Both democracy and rhetoric embrace the concept of the "holistic" nature of society; yet both continue to represent groups—of individuals, of interests, and of ideas. Both aim toward the achievement of consensus. Yet their effects are often to intensify contention among divisive groups.

Critics of democracy have often followed the theme set by Alexis de Tocqueville, who had a sharp eye for its flaws. "The very essence of democratic government," he wrote in 1853, "consists in the absolute sovereignty of the majority," which he held to be "an impious and detestable maxim." In his evaluation of it, "I found very few men who displayed that manly candor and masculine independence of opinion" that in the predemocratic era "constitutes the leading feature in distinguishing characters wheresoever they may be found."[2] His charge was that under a democratic system leaders fail to direct public opinion but instead try to reflect it. In short, egalitarianism denigrates judgment and undermines initiative and courage. Social values fall to the low level of the undistinguished average.

A similar charge has recently been made, on similar grounds, against the new rhetoric. "In the beginning," declares the critic, "there was rhetoric, the proper finish, discipline, and diversion of gentlepersons. Then there was social science, an academic wedge of the elite captured by discontented ethnics seeking to understand themselves, their new society, and their hopes of making it."[3] The evidence this critic cites are the rising demands in the mid-twentieth century of the poor, of women, of blacks, and of Hispanics for equality. The real beginnings of egalitarian rhetoric came in the earlier period, the mid-nineteenth century, when it was not minorities but the majority that demanded equal rights.

The reason rhetoric had to be recast as society was being restructured was well stated by Thomas Reid, a Scottish rhetorician who lived during the time when egalitarianism was first coming into consideration.

> Before men can reason together, they must first agree on principles; and it is impossible to reason with a man who has no principles in common with you. . . . Such common principles seldom admit of direct proof, nor do they need it. Men must not be taught them, for they are such as men of common understanding know; or such, at least, as they give a ready assent to, as soon as they are proposed and understood.[4]

It was precisely the breakdown of the long-held principle that good government results from rule by the best, not by the most, which led to confused communication as the democratic era was commencing. The new leaders had first to attain to their own new understandings of why egalitarianism must be accepted and of how to render it operable. How should the government be recast? The transformation of rhetoric to this new view was not quickly or readily accomplished.

It was a full two centuries after the time of Thomas Reid before Kenneth Burke, acclaimed as the prophet of the new rhetoric, formulated the new rhetorical principle that the dynamic power of persuasion derives from "identification." "You persuade a man only insofar as you can talk his language by speech, gesture, tonality, order, image, attitude, idea, *identifying* your way with his," wrote Burke.[5] Thus far had rhetoric moved from the time of Lord Chatham, Charles Fox, and Edmund Burke, when leadership meant that a man who knows the truth presents it with such confident assertiveness that it carries conviction. The new egalitarian rhetoric guided the retroactive flow of influence among and for equals. Identification, as Burke defined it, is another term for reflexive representation—which is what democracy means.

Both democracy and rhetoric are weighty influences because of what they do to reality. The objective world of facts that encloses us is one thing; how it looks to us, what we feel about it, and therefore what we think and how we act is something quite else. What we see depends to some degree on the kind of glasses through which we look. Democracy and rhetoric are like pairs of spectacles, each with its own lenses, with their own magnifications and distortions, through which we view the world in ways that make it real to us.

If we did not believe in democracy, and if democracy did not have its own special rhetorical needs and methods, the problems we perceive and the solutions we seek would be different from those that we have come to take for granted. Democracy is a symbol system and rhetoric is a process of putting symbols together in particular ways. The words we think with and communicate with are a forest of labels. It would be a confusing wilderness were not the symbols sorted out for us into sets of patterns that mark trails for us to follow. The paths discerned by democracy and charted by rhetoric are diversely pointed in varying directions.

The egalitarian nature of democracy is generally accepted, but there is far less agreement on what this means. One kind of meaning was indicated by John Locke and Thomas Jefferson, another kind by Karl Marx and V. I. Lenin. Democratic thinking stresses that government should equally serve the needs of all the people. But there are wide differences of opinion concerning how this should be done. In one view it is government of and by the people in order to ensure that it be for them. In another view, democracy takes the form of dictatorship, professedly in order to represent the needs and the desires of the masses better than they could do directly for themselves. In one view, communism is the antithesis of democracy, in that it orders what the people must do. In the other view, "capitalistic free enterprise" is a means of deluding the people into accepting the cunning machinations of the new propertied aristocracy. Variants of these two opposed views stress goals that are either narrowly nationalistic or inclusively international. Communism demands that the state own the natural resources and the means of fabrication, with the alleged aim of distributing goods equally; it determines what people are told to believe on the ground that this protects them from errors and disorder. On such grounds, communism claims to be the true democracy, through the agency of "the dictatorship of the proletariat." In noncommunist nations, democracy takes such diverse ways as presidential and representational government, or different forms of parliamentarianism. On one side of the curtain of division, political parties are either forbidden or sharply curbed and controlled on the ground that partisanship is dangerously divisive. On the other side, partisanship is fostered and encouraged as a means of representing and adjusting divergent interests. With such basic differences entrenched after several generations of experience with democracy, it is not strange that leaders confronted with newly emergent democratic feelings had to struggle first to attain to ideas of what democracy entails and, afterwards, had to contend among themselves while they sought to persuade the public to accept their formulations.

From the rhetorical point of view, what matters most is that egalitarianism became the major premise—the "first principle"—upon which all political thinking depends. Across the whole broad spectrum of world governments from the most compulsive dictatorships to the most chaotic free-will societies, comes the insistence: "It is the people who rule. It is the people we serve." Such has been the claim of Lord John Russell, and Disraeli and Gladstone; and also of Sun Yat-sen, Gandhi and Nehru; of Stalin and of Mao Tse-tung; of the dictatorial

Mussolini and Hitler; of Churchill and Roosevelt; of de Gaulle and Peron; and of Margaret Thatcher and Ronald Reagan. "The people reign" has been interpreted in many different and many contrary ways. But among them all, it is the premise from which leadership claims its sanction.

"The Emphasis Has Shifted"

How variously this new egalitarianism has been accommodated by the interpretative function of rhetoric may be illustrated by two different kinds of American rhetoricians. The one, Ralph Waldo Emerson, was a notable prophet of individualism. The other, Lincoln Steffens, was deeply committed to majority rule. Both of them recognized the new need for redefining the reciprocal relationship between the speaker and his listeners. Their interpretations of this relationship differed sharply.

In Ralph Waldo Emerson's view, the function of the democratic speaker is to look for individual differences in order that he may adjust them to his own concept of what they ought to become, what he could reshape them to be. In the lecture on "Eloquence" that he delivered to the Boston Mercantile Library Association in February 1847, he said:

The audience is the constant meter of the orator. There are many audiences in every public assembly, each one of which rules in turn. If anything comic or coarse is spoken, you shall see the emergence of the boys and rowdies, so loud and vivacious that you might think the house was filled with them. If new topics are started, graver and higher, these roisterers recede; a more chaste and wise attention takes place. You would think the boys slept and that they have any degree of profoundness. If the speaker utter a noble sentiment, the attention deepens, a new and higher audience now listens, and the audiences of the fun and the facts and of the understanding are all silenced and awed. There is also something excellent in every audience—the capacity of virtue. They are ready to be beatified. They know so much more than the orator— and are so just! There is a tablet there for every line he can inscribe, though he should mount to the highest levels. Humble persons are conscious of new illuminations; narrow brows expand with enlarged affections;—delicate spirits, long unknown to themselves, masked or muffled in coarsest fortunes, who now hear their own native language for the first time, and leap to hear it. But all these several audiences, each above each, which successively appear to greet the variety of style and topic, are really composed of the same persons; nay, sometimes the same individuals will take an active part in them all, in turn.[6]

In Emerson's second lecture on "Eloquence," first presented in Chicago in 1867, he further clarified his concept of the nature of the leader as the creator of the kind of audience he desired. The truly great speaker, he said, "gains his victory by prophecy." His listeners become "interested like so many children" because he "surprises them with his tidings, with his better knowledge, with his larger view, his steady gaze at the new and future event whereof they had not thought." Just as in the old rhetoric, oratory to Emerson meant the dominance of the speaker over his audience. As he phrased it, "Eloquence is the power to translate a truth into language perfectly intelligible to the person to whom you speak."[7] What made him, on the contrary, also the precursor of the new egalitarianism was his clear insistence that it is the people, the listeners, who must be the "meter" of the speaker.

Lincoln Steffens, more committed to egalitarianism than to individualism, still clung to the Aristotelian recommendation of adaptation to the audience; but he interpreted this in terms of representing the listeners rather than directing them. Citing his own experience as a popular lecturer, he explained:

> Now I know that a speech is a combination of the forces of the speaker and the audience. The speaker has the ideas and some feeling about them; a track is laid, an ordered, thought-through, more or less logical statement. . . . As I look over an audience, I get their status, mood, etc. As I go on, I see the audience laugh, frown, smile, shake their heads, applaud: signs of how they like it, how they feel, and I literally ride on that. I extend a statement to clear off a frown. I shorten a statement when I see they have got it. I feel my way.[8]

This appears to be a simple restatement of Aristotle's counsel to analyze the prospective audience and to adapt to it. But the emphasis has shifted. Instead of stressing the directive function of the speaker, Steffens recommends accommodation to the moods of the listeners. Under the egalitarian principle that it is the people who rule, in speaking to them, Steffens counsels, it is the feelings of the people that must govern. The speaker can only accomplish his chosen goal by adjusting to their responses. This conception denies or at least neglects the Emersonian view of the fundamental responsibility of the speaker to shape the feelings of the listeners. The basic Emersonian tone of "I say unto you" is transmuted into the Steffens tone that "This, then, is what you and I agree to believe." The difference is fundamental. And it is this difference that marks the transition to egalitarian rhetoric.

In general understanding, rhetoric is a process of interpreting meanings, which interpretation is essential for the functioning of society. In recent years the effective functioning of rhetoric has been vastly extended by such technologies as radio, television, films, the telephone, and global networks for the gathering and reporting of what managers of these processes estimate to be "news"—or the facts that matter. Societies exist as structures of coordinated and generally accepted views. The definition and interpretation of these views is the function of rhetoric. Accordingly, rhetorical processes are the fabricators of society.

The new rhetoric has been extensively analyzed. One of its early progenitors was Alfred Korzybski, the founder of General Semantics, who did much to establish the view that the "pseudo-universe" in which we most truly live is the linguistic universe of symbolic determinism.[9] Another is the Belgian philosopher and rhetorician Chaim Perelman, who demonstrated that it is not the certainties of scientific facts but the argumentation concerning their probable meanings by which thought and actions are governed.[10]

There is general agreement with the conclusion stated by Thomas Mann in his book, *The Magic Mountain,* that "Speech is civilization itself. The word, even the most contradictory word, preserves contact—it is silence which isolates."[11] Hugh Dalziel Duncan aptly summarized the general consensus of social scientists that "man as a social being exists in and through communication; communication is as basic to man's nature as food and sex."[12] The province of rhetoric, in this new view, has been posited by Ernst Cassirer: "Man lives in a symbolic universe. . . . He has so enveloped himself in linguistic forms . . . that he cannot see and know anything except by the interpretation of this artificial medium."[13]

Whether rhetoric is defined in old or in new terms, it remains clear that in the birthing of democracy rhetoric has been a major influence. It is no less true that as egalitarianism has become regnant, its excesses and its weaknesses as well as its accomplishments and its virtues continue to demand evaluation. The time span covered in this book is notably an age of discussion. Old limits of what could be discussed with propriety, or even with legality, have largely been swept aside. Almost nothing remains that cannot and often must not be publicly talked about. Even less remains that can be settled without discussion. This is why rhetoric has had an influential role in the shaping of democracy.

1
A CHALLENGE TO RHETORIC:
CONFRONTING THE IDEA OF DEMOCRACY

As the nineteenth century opened, it did not appear that democracy was an idea whose time had come. The evidence was against it. Its record was appalling. In America, democratic sentiments had resulted in rebellion against the king with severe loss to the empire. In France, the spirit of democracy destroyed all that was respectable. Religion was renounced and atheism was flaunted. The victims of democracy were ruthlessly guillotined. Monarchy and the aristocracy had been replaced with what looked like mob rule unleashed. In the wake of these disasters the newly formed French democracy yielded itself to a military dictator who set about attacking neighboring states and unsettling the established international order. England, too, had had its own experience with democracy, back in the seventeenth century, and there also it had led to regicide, the breakdown of the aristocracy, the unsettling of the society, and the imposition of an ineffective dictatorship. Such were the observable fruits of democracy.

Even so, the circumstances of the opening decades of the nineteenth century were bewilderingly mixed and so were feelings about them. English society from the earliest times had been structured on the principle of inequality, which in general had served the country well. Until the agrarian base of the society was disrupted by the industrial revolution, a tolerable degree of equity was maintained in the relations between the lords of the manors and their tenants. The abrupt intrusion of industrialism brought about changes that were hard to live with and not easy to interpret.

It was evident that traditional patterns of living had been disrupted, much for the worse. The miseries of the factory system aroused a widespread insistence on social and economic reforms. But what should the reforms be like? Unclear demands for change were countered by loyalty to old forms and manners. Initial efforts toward democratizing the society met strong and widespread resistance. How could the injustices of the system be rectified without weakening the bulwark of English culture?

There was urgent need for leadership that would be able to chart a new way into a new era. But from what source could the leadership take its cue?

The idea of democracy, in a limited form, originated in ancient Greece. Aristotle, in his *Politics*, book 4, chapter 4, wrote that "a democracy is a state where the freemen and the poor, being the majority, are invested with the power of the state." The suggestion was ominous. So were the outcroppings of democratic sentiment in earlier English history.

John Ball, at the time of the Black Death, and Sir Thomas More, in his *Utopia*, had advocated something like this in the thirteenth and the sixteenth centuries respectively. In 1683 Algernon Sydney, speaking from the scaffold on which he was to be beheaded for allegedly plotting to assassinate King Charles II and his brother the Duke of York (later to be King James II), denied defiantly that "all men are born under a necessity derived from the laws of God and nature to submit unto an absolute kingly government, which could be restrained by no law or oath."

About that same time, John Locke was arguing that all men are created equal. In the next century the Earl of Chatham, Charles James Fox, Richard Brinsley Sheridan, and Thomas Erskine (among others) eloquently pleaded for an equality of civil rights—especially the right to state and to defend unpopular opinions. Against all these pressures, the hierarchal structure of British society was entrenched and remained solidly in place not only in the legal and constitutional systems and in traditional customs but also in the prevailing favorable attitudes and opinions of the people.

Still, some far-reaching and fundamental changes obviously were needed. Concerning the need, there was not much argument. But what was it that could and that should be done?

"A Question the Wisest Cannot Answer"

The solution that was found and that was brought into effect was the Reform Bill of 1832. Lord Charles Grey was prime minister at the time and it was his basic strategy that won the necessary votes for it, so that in all justice this measure was then called and is since remembered as Grey's Reform Bill. He was far from being its only or even its principal champion. He was but one among many who perceived the need to find a form of democracy that would meet the urgent needs of the time, would satisfy the angry demands of the people, and would also preserve what was sound in the British constitutional system. After the plan was devised, the essential requirement was a persuasive campaign that would be effective in guiding the reform proposals between the Scylla of radicalism and the Charybdis of reactionary resistance.

It was the Whig Party, led by aristocrats and country gentlemen, all comfortably profiting from the old hierarchal system, that led the way to democratic change. The veteran liberal, Charles James Fox, eager to withdraw from public life into retirement, on 12 March 1803 wrote to the most promising of his younger followers, the twenty-nine-year-old Charles Grey, who was already in his seventh year as a member of the House of Commons, that if the Whig Party could be held together, "with you at the head of them, it might be a foundation for better things at some future period."[1] This general prophecy proved to be true. But what it meant was hazy, both to Fox and to Grey. The fruition was slow in developing.

The rhetorical problem was stated well by William Lamb, who is known to history as Lord Melbourne, and who like Grey was destined to become prime minister. Lamb was elected to Parliament in 1806, coming from a leading family. He had an indolent spirit but a fixed determination to do what he could to keep things as they always had been. In the diary that he kept throughout his career he showed his awareness of the importance of rhetoric and also of the difficulties of managing it. "Your friends," he observed, "praise your abilities to the skies, submit to you in argument, and seem to have the greatest deference for you." But this is all a surface show; for "in fact they all think themselves wiser than you, whatever they may say."[2] What Melbourne was pointing out is that there are few problems more difficult than changing convictions that are deeply held.[3] This was the psychological fact that proved the major barrier barring the advance of those who saw the need for fundamental change.

Where and how the impulse toward democracy originated cannot be precisely dated. The crumbling away of the old agrarian stability by the onslaught of industrialism brought such miseries and disillusionment that among the masses hope and comfort were smothered by despair. The poverty of the general populace was evident and so was their gradually growing spirit of rebelliousness. What could be done to remedy the situation was what had to be discerned.

The uncertainty concerning what could and should be done was exemplified in the views of a fierce-tongued Methodist preacher named Joseph Stephens, who became widely recognized as a champion of the poor. His wrath was directed most urgently against the middle class because it was receiving most of the benefits of the new industrialism. And he stormed violently against the Reform Bill, which carefully excluded the poor from its provisions. In Stephens' terms, "Those who are to go to Hell hereafter . . . are men of all lands, tongues, trades and politics, that have refused to clothe the naked, and that have not visited and sympathized with the sick."[4] The injustice of the prevailing system was clear to him, as were the inadequacies of the Reform Bill. But the need for a complete revision of the socio-political structure of society was beyond his vision. The best remedy he could conceive was paternalism—the shepherding care by those who enjoyed plenty of the masses who were deprived. It was difficult in that time for even the wisest to understand what a complete renovation was required.

The old domestic industries, along with small-plot farms, were ruined by competition from the new, large, and mechanized textile mills. Unemployment was not only general but its dire effects were made even worse by ruinous inflation. Wages, for those fortunate enough to receive any, were too low to pay for food, let alone for clothing and shelter. The figures for 1830 showed that "more than half the labouring population of the midland and southern farming areas were receiving some form of parish relief."[5] The relief they got came from the Poor Laws, which had been little revised since the time of Queen Elizabeth I. Parishes were required to make some provision for their own paupers, but only for their own—so that the poor dared not go elsewhere in search of work. In the mills, children as young as six formed a large portion of the work force. Their work day began at five A.M. and lasted until nine at night, with only thirty minutes off for rest, toilet relief, and eating. If they fell asleep or otherwise neglected their machines, they were flogged. Hope for improvement was scanty. As the House of Commons was told by a member from Carlisle: "There appears to me only a choice of evils—the children must either work or starve."

Thomas Malthus was gloomily "proving" that population must always grow faster than the means for supporting it. Adam Smith was urging that the system must be let alone to find its own solution through the balancing law of supply and demand. Jeremy Bentham argued for laissez-faire—by which he meant not to allow government to interfere with business. John Stuart Mill, in his essay *On Liberty,* agreed: "He who lets the world, or his own portion of it, choose his plan of life for him, has no need of any other faculty than the ape-like one of imitation." As late as 1867, Walter Bagehot was arguing in the introduction to his book on *The English Constitution,* that the franchise must be kept away from the "lower orders," for, "of Parliament these miserable creatures know scarcely anything; of the Cabinet they never have heard." He went on to warn leaders not to "raise questions which will excite the lower orders of mankind . . . on which these orders are likely to be wrong." To encourage them "will bind the poor as a class together . . . which will excite them against the rich."

The rhetorical challenge to find a way through these difficulties was not neglected, but there was no precedent for the forms that had to be worked out. Joseph Priestley stated the goal that was eventually to be pursued: that the proper aim for government was "the greatest happiness for the greatest number."[6] In consonance with this view, the elder Lord John Russell, then serving as lord lieutenant of Ireland, wrote to his eleven-year-old son that he had come to accept "the broad principle that all governments are made for the happiness of the many, and not for the benefit of the few."[7] But, as Disraeli wrote in his novel, *Tancred, or the New Crusade,* even the best of intentions had to await new insights:

> "The common sense of the country will carry us through," said the duke.
> "Through what?" inquired his son.
> "This—this state of transition;" replied his father.
> "A passage to what?"
> "Ah! that is a question the wisest cannot answer."

As Aristotle wrote, the very foundation for rhetoric is "invention"—the devising of ideas and plans. Leaders are expected to develop adequate policies.

But amidst new conditions, what should the policies be? On this question, the Tories and the Whigs turned in different directions. Generally, Tory spokesmen favored social reforms. The Whigs looked, rather, to such political measures as broadening the franchise and controlling or eliminating parliamentary corruption and influence based on annuities, grants, and sinecures. Neither party had much regard for democracy. The Tories clung to traditional forms of paternalism. The Whigs yearned for the quietism of the rural past and built strength through alliances with the rising middle class. A general spirit of humanitarianism animated both parties. "Something" needed to be done; it was difficult to know what it should be. The beginnings were not impressive.

"Contempt of the 'Civilized' for the 'Barbarians'"

Sir Charles Romilly studied law, went to France where reform had turned to rebellion, and came back home determined to reform the abysmal conditions of the English penal system.[8] On 26 January 1817, he made his most effective speech in the House of Commons against a government proposal to suspend the *habeas corpus,* on the ground that radicals were stirring popular discontent. "According to the account of Ministers," Romilly said, "the real evil is the extent to which the evil has spread and is spreading." He pointed out that the imprisonment of ten or twenty radical speakers would not allay public resentment against grievances that were real. He then implored the members "not to withdraw from the lower classes a protection to which they were as much entitled as the most exalted individuals in the State."[9] He could not prevail against the reactionism aroused by the excesses of the French Revolution.

The majority view was well stated by the Duke of Wellington, whose prestige as the victor of Waterloo led to his selection as prime minister. In the debate on the Reform Bill on 4 October 1831, he reminded the House that "England is one of the best governed countries in the world; and I am sure that for the past sixty or seventy years it has been the most prosperous." What he and his fellow Tories most feared was replacement of "rule by the best" with "rule by the most." In the words of a historian of the period, "The massive contempt of the 'civilized' for the 'barbarians' (who included the bulk of the laboring poor at home) rested on this feeling of demonstrated superiority."[10] In Wellington's view, if the franchise should be extended, "does any man believe that we should continue to enjoy these vast advantages?" He appealed to the proof of precedent: "A democracy has never been established in any part of the world, that it has not immediately declared war against property."[11] And protection of property, he reminded his hearers, was the basis on which the British Constitution existed.

Such were the obstacles against which reformist rhetoric had to contend: fear of mass discontent and the determination to maintain traditional superiorities. The brief experiment with democracy in England in the seventeenth century and the monstrous atrocities of the French Revolution were sufficient warnings against popular rule. In France it had resulted in atheism, in military dictatorship, and in the tumbling of all Europe into chaos. Why risk what it might do to England?

Against these obstacles a series of leaders contended, until gradually, over a span of decades, they found ways of modernizing and democratizing the nation. Their developing vision was necessarily limited and incomplete, for the problems were far more apparent than were available solutions. Gradually they clarified their own understandings and brought the country into its new age.[12]

"Reactionism Aiding the Cause of Reform"

An Intellectual Revolution, marked by efforts to understand and to adjust to the new conditions, accompanied the Industrial Revolution, out of which the disruptive influences had been spawned. In one aspect, it stimulated new international meddling. It led Lord Byron to dash off to Greece to join the Greek independence fighters, at the cost of his life. It animated the ingenious Earl of Dundonald, Thomas Cochraine, who distinguished himself in the House of Commons by his urgent advocacy of reforming the brutally cruel disciplinary practices in the navy. Dundonald was expelled from Parliament in 1814 for fraud in his stock exchange dealings. Then he won renewed acclaim for his naval services in Chile, Brazil, and Greece—which he undertook, he said, because "a British nobleman has the right to assist any country that is endeavouring to reestablish the rights of aggrieved humanity." Despite his reputation as a radical demagogue in politics, an illegal speculator in stocks, and a rebel against authority, he retained his popularity with the public and upon his death in 1860 he was honored by burial in Westminster Abbey. As will appear in a later chapter, another radical demogogue, Jack Lampton, who became Lord Durham, laid the foundations for dominion status for Canada.

Among the extremists who pioneered domestic democratic reforms, one of the most notorious was Henry (nicknamed "Orator") Hunt, whose career as a reform leader began in 1806. Hunt was a farmer who felt deeply the disruption of agriculture as its field workers left to take jobs in the new factories. Tall, bulky, rough-mannered, pugnacious, and vain, he was a "crowd-compeller" of considerable power. His most notorious speech was given to a huge audience that assembled in St. Peters Fields, in Manchester, on 16 August 1819 to hear his demand for the extention of the franchise to the poor. The 60,000 persons who assembled to hear him included a large proportion of women and children and their behavior was generally quiet. Nevertheless, the authorities were fearful of the radical tone of Hunt's speech and ordered an attack, in which at least six hundred unarmed listeners were killed. The public revulsion against this "Manchester Massacre" contributed to the adoption thirteen years later of the Reform

Bill. Aside from his oratorical abilities, Hunt contributed a significant symbol to the cause. He wore a white hat while giving that speech, which became notable when it was crushed by a militiaman's sword, and for years afterward the wearing of a white hat identified the wearer as one of the reformers, a defender of the poor and of the right. Hunt was imprisoned for two-and-a-half years. After his release he won election to Parliament, where he became an early advocate of women's rights, and where he joined the movement against the Corn Laws. In the election of 1833 Hunt lost his seat in the Commons, and he died on 15 February 1835. He is little remembered because there is nothing notable in the texts of his extant speeches. His appeal came from the strength of his personality and the power of his eloquent voice. Like the Earl of Dundonald, he was searching for an understanding of what democracy means.

Even more notable were William Cobbett, a hot-blooded journalist, and Richard Oastler, a Tory Radical, who became one of the master agitators of English history. It was the "out of doors" persuasion of these precursors of democracy that stirred public feelings that supported the parliamentary reform efforts of such political leaders as Lord John Russell, Lord Henry Brougham, and Earl Charles Grey.

William Cobbett was a journalist of such power and popularity that William Hazlitt coined the term "the fourth estate" to equate the role of journalism with that of the crown and the two parliamentary houses. Born in 1762, Cobbett's influence was at its height during the decades in which new democratic forms had to be found. So powerfully did he write and so well did he strike chords of feeling that appealed to his audience that he has been accounted as "perhaps the greatest popular journalist that ever wielded the resources of the English language."[13] His general tenor was negative—not for but against the tide of change. His recurrent theme was that "We want nothing new; we want only what our forefathers enjoyed." The vision that animated him was his memory (romanticized and idealized) of the England of his youth—"an England in which poor men ate meat regularly and wore gloves, in which a day's toil produced two or three times as much food and clothing as in his own time." He was also out of sympathy with internationalism and helped to create the patriotic zeal that so strongly marked the Victorian Age. As one historian phrased it, "he loved every acre of English soil with true Romantic ardour, and he loved with all his great heart, with all his terrific strength, that English people whose sorrows he understood so well, being bone of their bone and soul of their soul."[14]

Yet backward-looking as Cobbett was, the historian Somervell soberly judged that, "Of all the authors of the movement that drove the Whig Party into enactment of the Reform Bill of 1832, Cobbett was by far the most influential."[15] The paradox of reactionism aiding the cause of reform points straight to the heart of the rhetorical strategy that set England on the path to democracy. What Cobbett saw clearly and brilliantly popularized was that the common people had been relatively well off under the old agrarian system; that they were betrayed and despoiled by the new industrialism; and that "something" must be done to help them to regain a decent well-being. Since industrialism, once launched, could not be rescinded, new means must be sought that would restore the lost level of well-being. This was the underlying tenor of the inflammatory articles that Cobbett poured forth weekly in his *Political Register*—articles that were read avidly in both mansions and hovels—to strengthen the demands of the poor and to convince the regnant aristocrats that changes must be sought to remedy ills the people could no longer endure. In short, he did not suggest remedies but he did inflame rebellious discontent.

"Warmed by Humane Evangelism"

Equally paradoxical was the role of Richard Oastler, a platform agitator with a power equal to Cobbett's, whose reactionary views, combined with a virulent condemnation of the existing system and heated by compassion for the exploited poor, won for him the cognomen of *Tory Radical*. Like Cobbett, Oastler's vision was centered on memories of rural peace and tolerable good living, and it was fortified by positive horror of the evils of the industrial slavery that he knew intimately and portrayed in vivid detail.

Oastler was born on 20 December 1789 in Yorkshire; and both the date and the place were significant. Leeds, in West Riding, where his parents dwelled, had been a reasonably prosperous center of the domestic woolen homecraft industry that was destroyed by the new mechanized factories. It was a home warmed by humane and evangelical Christianity. When Richard was only a few months old, the Oastlers entertained John Wesley, who gave his blessing to the infant. The piety of the family was extended by a warm and practical sympathy for the poor. Richard's father was a convinced Tory who became so inspired by the new ideas of Tom Paine that he broke away from Wesleyan Methodism to join the movement known as the "New Connexion," influenced by the practical compassion of the Moravians.

Under this influence, Richard was brought up to value character, education, and evangelism. A major influence in shaping his career resulted from his father's abandonment of the woolen trade when he observed that the mechanization of the textile industry had resulted in the oppression and degradation of the factory workers.

By the time he was eighteen, Richard threw himself into politics, to join whole-heartedly in Wilberforce's anti-slavery crusade. He wanted to become a lawyer, but this his father forbade since he considered the profession to be immoral. Instead, Richard was apprenticed to an architect; and afterwards he took up his father's early profession as a woolens trader. Meanwhile, his evangelical faith, shaped by Moravian practicality in trying to direct Christianity toward the achievement of social improvements, led him to make regular visits into "the filthiest and most lowly hovels of the poor," to bring them aid and comfort. He also became a lay preacher for the "New Connexion," which gave him valuable experience in public speaking.

During the severe weather in the winter of 1815–16, Oastler began to develop new ideas concerning the urgent need for an organized social welfare program that would replace the outmoded "Poor Law." Once again he changed his vocation, this time to become as his father had the steward of a large estate. In this position he continued for eighteen years, animated by a determination to restore the "good old days" when landlords cared for the needs of their tenants.

After ten years as a prosperous estate manager, Oastler was "awakened" by an evangelistic and prosperous spinner, John Wood, to take an active part in seeking reform of the vicious industrial conditions. This personal campaign against "factory slavery" he initiated with a long letter to the Leeds *Mercury*, which proved to be "one of the most famous letters of the nineteenth century."[16] In this letter he depicted the suffering of children in the textile mills and exclaimed: "Would that I had Brougham's eloquence, that I might rouse the heart of the nation."

And rouse it he did. This first letter was succeeded by another, a month later, and they by a third in which he said: "The skill and ingenuity of man is now made to destroy the happiness and comfort of many merely for the gain of the few." These letters won such wide attention that Oastler began to be called upon to speak at mass meetings; and he spoke so well that his name became as prominent as Cobbett's. Because of the storm of public feelings that was launched, Peel was impelled in 1844 to introduce and win passage for a Factory Bill that reduced the workday for children to ten hours.

The program of the Whig Party to satisfy the rising surge of egalitarianism by extending the franchise to the middle classes was antithetical to Oastler's Tory convictions that government is most properly left in the hands of those of the upper class who are educated to govern. He considered an extension of the franchise as at best diversionary from the real issues and at worst a betrayal of past national experience. When the Reform Bill was introduced in Parliament in 1831, Oastler denounced it as "a revolutionary proposal to desecrate a constitution which the centuries have hallowed." What the poor needed, he contended, was not the right to vote but vastly better living conditions. He wrote more letters to the *Mercury* denouncing the division of England into "two nations," the rich and the poor. The factory workers, who were in any event to be excluded from the franchise, began to organize labor unions and in 1831 persuaded Oastler to assume leadership of their movement. Oastler accepted with the aim to convert the ruling class to a new conception of "minimal social decencies."

During the parliamentary electoral campaign of 1831, Oastler stood out as a prominent national leader in what he called a "straight fight between humanity and greed." It was during this campaign, when he was forty-two years of age, that

Oastler found his true "vocation" as a public speaker. He proved to have extraordinary power over an audience. As his biographer emphasizes, "He had in supreme degree the gift of the born orator for identifying himself with his hearers."[17] What this means is that he managed his ideas and language in such a fashion as to make his audience feel that he was the mouthpiece for their own sentiments. In this sense, he was more "discussant" than "orator." And he filled his speeches with vivid citations of facts that were meaningful in the experience of his listeners.

His central theme was a contrast between the miseries of the factory system and "the happier times that once had been." His open-field address at Huddlesfield to a crowd estimated at twelve thousand illustrates both the nature of his message and the conversational, audience-centered style in which he presented it. The central idea he developed was: "That machine which cannot afford good and comfortable wages to the man who works it is a curse to the country." In persuasively supporting this idea he was both specific and nostalgic:

> I am old enough to remember that there were thousands of respectable domestic manufacturers . . . who were able to make their cloth at home and go to sell it in the market. But they are now reduced almost to pauperism, or to the class of common labourers. They were the best masters the workmen ever had: these were the strongest bulwarks of the state, but they are now mixed amongst the paupers and labourers in one common class. I remember the time when there were happy companies upon a village green, as blithesome and happy as lambs, and I have gambolled with them. But they are now all gone and disappeared . . .; now they are locked up all day in a loathsome factory. . . . I feel that I am doing the work of God when I require the doors to be opened, and that these little ones should once more see the rising and the setting of the sun.[18]

The rhetorical importance of Oastler is how much he accomplished from so limited a premise. For him egalitarianism went no further than fairness of treatment for all. The poor were not to be exploited. But the remedy he saw was not the equality of rights—certainly not of the right to self-rule—but paternal responsibility of the fortunate and the capable to care for the distressed underlings. In retrospect this seems to have been a timid step wholly inadequate to the needs and the newly rising spirit of the times. But its effects were considerable. The public to which it appealed was still the majority, which did not disavow hierarchy but demanded that it be leavened by the spirit of *noblesse oblige*. This was the Old England as it was portrayed in the novels of Sir Walter Scott and as Oastler imagined it to have been. But even as his aim was a nostalgic return to a presumedly ideal past, his vivid descriptions of the injustices suffered by factory labor helped to build sentiment for finding new societal forms.

In his own mode, he went on from speech to speech. For Easter Sunday in 1832, a monster mass meeting was organized at Leeds for him to address. Many in the crowd walked as far as 120 miles at a pace of forty-six miles a day in order to hear him. And he produced results. The M. P. for Leeds, Thomas Sadler, was the member who introduced into the Commons the Factory Reform Bill, supporting it with a three-hour speech that Driver ranked as "one of the classics of British oratory in the nineteenth century." Sadler's bill failed, to be supplanted by a milder one favored by Lord Grey; but Sadler worked so hard for two years organizing support for it that he died from sheer fatigue.[19]

Factory reform was delayed as Oastler feared that it would be by the diversion of attention to electoral renovation on behalf of the middle classes. Oastler was dismayed, being utterly clear in his own view that to rectify the miseries of the workshops demanded primary attention. The granting of votes to the medium well-to-do would not remedy the primary evil. Oastler's speech became sharper as his anger grew. He came more and more to sound like the prophet Jeremiah.

"The only way," he trumpeted, "the aristocracy and clergy could regain the affections of the people and save themselves from ruin was that they should use their powerful influence to rescue the working class from the thralldom and delusion in which money and steam powers held them." Mill owners fought back by sending their agents to disrupt Oastler's meetings with jeers and hisses. In a burst of anger, Oastler cried out to them: "Silence, ye hissers, I tell ye, ye cowards, and ye may go and tell the tyrants by whom ye are employed, that ye may do your worst—that the Bill is safe—that WE WILL HAVE IT—that IT SHALL PASS!" But as we have noted, it did not.

Oastler's campaign continued for some eight years, until his physical strength and his personal resources were both exhausted. As his ability to continue the struggle diminished, so did his influence. His popularity oozed away, primarily for two reasons. One was that other rhetorical leaders developed a more forward-looking and more constructive set of proposals that transcended his remedy of a return to past simplicities. The other reason was that as Oastler declined in physical strength and became dejected and enraged by the failure of his crusade, he became so virulent in his speeches that he lost his audience. His new tone emerged notably in a speech he gave to a mass of 100,000 on 1 July 1832 in which he thundered that: "It is a question of blood against gold . . . if we are despised now it shall be a question of blood in another sense." Four years later, in a meeting in Nottingham called by the newly organized Chartist Movement, Oastler was relegated to a minor role and said haplessly: "I am now convinced that rights will only be granted to an armed force of free men." This was not a view that the English public was ready to accept.

In the election of 1831, Oastler's friend Sadler had to contest for his seat against Thomas Babington Macaulay, whose program was not factory reform but enlargement of the franchise—and Macaulay won. Lord Grey set up a Royal Commission on the Poor Laws to examine the nature of pauperism. To Oastler, there was no need for an inquiry about conditions that he described as "the horrors of uncivilized savagery and hopeless, abject misery." As events developed, Oastler was basically right. The extension of the vote did not bring about the reforms he saw as essential. This was left as a challenge to be met by the rising labor movement.

And how much did the impassioned rhetoric of Oastler and Cobbett accomplish? They were wrong in believing that the calendar could be turned back to the England of earlier times. They were not able to divert attention away from a broadening of the franchise and, instead, toward welfare reforms.

Very dramatically, however, the climate of opinion about the presumed values of the traditional hierarchal structure of British society was drastically revised. The laboring masses—no longer able to maintain decent living standards as small-plot farmers or as owners of cottage industries—were aroused. No longer were they contented; no longer did they feel that their lot in life was ordained and must be accepted. Their spirits were aroused to protest and to demand. The hierarchy was no longer secure.

In the meantime, more moderate and in some ways more perceptive shapers and leaders of governmental programs were guiding the nation's course toward the extension of the franchise to the broadening and prospering middle class. The groundwork laid by Orator Hunt and by Cobbett and Oastler, building a case for the needs and the rights of the exploited poor, also was to attain results. But the harvest from their labors was not to be garnered until a later time. The immediate future belonged to other leaders whom we have come to regard as moderates, although to their contemporaries they seemed to be radical too. They it were by whom democracy was introduced, even though their understanding of it remained incomplete.

2
THE OLD VERSUS THE NEW:
DEVISING FORMS FOR DEMOCRACY

In the early nineteenth century the idea of government by the people was regarded with dread. The English had not only observed the cruel excesses of the democratic French Revolution, they saw their own order challenged by French ideas. Their natural conservatism was enhanced by their being at war with France. Across the ocean, in republican America, they saw that even in that hotbed of innovation, democracy was carefully curbed. An electoral college prevented the direct election of the president; Senators were elected not by the people but by state legislatures; property was protected against majority encroachments; and a Supreme Court was set up to deny legislative adventurism. Elsewhere in the world democracy was seldom thought about. Ancient Athens and republican Rome had been in some degree democratic; but Plato wrote *The Republic* to portray the ideal state as totalitarian, and the Roman Republic was soon converted into an absolutist monarchy.

Democracy was neither inevitable nor were its advantages self-evident. There were sound reasons for favoring it, and other reasons for doubting its benefits. Whether good or bad, it had to be conceived before it could be brought into being.

Tom Paine, an Englishman with American and French connections and loyalties, was among those who envisioned it. But his atheism, irresponsibility, and lack of system caused him to be rejected in all three countries. Charles Fox, remembered as the chief of eighteenth-century liberals, never went so far as to believe in democracy. Sheridan came close to doing so, but he was too theatrical to win full respect. Edmund Burke, admired as a political philosopher, shrilly warned against it. William Pitt, the dependable statesman, did not recommend it.

The wonder is less that democracy was delayed than that it was accomplished. To "invent" it was a rhetorical triumph. To win support for bringing it into effect was even more so. The progression was both cautious and stumbling; but men of insight and courage guided it slowly and by partial steps as they worked it out in their own minds and started it on its historic course.

"To Defend Opinions They Did Not Think to Be True"

The progression of debate and discussion that led into the pathway toward democracy might be dated from the formation in 1776 of a nationwide network of Hampden Clubs by Major John Cartwright, which brought the subject of universal suffrage into the "realm of the discussable." For the generality of the people it remained a chimerical if not a nonsensical notion. The oft-quoted view of Bishop Horsley in 1797 that he "did not know what the mass of the people in any country had to do with the laws except to obey them," was more typical than eccentric. There was only limited questioning of the views of the influential Tory, Lord Eldon: that if Catholics should be allowed to vote it would mean the destruction of English society; that public safety demanded the death penalty for more than two hundred crimes and misdemeanors; that a fourteen-hour workday for children from the age of six was proper and necessary; that the chief purpose of government was to protect the property of the few from the greed of the many; and that the masses enjoyed such happiness as was available.

Happiness, however, was far from general. Even in the wake of the glorious victory of Waterloo, the public had much to feel discouraged about. Domestically, the people were oppressed by both unemployment and high prices. Internationally, the fruits of the long war were few gains and many losses. The Bourbons had been brought back to the throne of France. Autocracies ruled the principal English allies: Russia, Prussia, and Austria. Poland had been dismembered by England's beneficiary nations. Portugal, its most friendly ally, needed help in order to survive. Italy and Germany were searching painfully for unity. The spirit of idealism that sustained the English through the hard struggle against Napoleon soured into disillusionment as the freedom and justice they had fought for appeared to have been lost.

England's national leaders were challenged to repeal and revise a system that no longer served the country's needs. Inevitably their vision of the future was obscure. As Walter Bagehot summarized the problem: "Constitutional statesmen were obliged, not only to employ arguments which they did not think conclusive, but likewise to defend opinions which they did not think to be true."[1]

Under these circumstances rhetoric was not well employed. Following the last-ditch conservatism of Wellington, Parliament was guided by an Irishman, Castlereagh, even though he was accounted the worst speaker in it. Next came George Canning, who was acclaimed as its best speaker but was an injudicious leader. In succession afterwards came Lord Charles Grey, whose deepest yearning was for a quiet retired life, and William Lamb, Lord Melbourne, whose temperament was to pause, consider, reconsider, and then postpone. The leadership then devolved upon Sir Robert Peel, who was laborious, decorous, and dull. In the view of a respected historian, England surmounted its difficulties not by the quality of its leadership but because the natural conservatism of the national sentiment yielded ground only slowly to the newly forming liberal ideas.

"The fact that she did not plunge into the horror and disruption of violent revolution does not prove that she was lacking in ideas, but rather that her ideas were too deep-rooted in the soil of her past to be easily uptorn."[2]

In a time of uncertainty as to what to do, there is little need for speakers whose skill lies in emotional arousal. Problems that cannot be solved are best postponed. This is why Bagehot concluded that Peel's dullness was actually an asset. When delay is more needed than action, "there is nothing like the oratory of Peel—able but not inspiring, firm but not exalted, never great but adequate."[3] Since the people were fiercely discontented but unclear as to what they wanted and since the leaders were equally uncertain as to what policies they might devise, it was a time for debate rather than for action. In short, a workable consensus had to be maintained in a period when leaders scarcely knew what to think. Time was needed for ideas to develop. The governmental function was not to point toward new directions but rather to protect orderly processes. The leader who emerged fitted these needs.

"Too Lively a Sense of His Own Superiority"

George Canning was a product of the old school. His career illuminates the transitional nature of the time. Born in London on 11 April 1770 he grew up under the care of a widowed mother who supported her three sons by becoming an actress. Canning was sent first to Eton and then to Oxford by the generosity of an uncle, where he showed the effects of his mother's profession by shining in declamation and being outstanding in discussions and debates sponsored by school clubs. He proved to be not only a brilliant student but also a leader, winning his way by a combination of intellectual brilliance and hard work. Graduating with a law degree by the age of twenty-two, he was two years later brought into Parliament by William Pitt. He had from childhood been intimate with Richard Brinsley Sheridan, who taught him to favor Whig principles. However, on the issue of whether to favor Jacobin incitements for individual freedom or disciplined patriotism in opposing French excesses, he chose the latter and firmly supported Pitt. His first speech in Parliament, on 1 January 1794 displayed both brilliance and his inherent tendency toward sarcasm and the ridicule of antagonists. As Goodrich observed: "he knew how to play with an argument when he could not answer it; he had a great deal of real wit, and too much of that ungenerous raillery and sarcasm, by which an antagonist may be made ridiculous, and the audience turned against him, without once meeting the question on its true merits," so that, "during the first ten years of his parliamentary career, he never made a speech, it was said, on which he particularly plumed himself, without making likewise an enemy for life."[4]

His readiness in debate brought him too quickly into the cabinet, where he specialized in foreign affairs, and on domestic affairs he took strong stands against radical reforms. His fundamental theme was that England should intervene actively in international disputes, partly to defend justice and partly to ensure a dominant world position. His energizing drive was a combination of personal ambition and patriotic zeal. As he gradually matured in judgment, he became, as his biographer illustrates, "a New Man."[5] In the observation of Sir James Mackintosh, "He daily rose to larger views, and made, perhaps, as near approaches to philosophical principles as the great differences between the objects of the philosopher and those of the orator will commonly allow."[6] By the end of his life, when he died at the age of fifty-eight, on 8 August 1827 he was admired and praised even by opponents who had quivered under the severity of his sarcastic wit.

As secretary of foreign affairs and briefly in the few months preceding his death, as prime minister, he guided English policies to the support of the independence of Portugal, the liberation of Latin American provinces from Spain, and support for the independence of Greece. In domestic concerns, he took the unpopular liberal position of advocating emancipation for Catholics but strongly opposed the idea of broadening the franchise.

He had too lively a sense of his own superiority to be a good party leader. The basis for his strength lay not only in his intellectual abilities but also, in the judgment of Temperley, in his ardent patriotism and in his gradually evolving recognition of "that mighty power of Public Opinion, embodied in a Free Press, which pervades, checks, and . . . nearly governs the whole." His career is an epitome of both the harm and the good that rhetorical abilities may accomplish.

His devotion to the qualities of "Old England" animated his speech on 10 January 1814 to the electors of Liverpool. Napoleon had just retreated from his disastrous invasion of Russia, and Canning discussed what this meant for England:

> We behold a country inferior in population to most of her continental neighbors, but multiplying her faculties and resources by her own activity and enterprise, by the vigor of her Constitution, and by the good sense of her people; we behold her, after standing up against a formidable foe throughout a contest, in the course of which every one of her allies, and at times all of them together, have fainted and failed—nay have been driven to combine with the enemy against her, we behold her, at this moment, rallying the nations of Europe to one point, and leading them to decisive victory.[7]

His admiration for the "vigor of the Constitution" led him in this same speech to denounce the "excess of popular freedom" that refused support to the government "unless each individual interferes directly in the national concerns." To illustrate the evils of egalitarianism, he referred to the democratic "political David"—the United States—that should have joined to bring down the "Goliath of Europe," but that instead had "enlisted under the banner of the despot." Extension of the franchise in England, he thought, would similarly result in a weakening of the national purpose. The issue for every true Englishman was not "whether the political constitution of the state should be faultlessly perfect or not," but "whether the home in which he has dwelt from his infancy—whether his wife and children—whether the tombs of his forefathers—whether the place of the Sovereign under whom he was born . . . shall be abandoned to violence and profanation."

As an internationalist, when he stood for election in Liverpool, "I was an advocate of the war, because I was a lover of peace; but of a peace that should be the fruit of honourable exertion, a peace that should have a character of dignity, a peace that should be worth preserving, and should be likely to endure."

The Treaty of Vienna by which the Napoleonic Wars were concluded has been generally hailed by historians as having laid the basis for a century of peace. Canning, however, scathingly denounced it as a "piece of sublime mysticism and nonsense," which entangled England with allies whom the English neither liked nor trusted. His counsel was to avoid "entangling alliances" with despots.[8] But the treaty was affirmed and Canning turned his attention to domestic affairs.

As a public speaker, his supremacy over his associates was seldom questioned. His most striking characteristic was his boldness—a willingness to state extreme views in strong and unqualified terms. Like Lord Chatham of the prior generation whom he much resembled, Canning stood alone in the forefront of the verbal battles, willing to confront any antagonist, and doing so on his own terms, slashing away at opposing opinions as though they were unworthy of serious attention. His mode was not one of careful analysis and serious, sustained argument but of fierce assertiveness, reflecting the impression that what he believed and said was entirely right and that any who opposed him were simply incapable of understanding the subject under discussion. Despite this extremity of assertion, he managed to imbue his speeches with an appearance of reasonableness by inserting rhetorical questions amidst his statements—questions that answered themselves but seemed to do so on the basis of beliefs which his listeners fully shared. Similarly, he enforced his opinions by assurances that they were no more than reaffirmations of lessons learned in the long process of the nation's history. And he clothed his views in a vivid imagery that displayed the richness of his own imagination while engaging the imaginative interest and involvement of his hearers. Such was the nature of his oratory, which maintained its typical characteristics both in his parliamentary addresses and in his speeches to bodies of constituents.

He was appalled by the radical demands for "democracy," which meant to him the rejection of the "ancient constitution." Crowds numbering as many as fifty thousand, marching under banners inscribed "Liberty or Death!" frightened Parliament into enacting "Six Acts" that virtually established martial law. Canning supported this repression. In the election of 1820, on 18 March again in Liverpool, he exclaimed: "Do I exaggerate when I say, that there was not a man of property who did not tremble for his possessions?—that there was not a man of retired and peaceable habits who did not tremble for the safety of his home?—that there was not a man of orderly and religious principles who did not fear that those principles were about to be cut from under the feet of succeeding generations?"

He defined his own position as the speech proceeded:

Do I deny, then, the right of the people to meet, to petition, or to deliberate upon their grievances? God forbid! But the social right is not a simple, abstract, positive, unqualified term. Rights are, in the same individuals, to be compared with his duties; and rights in one person are to be compared with the rights of others.

"Tyranny," he went on, "is irresponsible power. This definition is equally true, whether the power be lodged in one or a majority; whether in a despot . . . or in a mob. Idle, therefore, and absurd, to talk of freedom where a mob domineers!" He concluded his speech with a burst of fury against the reformers:

Vain and hopeless task to raise such a spirit and then to govern it! They may stimulate the steeds into fury, till the chariot is hurried to the brink of a precipice; but do they flatter themselves that they can then leap in, and, hurling the driver from his seat, check the reins just in time to turn from the precipice and avoid the fall?
. . . May every man who has a stake in the country . . . see that the time is come at which his decision must be taken,—for or against the institution of the British monarchy!

In a speech at Plymouth in 1823 Canning turned again to his favorite topic of internationalism, again interpreting patriotism in conservative terms. England, he said, must never stand "isolated and alone. The situation which she holds forbids an exclusive selfishness; her prosperity must contribute to the prosperity of other nations, and her stability to the safety of the world." Neither, however, should the English "mix ourselves on every occasion . . . in the concerns of the nations which surround us." The steady aim of the government should be to "give to commerce, now reviving, greater extension and new spheres of employment."

When he died, he was acclaimed in the British press as a patriot fully the equal of Lord Nelson. His dying words are his suitable epitaph: "The country has had the best of me. I think it will do justice to my publick character."[9] As a Foreign Minister, Canning's contributions were great; as an opponent of rising democracy, he belonged not to the future but to the past. Among his contemporaries were others more inclined toward looking ahead.

"Composed of a Giant and a Little Child"

The instigation for electoral reform came most effectively from John Russell. In basic ways, he seemed unsuited for this or any other kind of leadership. The fact of his being born into the aristocracy did give him substantial advantages. But he had few of the other attributes (except sheer intellectual ability) that are normally required to attain success as a leader of men.

His birth was two months premature, which perhaps accounted for the ill health that plagued him all his life. He never grew to more than five feet five inches in height. Throughout his life his fund of energy was frail and uncertain. Despite his lifelong ambition for political power, during his early years in the House of Commons, ill health caused him to miss most of its sessions. It was only his determination to lead in bringing about a broadening of the franchise that kept him active in politics.

But if his body was weak, his spirits seldom flagged. As an opponent noted of him near the end of his long career, "J. R.'s power of self-assertion is one of the strongest points of his nature, which as someone has said is composed of a giant and a little child."[10] The strength that he possessed lay in his mind and in his need to lead. His weakness was not only physical but also temperamental. He was driven by a petulant and quarrelsome insistence on recognition, approval, and admiration. He aroused the jealousy of associates who viewed him as claiming credit that should be shared with them. He lacked that instinct for accommodation and compromise upon which political success commonly depends. Conciliation of those upon whose support he depended did not come naturally to him.

This was a weakness of which very early in life Russell became aware, even though he could not control it. While travelling in France as a youthful student, he wrote:

> France, perhaps, affords the best models for an agreeable man. In them we see the most refined politeness towards others, mixed with the most perfect confidence in themselves . . . a skill in placing every topic in the situation which alone can make it amusing in conversation—a grace in treating the most frivolous matters, a lightness in touching the most serious, and a quickness in passing from one to the other.[11]

The conciliatory skill that he admired he could not attain. He did, however, set himself seriously to work to master persuasive eloquence. And in this he was so successful that, as Gladstone estimated in his article on Russell in *The Dictionary of National Biography*, he became fully the equal of Edmund Burke as a masterful speaker. The comparison was apt, for he also shared in one of Burke's cardinal flaws: an inherent haughtiness that led him into unsocial aloofness.

It was this characteristic that was pinpointed by the astute Lord Holland, who in his estimate of Russell at the commencement of his career wrote that, "he is and must be a leader, and he has many of the best qualifications of one." But, as Holland qualified this judgment, he lacked the one quality that Holland believed to be indispensable: "He takes no pains, nor if he did, has the knack, to collect the opinions of others or to enlist their vanity, their ambition, their interests, and their affections in giving effect to them."[12]

As a party leader, Lord Russell was overbearing, too personally sensitive to imagined slights, and always confident that his own understanding was his safest guide. He believed that men are basically rational and hence that logical reasoning alone would finally lead them to right conclusions. Since his own views were right, they had to prevail. When he died at the age of eighty-six, in 1878, after fifty-five years in Parliament as a leader first of the Whigs and afterwards of the Liberals, he could look back over his many successes, realizing that they were marred and handicapped by unnecessary failures. In the common view of his contemporaries, he was not an effective party leader. Nevertheless, he was the instigator of fundamental reforms. He won them by his ability to convince.

His basic political conviction—which was early shaped under the influence of his Tory father, who had converted to liberalism through viewing sympathetically the impoverishment of the Irish while he served as Lord Lieutenant of Ireland—was that it was his duty to "add continuously and gradually to the power of the people," in order to enable them "to make head against the power of the crown." This was the tenor of his first major speech, delivered in the Commons on 25 April 1822 in which he developed the theme that, "We cannot confine liberty to one class of men." In his opinion, a broadening of the franchise had become a national necessity:

> The House of Commons does not possess the esteem and reverence of the people. . . . We have seen discontent breaking into outrage. . . . If we ask the causes, why a system of government, so contrary to the spirit of our laws, so obnoxious to the feelings of our people, so ominous to the future prospects of the country, has been adopted, we shall find the root of the evil to lie in the defective state of our representation. The votes of the House of Commons no longer imply the general consent of the realm.[13]

The motion that he made at this time to expand the franchise to include the whole adult population of the counties and the large towns was defeated. But the 164 votes supporting his motion signalled that the time for a change was close at hand.

The reform was delayed because the Whigs were disorganized and Russell lacked the talent for bringing them into unity. Neither was he able to please his own constituents. In the election of 1826 he lost his own seat and had to be returned to Parliament from a "safe" borough in Ireland. He continued to introduce electoral reform bills in the House. But he also continued to remain aloof from the tricky business of building a coalition broad enough to pass them.

And he persisted in scornfully rejecting any dealings with reform groups out of doors. In essence, Russell remained an aristocrat, less animated by a conviction of egalitarianism than by his sense of paternalistic *noblesse oblige*. It is largely because of his incapacity for leadership that not Russell but Lord Grey proved to be the father of the great Reform Bill of 1832.

"A Steadying and Renovative Role"

It was that "discontent breaking into outrage" that Russell had noted that provided the impetus that brought reform into effect. The demand for equality as a necessity to protect human rights was far from being confined to England. All Europe was being stirred by romantic idealism. In England, while the poor were restive with aroused resentments, English intellectuals were animated by such revolutionist poets as Byron and Shelley. Henry "Orator" Hunt was directing attention to the evils of industrial slavery. William Cobbett and Richard Oastler won effects for reform "by means of organized propaganda deliberately designed to bring upon Parliament the full pressure of an aroused public opinion."[14] Even though these men of incitive power looked backward to the quieter times of the eighteenth century for their inspiration, they also keenly felt the evils of industrialism and on this theme laid the groundwork for change.

Charles Grey matured into effective leadership more slowly than Canning and Russell and much more slowly than his admiring contemporaries expected. This perhaps was his great advantage, that he confronted the challenges of the post-Waterloo years with a maturity nurtured by long experience. He was born on 13 March 1764 the son of an able general who was not elevated to the peerage until 1806, the year also of the death of Fox and Pitt. Already Grey's qualities were so well recognized that he became foreign secretary and leader of the House of Commons. Just one year later his father died and Grey went from the Commons into the House of Lords.

Grey's career was well rooted in the classical tradition. At the age of nine he entered Eton, where he spent eight years before going on to Trinity College in Cambridge. As J. R. Butler wrote in his *Passing of the Great Reform Bill*, Eton was well suited for the training of statesmen. But it was not conducive to democracy. "Special attention was paid to oratory, and oratory of a particular type—large, dignified, lofty, appealing to the sense of honour and responsibility of a particular class. . . . Similarity of education combined with similarity of social position to produce a close society favourable to high spirit and intensity of life rather than to breadth of sympathy." Both Eton and the two great universities were recruiting grounds for Parliament, and at the age of twenty-two Grey was brought into the Commons. He was outstanding in school and quickly became prominent in Parliament. As Macaulay wrote in his essay on Grey, "At twenty-three he had been thought worthy to be ranked with the veteran statesmen who appeared as the delegates of the British Commons at the bar of the British nobility."

It was then that his democratic sentiments commenced to develop. Grey attached himself to the Foxite Whigs, and became one of the managers for the prosecution of Hastings. He also joined the "Society of Friends of the People," and in 1793 he presented a petition on its behalf calling upon the Parliament to approve a broadening of the franchise. Then, relegated to the Lords and submerged in the conservative reaction during the Napoleonic Wars, he "stood alone," as he said, in "the political world." It was not until 1830 that he emerged again into leadership.

Much more had been expected of him. Leadership of the Whigs had come to him almost by default after Fox's death. But he simply did not know in what direction to proceed. As a youth in 1794 he felt himself already committed to "the rights of men . . . but they do not consist in universal representation or in any particular form of government."[15] It was a confusing time and Grey was confused. When Pitt led the country to war with France, Grey opposed the war and went so far as to move the impeachment of Pitt. Then instead of building a strong parliamentary base, he advocated the secession of the Whigs from the Parliament.[16] Even his friends were disappointed by his indecisiveness and lack of vision. Sheridan, in a speech to the Whig Club in January 1802, denounced Grey scathingly as one of "those persons who, thrown by accident in the outset of life into situations for which they are not fitted, become Friends of the People for a time, and afterwards finding their mistake, desert the popular cause."[17]

For a decade after Waterloo, the Tories remained in power under Wellington, Castlereagh, and Canning. Grey was relegated to unprofitable impotence. As his biographer points out, "oratory requires an audience, and when the House of Commons was closed to him he could find none other. The electoral hustings were forbidden ground to a peer. . . . Henceforth his voice was scarcely raised in public except only in the House of Lords." Grey's own feeling about that forum was that, "It is impossible I should ever do anything there worth thinking of."[18]

For rhetoric to be productive, the speaker must develop an acceptable program and must find or shape an audience that he has the means to influence to adopt it. On 13 June 1810 Grey sadly commented to the House of Lords that, "I doubt very much whether there exists a very general disposition in favour of Reform." Even twelve years later on 9 February 1822 he was writing to Lord Holland that, "You may be assured that any nibbling at Reform will not now do." It was not until after the death of Canning that Grey was enabled to resume leadership and to commence the task of reuniting and inspiriting the Whigs. The elections of 1830–31 again gave the Whigs a majority and Grey was installed as prime minister. The test now was whether he did in fact have a workable program and whether he could maneuver the support to bring it into effect.

The country was not only ready but impatient for some broadening of the franchise; the question remained of how broad it should be and what form it should take. Whatever public opinion might be, the problem was how to persuade members of Parliament to vote for measures that would eliminate many seats and would change the conditions for election in many others. What Grey had to accomplish was to persuade the members to vote for changes that would be distinctly disadvantageous to many who must vote for them. To deal with this circumstance, Grey appointed a Committee of Four (including Russell but excluding the no-less-prominent Lord Brougham) to draw up a bill that would quiet public outrage and would win sufficient parliamentary votes. The bill that was devised was to eliminate no less than two hundred "safe" or "closed" borough seats. It also aimed carefully to restrict the poor from the electoral process and to win the support of the disenfranchised and clamorous expanding middle class. In addition to overcoming the self-interest of members whose own political careers were threatened, there also had to be satisfied the honest views of the many who agreed that reform was essential but who disagreed urgently on how far the broadening of the franchise should go. For this task of leadership Grey proved to be the right man in the right place at the right time.

Grey was well suited, both by his aristocratic status and by his convictions and temperament, to play the combined steadying and renovative role. He was far from being egalitarian in his views. He believed strongly that "rule by the best" must be preserved; but he was also well inclined to extend considerably the scope of those considered to be best able to govern. In short, he was less radical than moderate, and moderation provided the bridge over which both public opinion and the parliamentary majority could tread.

The Reform Bill that Grey guided to passage was little more than a shaky transition from monarchal and aristocratic rule toward eventual democracy. As John Bright was to say of it a generation later, "It was not a good Bill, but it was a great Bill when it passed." Bright went on to depict its limits: "The working men are almost universally excluded, roughly and insolently, from political power; and the middle class, whilst they have the semblance of it, are defrauded by the reality."[19] This was how Grey's reform appeared later, after democracy had become a tenable possibility. Nevertheless, the 1832 bill was a decisive step forward.

What Grey's bill undertook to rectify may be illustrated from the political status of Scotland, as that was summarized by Trevelyan:

> If ever an Act of Parliament saved a country from revolution, Scotland was so saved by the Reform Bill. Although in temper, creed, and outlook on life the people were less submissive than the English, the civil institutions of the country contained in 1830 no single element of self-government. . . . There was not even local self-government: all town councils were self-elected, and the Scottish Burgh Act of 1833, which remedied this state of things, was regarded in Scotland as second in importance only to the Reform Bill itself. As to Parliamentary representation, whereas in England the elections for most of the counties and a few of the boroughs were real popular contests, the

meagre handful of forty-five representatives that Scotland sent to Westminster were without exception chosen by small groups of privileged persons, generally sitting around a table. The total Scottish electorate was under 4000.[20]

In the Parliament, Grey had to win votes from two diametrically opposed groups: from radicals who demanded universal suffrage and from the larger group that feared even his moderate proposals. It was this latter group that Grey chiefly influenced. "Like the King, they were persuaded by Grey . . . to regard it as a conservative measure designed to save the threatened constitution and to put the question to rest."[21] The Reform Act was signed into law by King William IV appropriately on the very anniversary of the execution of King Charles II.

Grey's success in winning the necessary support for his reform came not through persuasive speeches to the Lords but through patient conciliatory discussions with the king and with parliamentary leaders. One by one, he won their concurrence that his plan was necessary to avert revolutionary disorders. In this role he proved to be unexpectedly adept. As his biographer notes: "He had cut out, in front of his party's march, a clear path through that Reform jungle in which both friend and foe had expected to see him miserably entangled. Men who had known him too well as the hesitating and pessimistic leader of opposition, always trying to avoid responsibility and action, could not believe that he had stepped quietly forward and plucked the flower safety from the nettle danger."[22]

Appropriately the leader of the transition was a prime exemplar of the great change taking form in rhetoric. Not oratory but discussion was his métier. Instead of proclaiming truth, he worked persistently to maneuver consensus. In this sense, he was a product less of the eighteenth century in which he grew to manhood than a prototype of the new kind of leadership that was to be typical of the twentieth century. But he also had qualities suitable to his own time. He was an aristocrat, and he dealt with aristocrats in a manner they could accept. "If they had not been aristocrats, they would not then have dared to side with democracy."[23]

Grey never relished the leadership into which he was cast by his exceptional conciliatory abilities. In January 1808 he wrote to his wife how much he missed her and his two daughters, exclaiming, "Oh that I could see them in reality!" In 1821 he wrote to her again: "To describe my melancholy at having left you all is impossible." In May of 1832 while the Reform Bill was moving toward adoption, when Lord Holland rebuked him for not making speeches in its behalf, Grey replied to him that, "never was captive more desirous of escaping from prison than I am from my present situation. But I will do my duty."[24] In July 1834, after the success of his bill, at the age of seventy he retired.

His influence was well stated by Trevelyan, who concluded that it was because of Grey that democracy "obtained its political rights without a convulsion. He had interpreted the need of the new, crowding generations, to the old generation of dignity and privilege, to which he himself belonged. He had stood between the living and the dead."[25] His role was the unsensational one of mediation. No statue has been erected in his honor, and this, in a sense, is fitting—for applause and approval were not what he sought. The satisfaction of serving his country well was his reward. His friend Thomas Creevey summed him up as a "most natural, unaffected, upright man, hospitable and domestic," and then, realizing that this was not enough, added that he also surpassed "all his contemporaries as a splendid public speaker."[26] Most assuredly he did not. How he did surpass them was in the rhetoric of accommodation, which was precisely what the circumstances demanded. He was not a man for all seasons but for the particular season in which he abode.

"On Bended Knees I Supplicate You"

When Grey was offered the prime ministry, he wrote to a colleague who was far more excitable, voluble, and steeped in the controversies that Grey avoided— Henry Peter Brougham and Vaux (known more simply as Brougham, or Broom)—saying: "How is a Government to be formed in the House of Commons, and who is to lead it? This question, I feel, can be answered by you alone; on you must depend, in the first degree, the efficiency of any Administration that can be formed, in whatever situation you might be placed."[27] It was an unexpected judgment. For one thing, the two were no more than casual friends and uneasy allies. For another, they differed widely in temperament, in reputation, and in their conduct: Grey avoiding controversy, Brougham glorying in it. Unlike Grey, Brougham was much less a man for the season in which they both lived, nor was he one for all seasons—but he was right for the oncoming season that was struggling to begin, at least in his views.

Leading rhetoricians have called Brougham a Renaissance Man, expansive in both his capacities and interests.[28] Walter Bagehot brushed him off as a "hundred-subject agitator." G. T. Garrat credited him with doing "more than anyone to free his countrymen's minds from the lumber of eighteenth-century ideas and inhibitions."[29] During his twenty years in Parliament he delivered literally hundreds of speeches, besides a vast number more that he spoke in the courts of law and to public assemblies during the fifty-four years of his active career. His speeches were typically polemical and marked by such sledgehammer force that he was generally accounted the most compelling orator of his time.[30]

Brougham was also a critic of oratory, authoring at least five major essays about it,[31] plus his book on the statesmen of his time. When he was named lord rector of the University of Glasgow, his inaugural address was an argument for the teaching of rhetoric as a fundamental need. For his own model he took Demosthenes, because the Athenian "kept the object of all eloquence perpetually in view, never speaking for mere speaking's sake." Yet despite his enormous abilities, oratorical power, and fierce drive of ambition, he did not attain the leadership for which he yearned. He remained to the end an orator of the old type. Although he matched John Russell's tendency toward egalitarianism, he sought to impose his own ideas rather than through coordinate discussion to find a midpoint of consensus.

He attempted too much: more than his auditors were able or inclined to comprehend and accept. As Goodrich properly stressed:

> He rarely puts forth a simple, distinct proposition. New ideas cluster around the original frame-work of his thoughts; and instead of throwing them into separate sentences, he blends them all in one; enlarging, modifying, interlacing them together, accumulating image upon image, and argument upon argument, till the whole becomes perplexed and cumbersome, in the attempt to crowd an entire system of thought into a single statement.[32]

In this he resembled Burke, although the two were virtually contrary in their views.

Brougham was aptly both compared to and contrasted with George Canning by an anonymous contemporary who had heard them often. Like Canning in his early period, Brougham lashed his antagonists with ridicule and sarcasm. But they differed not only in convictions but in style. "Canning marched forward in a straight and clear track; every paragraph was perfect in itself, and every coruscation of wit and genius was brilliant and delightful; it was all felt, and it was felt all at once: Brougham twined round and round in a spiral, sweeping the contents of a vast circumference before him, and uniting and pouring them onward to the main point of attack."[33]

Brougham's greatest virtue was also his greatest weakness. His rhetorical effectiveness was lessened by the sheer comprehensiveness of his mind and of his sympathies. Concerning many of the problems that engaged his vigorous attention, he was far in advance of his fellows. More than any of his contemporaries in Parliament, he sensed the fullness of the changes that were demanded by the new spirit of egalitarianism. What he demanded as essential was virtually the renovation of the whole society. Yet his instinct and experience as a lawyer served to discipline and shape his approach and to render effective what was diffuse. He piled up specific evidence in vivid detail to create a mammoth impetus that could neither be answered nor avoided.

He took all public concerns as his special province. He demanded that public education should become available to all: and he enforced his view by founding London University for the middle classes. He denounced the trading in slaves and then slavery itself. Military floggings, he insisted, should be abolished.[34] The Poor Laws should be fundamentally altered. Orders in Counsel, an executive prerogative, should be abolished; the marriage and divorce laws should be liberalized; freedom of speech and press must be extended. Religious discrimination against Catholics and dissenters had to end. Above all, the middle classes should be granted the vote.

In advocating such reforms, Brougham sought to overwhelm his opponents rather than to conciliate them. His energy was inexhaustible. In an age when three-hour speeches were commonplace, he often spoke for six hours or more. Nor was any topic beyond the reach of his mind.

In three speeches that represented his greatest efforts, he defended Queen Caroline against the charge of adultery; he detailed legal abuses that he demanded be eliminated; and he supported Grey's Reform Bill. In such speeches, as *The Times* editorialized on 8 October 1831: "he eclipsed every effort of oratory made within the walls of Parliament in the memory of the living generation." His delivery, as *The Times* continued, gave added weight to his ideas and evidence. "Even if we could give his words entire, where are the expressive looks, the commanding gestures,—above all, the emphasis, the sublime intonation of his various voice?" But in the view of a less admiring critic, his voice was too loud, his language sometimes "recklessly extravagant," his gestures tending to be "wild and absurd."[35]

Except for four years in office, his career was spent in opposition—much of it outside of Parliament and the latter portion in the House of Lords, which Grey accounted an irrelevant audience. The wonder is that he accomplished so much. He dared to undertake greatly. In his own view, "The history of empire is, indeed, the history of men, not only of the nominal rulers of the people, but of the leading persons who exerted a sensible influence over the destinies of their fellow-creatures."[36] In exemplifying this faith, "Brougham stood coiled and concentrated, reckless of all but the power that was within himself."[37]

Brougham was born to a Scottish mother and English father in Edinburgh on 10 September 1778. As a student at Edinburgh University he wrote three scientific papers that were published by the Royal Society. He helped to found clubs in which he gained practice and displayed brilliance in debate. After an unsuccessful effort to practice law in Scotland, he went to London and attended Lincolns Inn, then was admitted to the English bar in 1808. His many articles in the *Edinburgh Review,* of which he was a co-founder, and his charm in conversation won the friendship of Lord Grey and of Lord Holland, who brought him to the Whig cause. However, the Whigs neglected to bring him into Parliament; and after the subsequent eclipse of the Whigs, Brougham devoted himself to the law, in which he quickly won high repute. After serving two years in Parliament from a closed borough, he sought to extend his base of support by winning election from the prestigious borough of Liverpool in 1812 but was defeated by George Canning. Not until after the end of the war with France was Brougham again brought into the Commons, once more from a closed borough in 1816. Despite the general agreement that "he instantly resumed a commanding position," the Whigs refused to take him into their coterie of leadership. It was in 1820 that his reputation rose to tremendous heights because of his defense of Queen Caroline—climaxed with a peroration that he was said to have rewritten seventeen times. After that display, his income from the law amply provided for his needs.

His great speech on "The Present State of the Law" was delivered in the House of Commons on 7 February 1828. For six hours and three minutes his detailing of legal abuses held the close attention of the members. What he asked for he got. Some three-fourths of the abuses he described were rectified within a decade, and the remainder were eliminated in later years.[38] The printer of the speech properly termed it a "solid foundation" for legal reform. Brougham himself in his opening sentence called the problem he would discuss "one of the most important subjects that can possibly be submitted to the Legislature."[39]

In this speech, Brougham, profiting no doubt from his courtroom experience in appealing to jurors, made his closest approach among his political speeches to being a conciliatory discussant. He asked the aid of his listeners, while promising to give them his best:

> I pledge myself, through the whole course of my statements, as long as the House may honour me with its attention, in no one instance to make any observation, to bring forward any grievance, or to mark any defect, of which I am not myself competent to speak from personal knowledge. Be that as it may, whether I have the support of the Ministers or no—to the House I look with confident expectation, that it will control them, and assist me; if I go too far, checking my progress—if too fast, abating my speed—but heartily and honestly helping me in the best and greatest work, which the hands of the lawgiver can undertake.

Moreover, he asked also for the goodwill of the king, after a reminder that Augustus had found Rome of brick and left it of marble:

> But how much nobler will be our Sovereign's boast, when he shall have it to say, that he found law dear, and left it cheap; found it a sealed book—left it a living letter; found it the patrimony of the rich—left it the inheritance of the poor; found it a two-edged sword of craft and oppression—left it the staff of honesty and the shield of innocence.

Even though such a conciliatory relationship with those whose support he needed resulted in Brougham's greatest rhetorical success, he nevertheless reverted to his temperamental inclination toward sarcastic and vituperative attack. In consequence, his third great speech in the House of Lords on 7 October 1831 in support of the Reform Bill was only in its latter part aimed toward winning votes. Only then did it adhere to the conciliatory maneuvering led by Lord Grey. Brougham's speech is of rhetorical interest primarily for two reasons. One, it is an exceptional example of cutting the ground from under opposition through ridicule, sarcasm, and *reductio ad absurdum*. Second, it specifies the limitations of even so forward-looking a mind as his in the attempt to make a start toward transforming the aristocratic structure of the British government into a democracy.

Brougham made no pretense of attempting to win the consent of those who opposed the bill. In his opening remarks he flatly pronounced himself "careless whether I give offense or no."[40] The audience he sought to reach was in the Commons and in the public, not the peers whom he addressed. By making their reluctance to accept reform appear to be utterly ridiculous, he aimed to render their opposition bootless. What he pinpointed was the inconsistency of their claim to favor the principle of reformation while renouncing its implementation. In a paraphrase of their general position, he sneered at their praise of one another, which he summarized in a blistering sentence: "See such an one—*he* is a man of prudence . . .; he is not averse to all innovation, but dislikes percipitancy; he is calm, just to all alike; never gives a hasty opinion; a safe one to follow."

What he sought to establish was the "great principle" that the Reform Bill did not deviate from the long tradition that government should safely be left to men of property rather than to the propertyless mass. He pointed out that the vote would be restricted to men who paid no less than ten pounds annually as rental for their homes. It was "grievous unfairness," he said, to "insinuate that universal suffrage is at the root of the bill." Far from it: "The franchise is conferred upon householders only." He cited the evidence that this group was no more than a provident minority. "The whole foundation of the measure, therefore, and on which its parts rest, is property alone, and not population." No more than in prior history was the impoverished and incapable majority to be trusted.

What the bill did eliminate was government by "masters of rotten boroughs." On this point he was conciliatory, gently indicating that he would be pleased with all suggestions for safeguarding against its intrusion into affairs. He went on to clarify the principle that must be accepted:

> But if there is mob, there is the people also. I speak now of the middle classes—of those hundreds of thousands of respectable persons—the most numerous, and by far the most wealthy order in the community; for if all your lordship's castles, manors, rights of warren and rights of chase, with all your broad acres, were brought to the hammer, and sold at fifty years' purchase, the price would fly up and kick the beam when counterpoised with the vast and solid riches of those middle classes, who are also the genuine depositories of sober, rational, intelligent, and honest British feeling. Unable though they are to round a period, or point an epigram, they are solid, right-judging men, and above all, not given to change. If they have a fault, it is that error on the right side, a suspicion of state quacks—a dogged love of existing institutions—a perfect contempt of all political nostrums. They will neither be led astray by false reasoning, nor deluded by impudent flattery. . . . Grave—intelligent—rational—fond of thinking for themselves—they consider a subject long before making up their minds on it; and the opinions they are thus slow to form they are not swift to abandon.

Then he warned of the danger of rejecting so moderate a reform, for:

> Doubtless they are not the only classes who so felt; at their backs were the
> humbler and numerous orders of the state; and may God in his infinite mercy
> avert any occasion for rousing the might which in peaceful times slumbers in
> their arms!

So there came to England in the Great Reform of 1832, not democracy and
not even an ameliorative extension of the franchise by free choice, but from
necessity. As Brougham emphasized in continuing his address, the simple fact
was that the old establishment no longer could be maintained. "Whence the
congregating of 150,000 men in one place [Birmingham], the whole adult male
population of two or three counties, to speak the language of discontent, and
refuse the payment of taxes? I am one who never have either used the language
of intimidation, or ever will suffer it to be used towards me, but I am also one
who regard those indications with unspeakable anxiety."

His appeal was one his auditors could not deny:

> We stand in a truly critical position. If we reject the bill, through fear of being
> thought to be intimidated, we may lead the life of retirement and quiet, but
> the hearts of the millions of our fellow-citizens are gone forever; their affec-
> tions are estranged; we and our order and its privileges are the objects of the
> people's hatred, as the only objects which stand between them and the
> gratification of their most passionate desire.

Then he concluded with a warning: "beware of your decision!"

> Rouse not, I beseech you, a peace-loving but resolute people; alienate not
> from your body the affections of a whole empire. As your friend, as the friend
> of my order, as the friend of my country, as the faithful servant of my
> sovereign, I counsel you to assist with your uttermost efforts in preserving the
> peace, and upholding and perpetuating the constitution. Therefore, I pray
> and exhort you not to reject this measure. By all you hold most dear—by all
> the ties that bind every one of us to our common order and our common
> country, I solemnly adjure you—I warn you—I implore you—yea, on my
> bended knees, I supplicate you—reject not this bill![41]

In this spirit of necessitous adjustment to an aroused public opinion, the great
continental divide was surmounted. England adopted, not democracy, not the
principle that the people should and must govern themselves, but at least an
irretrievable step in that direction. The culmination did not come until a new
generation of leaders—Richard Cobden, John Bright, Gladstone, and Benjamin
Disraeli—learned to trust the people. But the decisive step was taken, and once
taken there could be no turning back. By the Reform Bill of 1832 the period of

modernization was set upon its course. This much is owed to the rhetorical efforts of John Russell, Charles Grey, Henry Brougham, and, in a partial sense, also to George Canning. It may be said of them that they interpreted conditions rightly and rightly guided a moderate step, the compromise that was politically attainable, into the future.

3
THE FOCUS OF ARGUMENT:
WHAT DIRECTION SHOULD GOVERNMENT TAKE?

The reshaping of both the government and the whole society was the great challenge that rhetoric confronted throughout the whole course of the nineteenth century. The rhetorical circumstances were difficult and progress was halting, coming rather in fits and starts than either steadily or in great leaps forward. One impediment was that the leaders who had to deal with the challenge had no more than limited vision concerning what needed to be done. Neither was public opinion either clearheaded or united. Amid the disruption caused by the industrial revolution, people at all social levels were beset by contrary sentiments. The solidly established traditions grown through centuries of experience in an agrarian and landlord system were unsuitable for the new industrial and commercial capitalism, yet they were too deeply and too broadly meshed into the life styles and thought patterns of the population to be easily discarded. Instead of the genteel hierarchy of prior times, what was happening was so rapid a compartmentalism of the rich and the poor that the term "two nations" came into general usage.

The functions of rhetoric—to define, to interpret, and to win support for available solutions—were almost too formidable for leaders to encompass. Yet however haltingly and however incompletely, those who accepted responsibility as leaders did provide sufficient guidance to bring the society through this dangerous transition. Instead of revolution, there was a gradual development of essential reforms.

The principal agency by which the changes were both directed and controlled was the Parliament. As Sir Ivor Jennings wrote in his monograph on *The Queen's Government:* "The task of adapting the laws and the system of government to meet the demands of electors and the changes brought about by economic development has fallen to Parliament. The volume of legislation passed in a single session is now far greater than the volume of legislation passed in a whole Parliament in the eighteenth century."[1] For an understanding of what rhetoric has meant in British history, a prior understanding of what Parliament is and how it operates is essential.

In earliest times, a parliament was simply a body of lords summoned by the king to give him such counsel as he might request. King Edward I changed this concept by providing for the election of members who were to meet and reach such decisions as seemed best. In the seventeenth century the House of Commons assumed clear ascendance over the House of Lords. Only in recent times has the Parliament been representative of separate constituencies and even today members need not have residence in districts from which they are elected. The Parliament is more truly a "national" body than is the Congress of the United States or most other legislatures.

The English Parliament is virtually unique in several respects. It incorporates the executive branch, rather than being "balanced" by it. Members of the cabinet are also members of Parliament and take their own regular part in the debates. In addition, a "question period" opens the daily sessions (except on Fridays), during which ministers are to be prepared to answer such questions as members may pose to them.

In many respects the eighteenth-century ideal of "clubbiness" continues to distinguish Parliament, both in the Commons and in the Lords. The chamber in Westminster Hall in which the Commons sits is small, only forty-five by sixty-eight feet. Majority members sit on benches on the Speaker's right, Opposition members on his left, separated by an aisle of about twelve feet. There is seating space for not more than half the membership. As in other legislatures, much of the work is done in committees. Britain's committees are large—with forty members or more—and reports are brought to the House after substantial debate. Even so, such reports are seldom accepted without spirited discussion. Perhaps not more than forty or fifty members of Parliament may attend sessions of the Commons, with the total membership summoned by a bell when a vote is to be taken. Party discipline is important and members typically vote as the leadership requests. Even so, the debates are important, for the dignity and independent spirit of the members requires that they be well informed. The complexity and enormity of business that must be conducted has required changes in rules that preclude the lengthy speeches of prior times and restrict speakers to a few minutes.[2]

Public opinion is a constant monitor over parliamentary actions. Formal recognition of such a monitoring influence commenced in 1834 when Sir Robert Peel issued his famous Tamworth Manifesto to his constituents and through them to the whole nation to explain what his policies would be if he were elected. After the extension of the suffrage, electoral campaign speeches by members of Parliament and other public addresses became increasingly significant, often eclipsing the speaking done in Westminster Hall. Concurrently, public speaking on political issues by individuals not members of Parliament, and other speaking on nonpolitical subjects also came to be extensive, reflecting the broadening of public interest in social and governmental questions.

"Voices of Discontent . . . Alarm Bells, Not Social Leaders"

The rhetorical processes that provided needed guidance cannot be traced in any steady or orderly sequence of development. The problems were multiple. Even the best minds that grappled with them were impeded by old ideas that did not readily yield to new approaches. Most of those who held power were more cautious than daring. Such progress as was made was forced upon the leadership rather than devised by it. In sum, the invention and the implementation of democracy was a gradual, retroactive, and cumbersome process. As is always true when problems that must be dealt with are both new and broadly inclusive, the search for solutions was largely by trial and error. A far clearer view of what was happening is granted to us by hindsight than it was to those who confronted the problems.

Rhetoric cannot accomplish more than it sets out to do. Without understanding, it cannot interpret. Without sympathy it cannot have purpose. Without purpose it cannot lead. Without leadership little is left but drift. The tendency to drift brought England dangerously close to disaster. Somehow this was avoided. Leaders accepted the challenge that confronted them. Their abilities barely but truly proved to be adequate to steer the deeply troubled society through its time of trial. It is their partial, divided, and gradually clarifying insight, brought into focus through their superb eloquence, that needs to be explored.

What must be remembered is that their minds and their feelings were products of their time. The political parties, both Tories and Whigs, represented a very limited base. They were land-holding aristocrats with their minds shaped by a long tradition of seldom-questioned superiority. They believed in public order, in low taxation, and in liberty for themselves. If the Whigs more than the Tories had come to question the dominance of the throne, neither group had come to believe in democracy. Their prototype was the gentlemanly squire, "picturesque in his thick-headedness and monumental in his complacency," with an aversion for "the strange and harsh" realities of their changing age.[3]

As the century advanced, the desperate plight of the poor was well illustrated in the enormously popular writings of Charles Dickens. But in the most popular of his productions, his pathetic hero Bob Cratchett expected little more of his exploitative employer Scrooge than a Christmas goose and a small increase in his miserably inadequate wage. The most urgent demands for reform came from outside the center of power—from newly organizing labor unions in the Chartist Movement, and from the Anti–Corn Law League.

The most inspiriting humanitarian thinkers of the period were the Utilitarian Jeremy Bentham, the philosophical anarchist William Godwin, and the founder of English socialism, Robert Owen. They and those whom they inspired were "liberals and almost all of them democrats who hated privilege and prejudice. . . . Unfortunately they differed so much in other respects that this community of ideals went for nothing." Consequently, "the only hope for the workers seemed to lie in class war and social revolution."[4] As the rising threat was viewed in 1844 by Charles C. F. Greville, "We are just now overrun with philanthropy, and God knows where it will stop, or whither it will lead us."[5]

Voices of discontent were numerous. Prominent among them though little remembered in later times were the Methodist preacher Joseph Rayner Stephens and such Church of England evangelicals as John Fielden, a radical reformist factory owner; an aristocrat, Anthony Ashley Cooper, Lord Shaftesbury; and Edwin Chadwick, director for a time of the Board of Health. Better remembered if less immediately effective in the reform movements were such intellectual and renovative thinkers as Coleridge and Southey, Carlyle and Ruskin, and the Utopian dreamer William Morris. None of them was a successful organizer; and their separated influence lacked the rhetorical point required to devise and win support for a program.

Such men were alarm bells, not social leaders. The most impressive intellectual understanding or the most urgently felt idealism cannot succeed without rhetorical effectiveness. Such men were exceptionally eloquent in their own spheres; but they lacked cohesiveness. The result was agitation that expressed despair and enhanced the bitterly seething discontent. But progress demands more. It requires an adequate and available mode of operation. This is what rhetoric had to provide.

"Not a Man among You Not Anxious to Elevate Himself"

Chartism and the Anti–Corn Law League were the nationwide social movements that most tellingly expressed the spirit of rebelliousness that was stirring among the masses. Both represented the needs of the poor but in divergent ways that prevented rather than aided unity of effort. The first aimed toward raising wages and improving work conditions in factories; the second to combat inflation, most especially the ruinously high cost of food. They had different leaders as well as different goals; and instead of unifying their efforts they impeded one another. Despite these difficulties, both attained a substantial degree of success.

The labor union movement made a truly sensational start. Considering that it started from base zero, without any guiding traditions, without legal recognition or protection, and with far more public animosity than support, the progress that it made in uniting workers and in establishing a basic program went far beyond any reasonable expectation. Trade union clubs there had been, mostly in London, but they were small groups of artisans who did not attempt either to unite or to extend their membership to other workers or to other sections of the country.

The broadening of the Chartist Movement stemmed from Robert Owen, the father of English socialism, who founded the first national labor union, The Grand National Consolidated Trades Union in 1834. The rhetorical goal that he set for it was far beyond possible attainment. As its charter proclaimed, it disdained "to obtain some paltry rise or prevent some paltry reduction in wages." More grandly, it posited a socialist state, with joint ownership and joint control over both the production and the distribution of goods in order to ensure "for the productive classes a complete dominion over the fruits of their own industry."[6]

Owen was more an aristocrat than a democrat. He owned a cotton factory at New Lanark in Scotland, where he established a school and provided housing for his employees in the mode of a benevolent despot. What he aimed for was the establishment of similar model communities, like his own and like the one in New Harmony, Indiana, which he went to America to assist. New Harmony was directed by a woman, Frances Wright, and from her Owen learned that women must have a role beyond that of being merely wives and mothers, though he stopped short of dreaming that they ought to be granted the right to vote.

Unlike such other revolutionary thinkers as Karl Marx, who was working out his own idea of communism through his studies in the British Museum, what Owen envisioned was not a war of class against class but rather a cooperation of social classes under the humane guidance of enlightened employers. In his ideal society he would eliminate such parasites as landlords, soldiers, and priests. Shared production with a just division of its fruits was his aim.

Because of reaching too far, Owen's rhetorical goal quickly collapsed. The trade union clubs held aloof and new factory workers were not attracted. When strikes were called to enforce demands, employers responded with lock-outs and strike breakers. When a group of Luddites in Birmingham expressed their hatred of their industrial enslavement by destroying machinery, the government put them down with harsh force. When a Friendly Society of Agricultural Workers was formed in Dorset, the government prosecuted its leaders and deported six of them to Australia. What Owen did accomplish was to bring from his social position a degree of respectability to the surging demand for social justice.

Other facets of Chartism took yet different forms, with different rhetorical goals and methods. At Rochdale in Lancashire in 1844, a group of twenty-eight weavers set up a cooperative grocery, a shoe factory, and a textile mill. Their Rochdale Society issued a prospectus stating its goal to be "the moral and intellectual advancement of its members." This moderate approach proved to be so appealing that by 1862 there were 450 such societies with some 90,000 members. Concurrently, Friendly Societies were organized nationwide to establish joint savings accounts to be used for the care of the workers' widows and orphans, a program that by 1847 incorporated a million-and-a-half members.

Rhetorical efforts were natural responses to circumstances. A great depression that commenced in 1830 resulted in multiple business failures that led to such vast unemployment as fifty thousand people in Manchester alone. Its harsh effects were aggravated by a series of poor harvest years on the farms. *The*

Condition of England came into nationwide discussion. Friedrich Engels (a German-born Manchester manufacturer), Thomas Carlyle, and Benjamin Disraeli emerged as prophets of doom who forecast disaster from the rapidly growing division of the population into rich and poor. Rhetorical point was given to the movement in 1837, when Robert Lovett, the head of the London Workmen's Association, induced several radical members of Parliament to join in the issuance of a People's Charter. It aimed toward political measures to effect such reforms as universal male suffrage, secret ballots, annual Parliaments, and the abolition of property qualifications both for voting and for membership in Parliament. Its charter claimed that "The House of Commons is the People's House and *there* our opinions should be stated, *there* our rights ought to be advocated, *there* we ought to be represented or we are SERFS."

It was an Irish Protestant landlord, Feargus O'Connor (1796–1855) who took command of the political phase of the movement. He established himself in Birmingham, which he represented in Parliament from 1832 to 1835—at which latter date he was unseated for lacking the requisite amount of property. His bombastic eloquence was brushed aside in the Commons; but after his dismissal from office he devoted himself to bringing into the Chartist Movement the Irish peasants and the English factory workers. Through his newspaper, *The Northern Star,* which built up the then-enormous circulation of fifty thousand, and through demagogic speeches to massed audiences of the unemployed and the hungry, he advocated "universal suffrage or death!" Under his guidance, meetings were held throughout England to elect representatives to a permanent "anti-Parliament," to convene in 1839, backed with the threat of a general strike and a promised outbreak of armed revolution.

For a brief time his efforts had impressive success. In June 1839 a monster petition with 1,280,000 signatures was presented to the House of Commons, which debated it languidly and defeated its demands by a vote of 235 to 46. O'Connor and at least five hundred local Chartist leaders were arrested; and O'Connor continued to edit his newspaper from his prison cell. A short upturn of the economy weakened the effect of his movement, but a drastic slide into the depression of 1841–42 again revived it. A permanent National Charter Association presented yet another petition, this one with 3,300,000 signatures; and again the House of Commons rejected it, by a vote of 287 to 59. Better times in 1843 again caused the protests to subside.

Chartism was too vague in its goals and too disunited to be rhetorically effective. As one of its speakers told his audience, "If a man ask what I mean by universal suffrage, I mean that every working man in the land has a right to a good coat on his back, a good hat on his head, and a good roof for the shelter of his household." The difficulty faced by the labor organizers was well stated by a speaker opposing Chartism, who told one of its meetings: "Denounce the middle classes as you may, there is not a man among you worth a half-penny a week that is not anxious to elevate himself among them."[7]

The socialism represented by Chartism proved to be a rhetorical goal around which not even the poor in England would rally. Parliament never took it seriously. Even so, it did not die easily or quickly. The European revolutions of 1848 along with yet another dismal downturn of the economy inspired the Chartists to call yet another national assembly that was to march upon the Parliament with a demand for universal suffrage. A heavy rain helped to keep the demonstration small and Feargus O'Connor was induced to call it off. In immediate terms, Chartism was no more than a frightening failure; in the longer term, its more basic objectives were brought into effect before the century closed. But such successes as it won were accomplished by other leaders who used other means.

"Luminously Clear and Pragmatic"

The Anti–Corn Law League was another response to the impoverishment of the masses that took a very different form and had a very different type of leadership. Its virulence derived from the miseries of the populace; but its philosophic underpinning was strongly influenced by a new view of economics that was presented by David Ricardo, a Dutch Jew who was born in London and converted to Christianity. He followed the pursuit of his father as a speculator in the stock market, thereby accumulating a considerable fortune. From this vocation he also converted. After reading Adam Smith, he designed an abstract and logical system of economics that Carlyle called "dismal" but that won so large a following as to result in its being termed "classical." Ricardo also won election to Parliament, where his views held respectful attention.

His economic theory denounced both "rental property" and "temporary as opposed to permanent" investment. What he proposed was that wealth should be "earned" rather than being an undeserved increment deriving from inheritance or from social developments. He did not oppose the accumulation of wealth. Quite to the contrary, in his system "Capital was visualized as the good fairy of industry; it was the capitalist who furnished the wage fund by which the employees were kept alive, which no strike action could increase and which legislative interference could only diminish. The one thing necessary to economic salvation was to give capitalism as free a hand as possible."[8]

Ricardo's view of capitalism provided a base from which partial and ameliorative reform measures could be developed and could win support. Its fruits were the Factory Law of 1833 (reducing the workday to twelve hours), the new Poor Law of 1834 (extending welfare benefits to the unemployed), and formation of the Anti–Corn Law League during the depression of 1837–39. Each of these reform measures and movements resulted from the setting of rhetorical goals that were sufficiently restricted and pointed to attract support.

The problem to be solved as the reformist speakers defined it was poverty. More specifically, it was the high price of food, and particularly the price of grain, which was kept high by the "Corn Law" tariff enacted in 1815. The two

leaders who brought this issue into clear focus were two Manchester industrialists: George Wilson, a canny organizer, and Richard Cobden, an eloquent
persuasive speaker who was designated as the chief spokesman for their effort to
eliminate the tariff.

Both Wilson and Cobden well understood that the high price of grain was
only one facet of the problem of poverty. But, as Cobden explained to justify the
narrow focus of their movement, "The English people cannot be made to take up
more than one issue at a time with enthusiasm." What he undertook was to deal
with that one topic in a way that would spread the reform as broadly as possible.
The theme he decided to pursue was to make the Corn Law "the symbol of
aristocratic misrule."

This rhetorical strategy proved to be sound. It succeeded largely because of the
persuasive campaign that was waged first by Cobden and then even more
effectively by his fellow townsman John Bright, whom he enlisted in the
campaign. What they said was rendered especially effective by the poor harvest
years of 1845–48, which devastated Ireland and had almost as severe effects upon
the poor of England. As is always true, persuasive speaking did not operate in a
vacuum. It was adjusted to and took advantage of emergent and changing
conditions. Poverty was the prime motivater, but the speeches had to point the
way through the problems to a solution. The solution the speakers sought and
won was to substitute an income tax for the tariff revenues and thereby to bring
down the price of food.

Richard Cobden, the chief architect of the persuasive strategy for the movement and its first major spokesman, commenced his parliamentary career in
1841. As a businessman he had travelled extensively throughout England and in
Europe and America with the result that "No man of his time entered the House
of Commons with so sound a knowledge of the world at large as Cobden brought
when he entered Parliament at the age of thirty-seven."[9] His conviction based
upon his own experience and sympathies and enforced by Ricardian economic
theory was that property creates responsibility and that the only avenue to
reform was by the enlargement of the property of the middle classes. He was
devoted to "self-regulation" as encompassed in the general principles of laissez-
faire. The best that government could do was to stand aside. "Government," he
told his audiences, "was a bad thing in itself, always oppressive to individuals,
frequently unjust, nearly always expensive and inefficient."[10]

Despite his "one issue" emphasis, Cobden was also a passionate advocate of
international peace. In his judgment the tariff system not only robbed the poor
and handicapped business but also was the leading cause of war. In a speech in
the Covent Garden Theater in London in September 1843, he explained why:

Free trade—what is it? Why, breaking down the old barriers that separate
nations; those feelings behind which nestle the feelings of pride, revenge,
hatred and jealousy, which every now and then break their bonds and deluge

whole countries with blood; those feelings which nourish the poison of war and conquest, which assert that without conquest we can have no trade.[11]

His speeches both in Parliament and to public audiences were conciliatory, luminously clear, and pragmatic rather than ideological. His listeners had the feeling that he was of their own kind, not radical but practical. As Lord Morley described their responsiveness to Cobden's appeals: "They were delighted by mingled vivacity and ease, by directness, by spontaneousness and reality, by the charm so effective and so uncommon between a speaker and his audience, of personal friendliness and undisguised cordiality."[12] In short, Cobden was the new egalitarian type of rhetorician, talking not so much to as for his listeners, not forcing his views upon them but professing to present their own. This does not mean that he was in our modern sense democratic. Like the general leadership of his time he believed not in democracy but in paternalism. As he said to the Commons on 13 April 1857: "I have faith in great multitudes when appealed to perseveringly and honestly," but he did not believe in universal suffrage. This represented too great a break with the past. As his biographer asks, "Why should Cobden be blamed for not perceiving what nobody of his time perceived?"[13]

He was ahead of his time in his insistent reiterations that peace depends upon international laissez-faire principles. The effort to bolster national well-being by the seizure of colonies he considered a form of folly that was close to madness. Commenting on England's Opium War against China in defense of its privileges of extraterritoriality, he exclaimed, "God help the *Christians* who think of making their religion acceptable in the rear of an opium war."[14] In reviewing England's troubles with India, he asked: "Has not our conduct been such as to imbue the minds of the native population not only with hatred but contempt for us?"[15] Rejecting the notion that England ought to intervene to assist foreign revolts against tyranny, he said scornfully, "The truth is, and must be again and again told the English public and the world that our own aristocratic politicians make political capital out of the Italians, Poles, Circassians, etc., for purposes of their own . . . instead of *doing the work* of liberty at home."[16]

The "liberty at home" to which he chiefly devoted himself was to accomplish repeal of the tariff on grains. His basic arguments were that this tariff not only impoverished the masses but also was an unjust and harmful intrusion by government into individual enterprise. His speech on this subject in the House of Commons on 13 March 1845,[17] was a model of rhetorical strategy: well-reasoned, factually sound, and well-adjusted to the basic views of his listeners who had to be induced to vote as he wished. His own views on the subject were already well known, as was his guiding philosophy. What he undertook in this speech was to show that what he advocated was precisely what his auditors also believed and what it was their own interest to accomplish.

The first part of his speech was an elaborate discussion of economic theory, on the theme that governmental interference with free trade is self-defeating. The professed intent of the Corn Law was to protect the farmers; but the farmers continued to be the most distressed portion of the population—and the tariff was the cause. Their natural customers could not afford to pay the high prices of food; their farm workers had to be paid at a higher rate; the price of grain made it unprofitable to raise cattle. Because of such problems, the capital that was essential to improve agriculture flowed away from the land rather than to it. The high price of food forced a rise in factory wages—never enough for the workers but an added expense for the owners, who consequently raised the prices that their customers had to pay. Everyone suffered: farmers, landlords, city workers, industrialists, and the public. All this was argued with spirit and supported by the citation of specific facts. The tone was consistently conciliatory with frequent statements that Cobden understood he was telling his listeners only what they already knew and believed.

In the latter portion of his speech his tone became quite different—sharpening into attack. Members of the House, he said, were divided into two groups: "politicians," whom he refrained from identifying, and those whose sole aim was to serve the needs of the nation. The votes of the first group he could not win. To win the others he shifted for the first time into denunciation of the ministers' supporters:

> This cry of protection has been a very convenient handle for politicians. The cry of protection carried the counties in the last election, and politicians gained honours, emoluments, and places by it. But is that old tattered flag of protection, tarnished and torn as it already is, to be kept hoisted still . . . or will you come forward honestly and fairly to inquire into this question? . . .
>
> No! You are the gentry of England who represent the counties. You are the aristocracy of England. Your fathers led our fathers; you may lead us if you go the right way. . . .
>
> The English people look to the gentry and aristocracy of their country as their leaders. . . . But you never got it, and you will not keep it, by obstructing the spirit of the age. . . .
>
> . . . you stand now in a very critical position. . . . Everywhere you are doubted and suspected. . . . Well, then, this is the time to show that you are not the mere party politicians which you are said to be.

The speech had an effect so powerful that Prime Minister Peel confessed his inability to reply to it. The Corn Law was repealed, and an income tax was adopted to shift the revenue base from the poor to those with income to spare. For seven years Cobden had given his best efforts to this cause. For the next twenty years, before his death, he devoted himself unsparingly to the cause of peace. In this campaign, as also in his fight against the Corn Law, the associate upon whom he chiefly depended and whose eloquence and effectiveness even surpassed his own was the Quaker orator, John Bright.

"Like the Surge of the Swollen Tide"

Trevelyan's biography of John Bright celebrates him as "the rallying-cry of the masses" and "the symbol of an honest man in politics."[18] Ausubel in his revisionist biography points out that "he became one of the most hated men in early Victorian England." His conclusion is that "Bright was neither the saint his admirers found him to be nor the monster his enemies were certain that he was." On balance, "the saint in him far outweighed the monster." As Ausubel's masterly analysis demonstrates, the "myths about him continue to be far more influential than the truth."[19]

The difficulty was that in that time of fundamental transition, no leader could either cast aside wholly the encumbrance of tradition nor clearly see the needs of the future. Bright had the additional problems of having been inspired to oppose evils by the moralism of his faith and his having been handicapped by his Quaker tradition of quietism and dislike for controversy. His abandonment of quietism in favor of political action dismayed his Quaker family and associates, and his campaign to end aristocratic control brought against him a storm of denunciation from the establishment. Nevertheless, he won such public support that he became the first religious Dissident ever to hold a position in the Cabinet. And what he fought for generally came to pass.

His greatest single asset was his oratorical power. In Trevelyan's judgment, his public speeches were "his one form of perfect achievement . . . his one great political weapon."[20] In Ausubel's terms, "Bright started out as an angry young man. But his distinction was that he lived to become both an angry middle-aged man and an angry old man. What sustained his anger was his sense of the slowness of the change from the old social order to what he regarded as a wholesome modern society."[21] He rejoiced in the Reform Bill of 1832 (which was adopted before his entry into politics) while fighting for still further extensions of the suffrage; and he staunchly supported the repeal of the Corn Law. He denounced England's drive for empire and demanded that it cease trying to be "knight-errant of the human race." If Great Britain had merely minded its own business, he declared: "This country might have been a garden, every dwelling might have been of marble, and every person who treads its soil might have been sufficiently educated."[22]

In using his "great weapon," he spoke with "plain simplicity . . . His voice had a bell-like clearness. . . . The sound of it was music and poetry. He was singular among orators for his absence of gesture; there he stood foursquare, and sometimes half raised his arm. His oncoming was the surge of the full swollen tide, not of the sea in storm; he awed his listeners by the calm of his passion, a terrible steed restrained by a yet stronger hand. . . . He flattered no one, great or small, man or woman, in politics or in private life."[23] "Making masterly speeches" was "his chief contribution," as Ausubel too agreed. "One of the most vital roles he played was that of morale-lifter."[24] Bright's own view of his role was explored in a letter he wrote in 1842 to his mother-in-law: "seeing that I have some power, very feeble when compared with that of some others . . . I should feel myself guilty, as possessing abundance and leaving others to hunger, nakedness and immorality and deepest ignorance and crime, if I were to retire into domestic quiet and leave the struggle to be carried on entirely by others."[25]

Bright was born on 16 November 1811 and died on 27 March 1889. His early years were devoted not to politics but to his father's business. During the forty-seven years that he served in Parliament he remained firm in the moral principles he had learned at home. More than his associates, he believed in equality of rights—but not in equality of participation. Like his peers, his highest vision was that of enlightened paternalism: As he said during the campaign of 1843 that won for him a seat in Parliament:

> High and great people can take care of themselves; but the poor and de-fenceless—the men with small cottages and large families—the men who must work six days every week if they are to live in anything like comfort for a week—these men want defenders; they want men to defend their position in Parliament; they want men who will protest against any infringement of their rights.[26]

It was only after the death of his first wife that Bright shook off the insistence of his Quaker faith on standing aside from controversy. His first speeches were in Quaker meetings and were directed against the Corn Law. The effect was described by one of the members:

> The presence of John Bright at gatherings of the Friends in those days was not always a source of unmitigated gratification. What had they done? those gentle, soft-voiced people, who never imputed a motive, passed a hasty judgment, or made a rash promise, . . . who were above all peace-makers—that from their midst should come a young man whose words smote like sledge-hammers; who . . . was always quite sure that he was in the right; who set himself in opposition to the prejudices of whole classes of English people.[27]

Like Cobden, Bright was an "outsider" amidst the aristocrats who governed. As much as twenty-three years after his entry in Parliament and after he had become one of the most noted statesmen of England, the aristocrats were shocked that Lord Russell actually invited him to dinner in his home. But by them Bright was never overawed. As he wrote to his sister concerning his advent into the House of Commons, "The great ones of the earth are not very great after all. I felt as if I knew all about them, their schemes, their capacities and all."[28] His Quakerism sustained him to trust in his own inner strength.

After the repeal of the Corn Law, Bright turned his attention to the deplorable conditions of Ireland and then to England's meddlesome interference in foreign affairs. He scorned to associate himself with either party, despising the Whigs and the Tories alike. As a product of the new industrialism and in general an advocate of laissez-faire, he fought against the Factory Act on the ground that the poor needed to work long hours to earn more pay. Disliking the aristocrats in Parliament, he spoke often in public meetings. After a decade of ceaseless agitation his health broke and he was forced to retire. But in 1858 he returned to his seat in Parliament with his zeal unconstrained. When the Civil War broke out in America, he supported the North against the feelings of his own constituents, who depended upon cheap cotton from the South. On this theme he made some fourteen speeches, of which the one he gave at Rochdale on 4 December 1861 is representative. During his latter years he continued his fight in Parliament for Quaker principles of brotherhood and mercy, including an attack on 3 May 1864 against capital punishment. These speeches well illustrate the nature of his rhetorical skills and his mode of employing them.

On the topics he chose to discuss, Bright made sure that he was well informed; and one of his rhetorical methods was to assure his listeners that his own knowledge and understanding surpassed theirs. In the introduction to his Rochdale speech in 1861, for example, he commented that, "I always find that the subjects for discussion appear to be infinite, and far more than it is possible to treat."[29] Like Lord Brougham, he crowded his speeches with precise factual data drawn from multiple sources to make manifest his depth of preparation and mastery of the problem he was discussing. In his speech denouncing capital punishment, for example, he cited the experiences of many nations and the opinions of many highly respected authorities before ending with a Quaker-like appeal to the consciences of his hearers (which also was one of his customary rhetorical methods):

> I should be glad indeed if it might be said of this Parliament at some future time, that it had dared to act upon the true lessons, and not upon the—what shall I say?—the superstitions of the past; and that this Parliament might be declared to be the Parliament which destroyed the scaffold and the gallows in order that it might teach the people that human life is sacred, and that on that principle alone can human life be secured.[30]

In addition to making clear the superiority of his own understanding and the moral basis for his judgment, Bright always spoke with a plain simplicity and restraint that indicated his intention of convincing his listeners with facts rather than overwhelming their intellects with emotionalism. In consonance with this rhetorical mode, he interlarded his speeches with frequent assurances that what he was saying was neither more nor less than his listeners knew from their own experience, with such comments as "you recollect, many of you," "You know perfectly well," ".Well we know," "I have no doubt you have seen" and "Therefore, you will see at once."

Yet another of his devices was to ask his listeners to have in mind what posterity would say about their decision. This was illustrated not only in the conclusion just quoted from his 1864 speech but also in his closing remarks in the 1861 appeal that England support the North in the American Civil War:

> When that time comes I pray that it may not be said among them [the future generations of Americans] that in the darkest hours of their country's trials England, the land of their fathers, looked on with icy coldness, and saw unmoved the perils and the calamities of her children.[31]

Further, he insisted ever so gently that from the depth of his own knowledge he was sifting out for his audience what was most essential for them to know. Typical is his comment in a speech favoring further electoral reform, delivered to a meeting of citizens in Birmingham on 27 October 1858 just after an improvement in his health made possible his return to the platform: "I will not trouble you with a heap of statistics which you cannot remember, but will give you as a proof one or two cases."[32]

As Trevelyan properly said, Bright's speaking was like "the surge of the swollen tide," not marked by great outbursts of emotion at intervals but gradually gathering irresistible force from accumlated evidence and from a depth of quiet but deeply felt moral conviction. In a speech to the Commons on 27 April 1860 for example, on one of his favorite topics, the necessity of religious toleration, and in asking for parliamentary action to end the general tax for support of the Church of England, he concluded: "I ask the House to consider whether it not be to the advantage of the Church, of morality, religion, and the public peace, that it should now be set at rest once and forever."[33]

Saint or monster? A review of Bright's more than half a century of public leadership shows him to have stood courageously against class privileges, thereby enraging those who enjoyed power, and always in favor of peace, justice, and protection of the rights of the helpless mass of the people. He was sufficiently honored in his own day along with being mercilessly attacked; and he is well remembered as a kindly and determined man who did much to assist in the transition to the new era in which government came to be viewed as an instrument for the well-being of all. He was buried not in Westminster Abbey but in the quiet cemetery of his home town. In reviewing his own life, he was content to think of accomplishments that were unsensational but fundamental: "The children are better fed, and their education is more complete."[34]

"A Whirlwind of Ideas and Emotions"

One more powerful speaker whose role was important in the great transition was Thomas Babington Macaulay—a brilliant rhetorician who along with his great peers had at least (and only) a partial understanding of what had to be done to deal with the urgency of the problems of his time.

Born in 1800 as the son of Zachary Macaulay, who hated slavery from the bottom of his soul, young Macaulay was reared as a Church of England Evangelical. He was an infant prodigy, spouting Latin at the age of four, who at the age of eight wrote a universal history of the world. At Cambridge he won the highest awards for poetry, was a charming and indefatigible conversationalist, and developed high skill in debate. When he entered Parliament in 1830, his first speech was a demand for an end to restrictions against the Jews, marked by a "whirlwind of ideas and emotions" that "held every listener on tiptoe."[35] Like Brougham and Bright, his mind was astonishingly inclusive and his energy was inexhaustible. Above all his contemporaries in public life, he was an optimist who believed passionately in the need for and the possibility of social improvement.

His fame and his influence stemmed from his poetry, his speeches in Parliament, his essays, and his remarkably popular *History of England*, which was a celebration of the virtues of Whiggery during the forty years after the accession of King James II. The most famous part of this history, chapter 3, ends with a ringing declaration of his abiding faith:

> It is now the fashion to place the golden age of England in the times when noblemen were destitute of comforts, the want of which would be intolerable to a modern footman; when farmers and shopkeepers breakfasted on loaves, the very sight of which would raise a riot in a modern workhouse; when to have a clean shirt once a week was a privilege reserved for the higher class of gentry; when men died faster in the purest country air than they now die in the pestilential lanes of our towns. . . . It may well be, in the twentieth century . . . that labouring men may be as little used to dine without meat as they now are to eat rye bread; . . . that numerous comforts and luxuries which are now unknown or confined to a few may be within the reach of every diligent and thrifty working man.

Progress, he believed, was not only attainable; it was to be brought about by government, for government alone could avail. But in the speech he made in the House of Commons on 2 March 1831 in support of the Reform Bill—generally accounted the equal of Brougham's as a vote-winner—he showed the limits of the Whig vision. In accord with the strategy directed by Lord Grey, he represented the proposed bill as being fundamentally conservative. His theme was, *Reform, that you may preserve.* "Now, therefore," he told the members, "while everything at home and abroad forebodes ruin to those who persist in a hopeless struggle against the spirit of the age, . . . now, while the heart of England is still sound, now, while old feelings and old associations retain a power and a charm which may soon pass away, . . . take counsel, not of prejudice, not of party spirit, not of ignominious pride of a fatal consistency, but of history, of reason, of the ages which are past, of the signs of this most portentous time."[36]

If his persuasive strategy was that counselled by Lord Grey, his eloquence supplied a driving force of emotionalism equal to that of Brougham. Unlike

Brougham, however, Macaulay identified himself with his listeners, even while he exhorted them to support the reform basically in their own behalf:

> Renew the youth of the state. Save property, divided against itself. Save the multitude, endangered by its own unpopular power. Save the greatest, and fairest, and most highly civilized community that ever existed, from calamities which may in a few days sweep away all the rich heritage of so many ages of wisdom and glory.
>
> The danger is terrible. The time is short. If this bill should be rejected, I pray to God that none of those who concur in rejecting it may ever remember their votes with unavailing remorse, amidst the wreck of laws, the confusion of ranks, the spoliation of property, and the dissolution of social order!

He did not argue for democracy; this was not envisioned by his optimistic preview of the future. On the contrary, "My firm conviction is that, in our country, universal suffrage is incompatible, not with this or that form of Government, but with all forms of Government, and with everything for the sake of which forms of Government exist; that it is incompatible with property and that it is consequently incompatible with civilization."

Even sixteen years later, in 1857, just two years before his death, he was still warning of what dire evils would result if democracy should triumph: "Either the poor will plunder the rich and civilization would perish; or order and prosperity would be saved by a strong military government, and liberty would perish!"[37] As is illustrated in the military totalitarianism that came in the twentieth century to Germany, Italy, Japan, and many smaller countries, even in this judgment he proved to have substantial discernment.

But, if not democracy, what was the best course for England to pursue? Like most of his best contemporaries, what Macaulay advocated was paternalism: that the rich and the powerful should care for the poor and the weak. It was on this hope that his optimism was based. While the Luddites were wrathfully destroying machinery in Nottinghamshire in 1811–16 during Macaulay's youth, he saw the folly of trying to reverse the growth of technology. But his abiding faith in progress enabled him to avoid the pessimism that beset such other prophets of change as Carlyle and Ruskin, William Morris, and Matthew Arnold, and the general leadership of the government. What he failed to perceive was that the governmental goal of preserving property was inconsistent with its broader duty to preserve the dignity and rights of individuals. His humanitarianism stretched as far as it could go; but it did not go far enough. Hence he remained a partial prophet. Liberty he staunchly defended; but equality he did not trust. In this cardinal respect, his rhetorical goal was derived less from the future than from the past. His great eloquence was devoted, like that of his peers, to amelioration rather than to fundamental change.

The major rhetorical achievements of this mid-period—between the adoption of the Reform Bill of 1832 and the new reforms yet to be enacted in 1867—were momentous, considering the weight of tradition and custom that had to be overcome. They included the enfranchisement of the middle classes, improvements for factory laborers, a vital shift of taxation from the poor to the well-to-do, and improved welfare support for the poor. In the international sphere, the major speakers, Robert Owen, Richard Cobden, and John Bright, launched a prolonged and solidly sustained educational campaign, aiming to teach the public and the government alike that to meddle with the internal affairs of other nations is dangerous and counterproductive; that empire-building ought to be curbed by ethical principles; and that the maintenance of international peace requires not only good will but also such practical matters as free trade and the free flow of communication. What they did not accomplish and what only Owen envisioned was the uprooting of the entrenched hierarchal nature of the society. That was the challenge left to be met by the next generation, which gradually and uncertainly came to hold and to champion egalitarian views.

4

UNCERTAIN RHETORIC:
WHAT TO DO ABOUT IRELAND AND THE COLONIES?

A difficult problem to be dealt with in the age of transition was: What to do about the colonies? And, most pressingly, what to do about Ireland?

These relationships were plagued by issues of the sort that precipitate wars. Bitter feelings were as explosive as is usual on the eve of war. The possibility of reaching reasonable agreements through rational compromise appeared to be remote. Nevertheless, these issues were talked out rather than fought out. The Irish leader Daniel O'Connell restrained his followers, who were eager for rebellion, by assuring them that to fight is less wise than to discuss. And this was the view that prevailed.

Meanwhile, colonial problems were blotting out the enthusiasm for empire that had reached its heights in the triumphs in Canada and India during the time of Lord Chatham. Profits brought home from overseas possessions were proving to be both smaller and harder to get than those that could be won in fair competition in what was coming to be called "the empire of free trade." Moreover, colonialism itself was falling into disrepute.

The moral feelings of the English were being ravaged by reports of harsh measures used to restrain revolutions in India and by a war waged against the Chinese to force them to buy English opium. Canada was ruinously mired in debt from building the two longest railways in the world through largely uninhabited areas. It was also split apart by cultural, linguistic, and religious animosities. It was abuzz with annoying border threats and even invasions from its much stronger southern neighbor. The disillusionment with empire was well indicated by Benjamin Disraeli when he said: "It can never be our policy to defend the Canadian frontier against the United States. What is the use of colonial deadweights which we do not govern?"[1]

The leaders who used rhetoric as their instrument for dealing with Ireland and the overseas possessions included such sober statesmen as Palmerston and Gladstone, the sparkling Disraeli, an erratic demagogue known as "Radical Jack" Durham, and two enigmatic Irishmen, O'Connell and Charles Stewart Parnell. Gladstone and Disraeli will be discussed in a later chapter. What all these leaders shared was their determination to solve the colonial issues through persuasion rather than by force. Basic (if only partial) reforms were initiated—and revolu-

tion was avoided. The personalities and the rhetorical strategies of these speakers were reflective of the changing character of their time. Tradition was giving
way to innovation. It was a transition that they helped to guide.

"Mediation—the Most Difficult of Rhetorical Goals"

Irish-English relations were mired in a bitterness that had brewed for centuries. The feelings on both sides are portrayed in a quotation from the young
Disraeli published in the 18 April 1836 issue of the London *Times:*

> They hate our order, our civilization, our enterprising industry, our sustained
> courage, our decorous liberty, our pure religion. This wild, reckless, insolent,
> and superstitious race have no sympathy with the English character. Their fair
> ideal of human felicity is an alternation of clannish broils and coarse idolatry.
> Their history describes an unbroken circle of bigotry and hatred. . . . My
> Lords, shall the delegates of these tribes, under the direction of the Roman
> priesthood, ride roughshod over our country—over England—haughty and
> imperial England?

The Irish had neither the ability nor the intention of trying to dominate
England. What they did want was to escape from conditions of exploitation so
dire as to cause even so doughty an imperialist as Winston Churchill to look
back at them as "The greatest failure of British Government."[2] Some basic
reforms were accomplished at the close of the eighteenth century. But the vast
Catholic majority in Ireland was excluded not only from political office but also
from advanced schools; farm rental charges were impossibly exhorbitant; Irish
commerce was strangled by English domination; underemployment was endemic
across Ireland; hunger to the verge of starvation was recurrent; and the Act of
Union of 1801 dismally failed to produce the domestic self-rule that it professed.

These were problems that Daniel O'Connell sought to solve—not through
rebellion but through discussion. To the distraught and angry people of Ireland
his message was: "As long as truth and justice should be supposed to influence
man; as long as man is admitted to be under the control of reason; so long must
it be prudent and wise to procure discussions on the sufferings and rights of the
people of Ireland." And to the English his appeal was to their moral sentiments,
reminding them sternly that, "England alone, of all the states pretending to be
free, leaves shackles upon the human mind."[3] As O'Connell viewed the circumstances in 1814 with the long Napoleonic Wars nearing an end, he confidently
gave his Irish followers an optimistic assessment of "our present prospect of
success":

> First, man is elevated from slavery everywhere, and human nature has become
> more dignified and, I may say, more valuable. Secondly, England wants our

cordial support, and knows that she has only to concede to us justice in order to obtain our affectionate assistance. Thirdly, this is the season of successful petition, and the very fashion of the times entitles our petition to succeed. Fourthly, the Catholic cause is disencumbered of hollow friends and interested speculators. Add to all these the native and inherent strength of the principle of religious freedom, and the inert and accumulating weight of our wealth, our religion, and our numbers, and where is the sluggard who shall doubt our approaching success?

The favorable factors that O'Connell cited were real; but there were others that he failed to include in his optimistic assessment. Among them were the profits received by absentee English landowners of large Irish estates; the fact that from "time immemorial" many English aristocrats lived on their Irish incomes and owed their status to their extensive Irish holdings. He neglected to mention that the close geographical proximity of the two islands made it difficult for England to risk allowing the Irish to be independent. Nor did he speak of the combination of English contempt for presumed Irish inferiority and Irish hatred nurtured by centuries of oppression. In O'Connell's time, following the reforms won by Curran, and Grattan, and Pitt, leaders in both islands expected a relaxation of the long standing mutual bitterness. But for the Irish masses conditions were not better but worse: conditions of poverty to the verge of starvation aggravated by increasing population and a succession of poor harvest years. O'Connell felt deep sympathy for the sufferings of the peasantry, was well aware of the frustration that was breeding a reckless spirit of armed revolt, and sought to play the role of mediator.

Mediation is precisely the most difficult of rhetorical goals. Rhetoric requires a clear definition of purpose, the organized presentation of evidence adequate to support it, and the arousal of strong feelings to impel acceptance of the speaker's goal. The qualifications and ambiguities of a median position between two opposing choices lead to confusion and uncertainty rather than to united action. This was the rhetorical circumstance with which O'Connell had to deal.

What O'Connell sought to accomplish was to harmonize two incompatible processes: to unify and to intensify Irish resentment and demand for reforms while also holding these feelings in check and appealing for settlement of these problems through rational discussion. Because of this intermingling of contrary messages, the responses he got consisted of both admiration and hatred from both sides. The English condemned his arousal of Irish unrest while appreciating his call for patience. The Irish hailed his championship of reform and denunciations of English injustice but were puzzled and angered by his conciliatory avoidance of confrontation.

Interesting and suggestive parallels may be drawn between the rhetorical strategies of O'Connell and those employed by Mahatma Gandhi in India more than a century later. Both denounced abuses, demanded self-rule, and refused cooperation; both renounced force and appealed to the English moral sense and self-interest as the means of redressing similar evils. Their results as well as their methods were also similar. Gandhi's followers got out of his control and engaged in such widespread violence that for several years he withdrew from pursuit of his mission; and afterward he was killed by one of his own disappointed followers. O'Connell was not assassinated, but he was deserted and denounced by those whom he sought to lead as well as by leaders on both sides.

He was also praised, even extravagantly, especially after his death. Gladstone, attempting to use O'Connell's repute to support his own program for limited home rule for Ireland, called him "the greatest popular leader the world has ever seen." Echoing this phrase, the Irish-American historian Claude Bowers praised O'Connell's eloquence as "one of the most marvellous the world has known . . . with its power of appeal that no other leader had ever possessed."[4] A later enthusiast, Seàn O'Faolàin, called him "the greatest of all Irish realists, who knew that if he could but once define he would thereby create."[5] Arguing that O'Connell defined the only feasible policy for his time, O'Faolàin concluded that, "He left his successors nothing to do but to follow him."[6] He should have added, "partially," and with "significant exceptions." O'Connell was never as successful as he sought to be nor as much as the situation demanded. To a degree this was because of his own limitations.

The Anglo-Irish William Lecky was puzzled by the paradox of contradictory reactions to O'Connell. Admitting to his own "difficulty of painting the character of O'Connell with fairness and impartiality," he cited as the reason that no "public man of his time was the object of so much extravagant praise and blame."[7] Lord Melbourne had no such doubts. He branded O'Connell as "a braggart and bully, whose word was worth nothing, and whose objective was to make good government impossible." But he also confessed that O'Connell's influence was too great for him to be ignored.[8] More explicitly, the diarist Charles Greville, an astute observer of the political scene, judged that, "His violence, bad taste, and scurrility have made him 'lose the lustre of his former praise'"; but he also noted that "he must be conciliated" and that "but for him the Catholic question would never have been carried."[9]

Examination of O'Connell's speeches eliminates any puzzlement about the diversity of reactions toward him. The sincerity of his patriotism was supported by an overpowering eloquence. But despite being a very good lawyer, O'Connell was habitually careless in his use of facts. Especially in his stump speeches he magnified his theme by simply sweeping aside objections and by distorting or even fabricating evidence. He was Irish to the core: impetuous in manner, clear in purpose, careless of detail.

O'Connell's influence derived from the two factors upon which leadership depends: he truly represented the people while greatly transcending them in ability. He was born on 6 August 1775 into the middle class, the son of a small landholder. While he was a youth in school, the government (in 1792) granted to Catholics the right to practice law and O'Connell became a lawyer. His superiority of intellect and eloquence in courtroom pleading brought him both wealth and fame. In 1813 he made the crucial decision to become a political activist.

The purpose O'Connell sought to achieve was to bring the power of public opinion both in Ireland and in England to bear upon the government with strength sufficient to force reforms that would allow the Irish to live free and to live well. The three goals he had specifically in mind were: repeal of the Act of Union to permit the Irish to govern themselves in their domestic concerns; repeal of the legal restrictions against Catholics; and reform of the ruinous land rental system. His first and most immediate aim was to unify the Irish people; and the second and also indispensable one was to appeal to the moral sensibilities of the English. Each goal was difficult enough in itself; since in crucial ways they were antagonistic to one another, how to reconcile them posed a rhetorical dilemma.

Disunity among the Irish derived in part from a long history of bitter rivalry among the clans. In even larger part it was caused by the impoverishment of the peasantry. Since farm plots were both essential to survival and inadequate in number, the desperate peasants viewed one another as competitors and allowed the landlords to impose larger and larger rental charges. As the rents increased and living conditions worsened, the competition to get land became increasingly fierce. It was a self-perpetuating endless circle of misery. To reverse the trend, O'Connell realized that he must arouse a hatred of English exploiters sufficiently strong to submerge the rivalry among Irish individuals and communities. The first step in the solution he devised was the organization of the nationwide Catholic Association in 1814. The dues he set for membership were so low, just a penny a month, that all could afford to join. His next step was to initiate the holding of mass meetings, sponsored by the association, which he and his lieutenants addressed. What the speeches aimed for was to induce the listeners to turn from distrust of one another by directing their hatred against English injustices.

In his speeches to these mass audiences, O'Connell displayed a self-assurance so marked that it approached arrogance. He sounded not like a lawyer marshalling evidence to prove a case but like a prophet announcing truth. This role would have been easier to maintain had his vision of truth not been two-sided: condemnation mingled with conciliation. To build the force of a favorable public opinion, O'Connell realized, he must not only arouse resentment (to unify the Irish) but also divert it from armed rebellion and hold it in check (in order to win sympathetic support among the English). How could he do both at once? A student of O'Connell's rhetoric cited as typical of the solution he devised the following appeal he made to his Irish listeners: "not to violate the peace—not to be guilty of the slightest outrage—not to give the enemy powers by committing a crime, but peacefully and manfully to stand together in the open day—to protest before man, and in the presence of God, against the iniquity of continuing the

Union."[11] In essence this was indeed O'Connell's central theme. But it represents only one aspect of his rhetoric. He wooed one segment (the Irish) of the broad audience he needed to reach while antagonizing the other (the English) with such statements as the following, taken from his most famous speech, the one at Tara: "I have no higher affection for England than for France; they are both foreign authorities to me"; and "Torture, flogging, pitch caps, and imprisonment were the congenial agencies whereby England endeavored to carry her infamous designs."

The most critical act in O'Connell's career was his decision in 1828 to stand for election to Parliament from County Clare. Catholics were forbidden to hold office, but with his lawyerly acumen O'Connell noted that the law did not specifically forbid them to stand as candidates. His Catholic Association brought sufficient voters to the polls to win the election for him; and the British Government recognized that the election created a new situation. As Prime Minister Wellington and Home Secretary Peel agreed, "The excitement among Irish catholics after their victory was so intense that there was no telling what else might happen."[11] They introduced a Catholic Emancipation Bill in Parliament, which became law on 13 April 1829 thereby making it possible for O'Connell to take his seat in the House of Commons. He had found a right method for bringing public opinion into such focus that it had to prevail.

The rhetorical campaign that O'Connell conducted ran through all the years from 1813 until his imprisonment for treason in 1844. The most sensational of his speeches, which well illustrates his diverse methods, was given at Tara, the seat of the ancient Irish monarchy, on 15 August 1843.[12]

The purpose of his speech was to renounce the Act of Union, which professed to grant "equality" to the Irish by enlarging their representation in the English Parliament, but which also reduced their own Irish Parliament to a minor body debating local concerns.

The crowd that assembled at O'Connell's call was immense. According to the London *Times,* it was a full million. As O'Faolàin described it: "All night long the crowds poured across the plains, camped on the hillsides, slept under the hedges; and when dawn lit the countryside there was not a road around but was black with trudging men." The setting was grandly impressive. A huge platform had been erected on the top of a small central hill. On this platform O'Connell stood surrounded by a "thousand" dignitaries. The massive audience stretched around him on all sides as far as his eye could see.

Of course most of them could not hear his words. But they could see him, as his commanding presence swayed with emotional intensity. Highlights of the speech O'Connell presented in rhythmic phrases that were chanted as a refrain, like the words in a Greek chorus, by listeners close to the platform and then reverberated in waves of repetition that rolled back through the crowd.

He began by asserting that it would be "drivelling folly, if I were not to feel the awful responsibility of the part I have taken in this majestic movement." He referred then to "the historical importance of the spot on which we stand." This he followed with the statement of his theme: "to protest in the face of my country, in the face of my Creator—in the face of Ireland and her God, I protest against the continuance of the unfounded and unjust Union."

The union had been imposed upon Ireland, he went on, "not only by physical force, but by bribery the most unblushing and corruption the most profligate." In contrast, the Irish conduct had been exemplary. "Had it been a fair bargain, the Irish would have continued faithful to the last, regardless of the injuries which it might have entailed upon them—for the Irish people have been invariably true to their contracts; whereas England never yet made a promise which she did not violate, nor ever entered into a contract which she did not shamelessly and scandalously outrage." On the grounds that the Union had been procured by deception and that its presumed benefits were "a living lie to Ireland," he declared, "I proclaim, in the name of the Irish nation, that it is null and void."

His rhetorical question, "Are you and I a bit more Englishmen now than we were twenty or forty years ago?" aroused jeers, cheers, and laughter. He rushed on to magnify his denunciation, pronouncing that "no nation on the face of the earth ever committed so much of injustice, fraud, and iniquity, as England." The "financial robbery" of Irish farmers he described as "iniquitous, fiendish, and harsh."

From his extremity of denunciation he built a bridge of humor that brought gales of laughter, over which he crossed to conciliation, praising "the brave, the gallant, and the good-conducted soldiers that compose the Queen's Army." But he added that, "if they made war upon us," the Irish would "furnish enough women to beat the entire of the Queen's force." Fortunately, however, he concluded, war was not to be expected. England would withdraw from Ireland rather than fight to maintain control over it, for "it is idle to imagine that any statesman ever existed who would resist the cry that Ireland makes for justice."

The speech well illustrates the juxtaposition of violent and of conciliatory language that confused his immediate hearers as well as more distant observers, critics, and historians. His vigor in denunciation was followed by an appeal for patience: "We will break no law." He assured his emotionally aroused listeners that "though they have force sufficient to carry any battle that ever was fought, they [will] separate with the tranquillity of schoolboys breaking up in the afternoon." As the crowd realized that his climax was actually the anticlimax of asking for restraint and more patience, there arose murmurs and cries of dissent. To these O'Connell responded with his closing words: "I wish you could read my heart, to see how deeply the love of Ireland is engraven upon it, and let the people of Ireland, who stood by me so long, stand by me a little longer, and Ireland shall be a nation again."

Judged by artistic standards, the speech was weak in organization, marred by misstatements of fact, exaggerated charges, and confusion in its theme. In his opening words O'Connell warned that "I am not here for the purpose of making anything like a schoolboy's attempt at declamatory eloquence." What he did aim to accomplish was the difficult goal of arousing such an emotional intensity as would convince the English of Irish determination while, concurrently, holding Irish resentment in check. This rhetorical goal was admirable but too subtle to admit of accomplishment. The English reaction is illustrated in Charles Greville's comment to Queen Victoria that O'Connell's speech was indeed "violent and factious," but that it would be injudicious to bring him to the bar of justice.[13] This advice she did not take; O'Connell was brought to trial for treason and Ireland was swept by disorder. "In the end, order was restored by force; . . . and famine came to rob the Irish of capacity to accomplish much save ward off death."[14]

This climax did not come however for another year, when O'Connell called for another gigantic assembly to demand reform of the land tenantry system under the pressure of a tragic potato famine.

The lot of the Irish peasantry even in the "good years" was, in the words of the English historian Wingfield-Stratford, "hopeless beyond belief." Land rentals were high, sometimes even more than the total year's harvest. There was not good land enough to go around. When a farmer ventured to improve his plot by irrigation, fertilization, or rotation of crops, he was charged a higher rent for it. A major problem was that the Irish planted little except potatoes, since that was their most nutritious available food, and potatoes are peculiarly liable to plant disease and insect damage. It was against these combined evils that O'Connell proposed another major protest. Irish historians have blamed the "falsity" of his "basic assumption"—namely, that "the peaceable combination of a people" would by itself prevail to induce reforms.[15] O'Connell's leadership was handicapped by his realism, his reasonableness, or his caution—whichever term seems most appropriate. Probably all of them were his guides for judgment. To his desperate Irish countrymen they were lumped together as sheer timidity.

To the English government, O'Connell's demands and incitements appeared to be a compound of bluff and bluster. The ministry commanded him to call off his proposed monster assembly—and he did so. Wingfield-Stratford summed up the circumstances fairly: "O'Connell had used the most violent language and plainly threatened to meet force with force, but he was really bluffing, and this time it was evident that his bluff would be called. Ireland was in no state to withstand the wealth and manpower of Britain, and O'Connell was never more a patriot than when he decided to draw back and save his countrymen. . . ."[16] The issue was postponed until a later generation when new leaders under new conditions again confronted it.

"Public Opinion Properly Mobilized"

The "new conditions" were a complex of contradictions that no leader proved capable of synthesizing into a clear pattern. The one who came nearest to doing so was John Henry Temple, Lord Palmerston, an Irishman of a Celtic temperament, the scion of a wealthy and prestigious family, whose ability to clarify and to imprint his own definition of circumstances made him the dominant figure in English politics during the middle years of the century. He was loved by the middle classes, who called him "Old Pam" and trusted him to keep English trade prospering. He won the hearty dislike of Queen Victoria and her Consort Albert and the active enmity of many of their aristocratic associates. And he kept himself in power largely through his skill in persuasive speech.

Following the Reform Bill of 1832, the coming to the throne in 1836 of the well liked girl Queen Victoria, and strengthened by a succession of able administrators as prime ministers, England achieved a stablility and prosperity (except for the lower classes) that brought the small island nation unrivalled worldwide prestige. Its merchant marine amounted in 1850 to some 60 percent of the world's tonnage. The English pound was universally accepted as the soundest monetary standard. And English interests controlled at least one third of the world's trade.

The situation in Europe presented particularly difficult challenges to English leadership. The Peace of Vienna, engineered by Metternich, allied England with such autocracies as Austria and Russia, while her sympathies were attracted by the new liberalism that had commenced in France in 1830 and that was exemplified in the central Euopean revolutions of 1848–49. Formulation of any clear and consistent foreign policy was virtually impossible. Palmerston was by far more successful than his rivals in shifting nimbly from one stance to another while explaining the tangled skein as an exercise in reasonableness.

In his early life he showed litle brilliance or promise. His education in Edinburgh and Cambridge universities was undistinguished. In his bid to enter public life he was defeated in three elections before winning his seat in the Commons in 1807 at the age of twenty-three. There his maiden speech in defense of the policies of George Canning was well received. It was a decade, however, before he found a place for himself. He made a series of ineffective and unappealing speeches on behalf of Wellington's Tories before he finally switched in 1826 to the Whigs. In a speech to the Commons he explained that he was leaving "the stupid old Tory party" because "on the Catholic question; on the principles of commerce; on the corn laws; . . . on colonial slavery; . . . on all these questions and everything like them, the [Tory] Government find support from the Whigs and resistance from their self-denominated friends."[17]

During the next two-and-a-half decades Palmerston served several terms as foreign minister. His clarity of mind and his personal courage in asserting and defending shifts of policy won him notoriety and general public approval. But his lack of tact in dealing with his political associates and opponents and with the Queen built a body of opposition that in 1850 threatened to bring his career to an abrupt end. The immediate issue was Palmerston's support for Prussia and Austria, in which he was opposed by Queen Victoria and by such influential Parliamentarians as Peel, Disraeli, and Gladstone. Lord Russell, the prime minister, wanted to keep him but felt impelled to let him go.

Palmerston saved himself with a masterful speech that commenced about 10 P.M. in the Commons on 25 June 1850 and continued for four hours until 2 A.M. At its conclusion, as his biographer Herbert Bell describes the scene, "The House found itself cheering until it seemed that the cheering would never stop. . . . It would be difficult to exaggerate the effectiveness or the effects of this amazing speech." He tells how it happened:

> The very acme of political drama was reached when, a little before ten o'clock on the evening of June 25, Palmerston, the most feared, the most hated, and the most admired statesman of Europe, rose before the world's greatest court to plead for his political life. A crowded House watched him tensely as he stood, with half a sheet of paper, jotted with headings, in his hand. Were they to hear new levities and impertinences, new accusations and defiances, flung recklessly at adversaries in England or abroad? They heard nothing of the sort. Instead, they listened to a calm and reasoned defense of all his foreign policy from the time of Canning's death, . . . to a flow of facts perfectly marshalled and arranged, punctuated by explanations and justifications of his principles.

The kind of "justifications" he presented may be illustrated by his defense of harshness in dealing with colonials in Africa and the Orient:

> These half-civilized governments all require a dressing every eight or ten years to keep them in order. Their minds are too shallow to receive an impression that will last longer than some such period and warning is of little use. They care little for words, and they must not only see the stick but actually feel it on their shoulders before they yield to that only argument which brings conviction, the *argumentum baculinem.*

Lord Clarendon, who heard the speech and commented on it, "marvelled at the exhibition of 'physical and mental power almost incredible in a man of his age.'" As for the effect resulting from the speech, Bell also quoted Lord Clarendon's further judgment—that "It will place him on a pinnacle of popularity at home, whatever it may do abroad, and completely settle the question about which I never had a doubt, that no change at the F. O. is possible, and that Lord John must either go *on* with him or go *out* with him."[18]

During the remainder of his life until he died on 18 October 1865, Palmerston conducted a continuing and successful battle defending the constitutional principle of the supremacy of the Parliament over the throne. Queen Victoria was determined that she would be the shaper of foreign policy. On this great issue, Palmerston prevailed—and he did so primarily because of his rhetorical skills. He was particularly attentive to newspaper reporters, who helped him to maintain the confidence and support of the public. Bell describes his relations with the newsmen as follows:

> His affability and genuine kindness warmed their hearts; his playfulness in telling amusing anecdotes, even when times were critical, brightened up

tedious and anxious hours. Best of all, he filled the reporter's greatest need, the need for accurate and early news. Men believed, at least, that he timed his speeches with reference to the hours when the great dailies went to press; and, when such timing was impossible, provided outlines which could be embellished in his well-known style. [19]

On the basic issues concerning the development of democracy, Palmerston's positions were mixed. He detested slavery and did much to end the trade in slaves. Concerning the domestic "factory slavery," he stood inflexibly with the laissez-faire principle of leaving the problem to be solved by the competition between capital and labor; accordingly, he detested and opposed Chartism. He also stood stoutly against further enlargement of the franchise. On the question of reforming the land tenure system in Ireland, his epigrammatic dismissal of reform was in the form of a widely quoted quip: "Tenant right is landlord wrong."[20] His conviction was that the best solution for Ireland was for its surplus population to emigrate to America, after which rental charges would naturally decline, since competition for rental properties would subside. The real issue, he thought, was religious: "The fact is that the Catholic priests see that their fees and endowments are dwindling with the decrease of the population . . . and their object is . . . to transfer the lands in Ireland from Protestant landlords to Catholic middle-class men, and thus to lay the groundwork for abolishing the Protestant Church and setting up the Catholic Church in its stead."[21] On these basic issues, as Bell concluded, "he was still a child of the early nineteenth century."[22]

Still, although opposed by the crown and by the major political leaders of his time, Palmerston held his position of predominance for reasons that Lord Russell explained to the Commons during the days of Palmerston's final illness.

He had the resolution, the resource, the promptitude, the vigor which befitted war; and, when peace arrived, he showed that he could maintain internal tranquillity, and, by extending our commercial relations, could give to the country the blessings of peace. The reason why he could do this is plain . . . his heart always beat for the honour of England.

In his biographer's final estimate:

the pre-eminence he coveted for his country was not only material, but even more, perhaps, moral. England should cast the bread of her public opinion upon continental waters, and reap the reward in the respect and affection of those peoples whom it might sustain. It has been said of him that he found the force of public opinion a great fact and made of it a great doctrine. . . . Be this as it may, there is no question as to his belief that public opinion properly mobilized, directed, and sustained, would ultimately triumph over physical force. [23]

This judgment is sustained by the most careful student of Palmerston's policies, who concluded concerning the difficult circumstances of 1848 to 1850 that

"Palmerston had long ago lost the Palace. He recently lost the premier. But he had won the public."[24] When he was buried by public insistence in Westminster Abbey, his crypt appropriately was placed close beside those of Lord Chatham, William Pitt, Castlereagh, Canning, and Wilberforce—others who like him helped to bring the great transition to pass, even though their vision of democracy like his, was less than complete.

"An Autocrat at Home and a Democrat Abroad"

The champion of reform of the colonial system as it operated in Canada was a most unlikely type of rhetorical persuader. An unfriendly but scarcely unfair historian describes him:

> Black-browed "Radical Jack" Durham, the champion of left-wing ideas in the Government, was . . . sure he was right. But he was less successful in persuading others to share his belief. The rich radical seldom carries conviction, especially if he is as fantastically rich as Durham. Justly or not, it is hard to accept, as spokesman of the poor, a man who is reported to have spent £900,000 on doing up his house. Besides, Durham's character was even more paradoxical than his political position. Independent, courageous, and with fitful gleams of political vision, he was also a theatrical, unbalanced egotist whose infirmities of temper had been developed to the highest pitch by bad-health, bad nerves, and too much money. Accustomed to indulge every changing mood, to follow every impulse, his character was a bundle of inconsistencies. He was an autocrat at home and a democrat abroad, spoiled his children and cuffed his servants, was delightful to his friends one moment and insulted them the next, gave magnificent dinner parties through which he himself sat in sullen silence, risked his reputation to serve the cause of liberty and equality at the same time as he was pulling every string he could lay hands on to get himself made an earl. As a member of the cabinet, Durham was impossible. . . . He stormed, he sulked, he made scenes, he burst into tears, he flung out of the room, he squabbled incessantly . . . . Outside the cabinet, Durham intrigued with disaffected members of his party against his own leaders and made public speeches of extreme indiscretion.[25]

This was a portrait with which there was little disagreement. Yet despite his very obvious disabilities, Durham won for himself sufficient public support so that in the ruling circle he was feared rather than ridiculed or ignored. As another student of the times points out, "Durham was the only man who could have welded radicals and liberals into a serious challenge to the Whig leadership and he was too impatient and egocentric to take advantage of his opportunities. But he was always a bugbear in the minds of the traditionalists. Palmerston urged Melbourne to come back to London: 'You ought to be looking after your stray sheep. That wolf Durham is prowling about the fold.' "[26]

Greville, who was a schoolmate of Durham and observed him closely throughout his career, thought him so careless a gossip that he should have been gagged—except that when he was appointed Ambassador to Russia his language and his conduct were very moderate. In short, he could and did adjust himself to circumstances. This was a wealthy aristocrat who won a great following among the masses by making reckless speeches to them about their rights. But few doubted his mental abilities or his patriotism. Lord Grey felt impelled to appoint him as one of the Committee of Four that drew up the Reform Bill in 1831. Afterwards, Durham had one more great opportunity for public service when he was appointed Lord Lieutenant of Canada in 1838. He remained there only four months, during which time he insulted Canadian patriots and threatened to imprison or to execute them without trial. Then, being displeased with criticism of his conduct by his Government and even more so by the lack of his accustomed luxuries, he resigned in a huff and returned home. During the homeward voyage he (or his secretary) composed an impressive Report on Canada that laid the basis for creation of the British Commonwealth. Greville, in his diary entry for 10 December 1838 describes the sequence that led to this result:

> Nothing can illustrate more strikingly the farcical nature of public meetings, and the hollowness, worthlessness and accidental character of popularity, than the circumstances of Durham's arrival here. He has done nothing in Canada, he took himself off just as the fighting was going to begin, his whole conduct has been visited with universal disapprobation, and nevertheless his progress to London has been a sort of triumph; and he has been saluted with addresses and noisy receptions at all the great towns through which he passed. . . .
>
> His speeches in reply to the addresses are most extraordinary performances, unbecoming in tone, contradictory, inconsistent, and inflated; for as to disclosures he has none to make of any sort or kind. He had the finest game to play in Canada that could be placed in his hands, for the proceedings here gave him a legitimate grievance, and would have enabled him to claim double credit for success, and exemption from any blame or discredit from failure.[27]

Greville's claim that the government was neglectful of Canada is supported by Disraeli's comment: "These wretched colonies. They are a millstone around our necks."[23] Greville's charge was that Durham's rhetorical strategy was weak. More accurately, it was faulty in significant ways but strong enough in other respects to make it effective. His *Report on the Affairs of British North America* derived more from ignorance than knowledge. As Callwood properly notes, he "had formed his judgments in the manner of those who don't stay long enough to be confused by complexities."[29] Even so, he managed to pinpoint the essential fact. "I expected to find a contest between a government and a people. I found two nations warring in the bosom of a single state; I found a struggle, not of principles, but of races."[30] His recommendation was that Canada be divided into two provinces, English and French—which, he cannily concluded, would be dominated by the more populous English. The government that he proposed should be representative, to be elected by the whole adult male population. Lord Russell, then Home Secretary, proposed a bill that granted Canada self-rule but rejected the democratic electoral base for it.

This bill was adopted. Five days afterwards, Durham died. His place in the history of British public speaking is enigmatic. His speeches were recklessly sensational; he was a poor statesman. Even so, he made a contribution that proved to be lasting; and he did it primarily by maintaining public support. His reputation in his own time equalled or surpassed that of many who must be accounted better, wiser, and abler men. But more than most of them, he won the affections of the people. When he spoke on the Glasgow Green in October 1834, a hundred thousand gathered to cheer and to hear him. More also than most, he believed in democracy, at least to the extent of extending the franchise to all who owned property. His greatest failing was his demagogic habit of exaggeration and his egocentrism that repelled many whose support he needed. Many of his contemporaries including his sharpest critics expected him to attain top leadership in the new Liberal Party—and he might well have done so had he not died unexpectedly at the age of forty-eight. Like John Wilkes of an earlier generation, his chief significance was as a symbol of discontent that made him a rallying point for public feelings. Because of his report on Canada, he merits more than a footnote in a review of rhetorical influences in English history.

"The Uncrowned King of Ireland"

If Durham seems dubious as a claimant to rhetorical fame, so too does the great Irish spokesman of the latter part of the century when home rule for Ireland was at least partially attained. Charles Stewart Parnell was in basic ways almost the antithesis of Daniel O'Connell. Parnell was a poor speaker, a poor organizer, and a scorner of conciliation, cooperation, and compromise. Yet so effective were his political efforts, and so dominant his hold on the affections of the Irish people that he came to be called "The Uncrowned King of Ireland." Considered rhetorically, he was a puzzle and a paradox.

By usual rhetorical standards he was beneath notice. He lacked both fluency and verbal artistry; neither his voice nor his manner of speaking was impressive; and he made little effort to establish rapport with his listeners. His speeches display neither a masterful array of arguments nor imagery nor a skillful organization of evidence. His style is commonplace, without pictorial embellishment and it lacks the surge of powerful emotions. Yet his strength of leadership made him outstanding among contemporaries of great eloquence; and since he remained coldly aloof from personal relations and from political maneuvering, it was from his speaking that his influence derived. More than of any other public leader, it may be said of Parnell that he was eloquent in spite of what he said and in spite of how he said it. It was for this reason that the astute John Morley, who was particularly sensitive to the rhetorical role in the shaping of history, called Parnell "unique."[31]

Seeking to unravel the riddle of Parnell's effectiveness, Morley turned for help to Gladstone, who had every reason to know well the nature of Parnell's influence in Parliament. Gladstone's reply was: "I say he is a political genius—a genius—a genius of a most uncommon order." But do you find him to be a good speaker? Morley persisted. "Indeed I do, for he has got the rarest of all qualities in a speaker—*measure*. He always says exactly as much as, and no more than, he means to say." From another member of Parliament Morley secured the opinion that Parnell's greatest virtue as a speaker was that he was "free of the evil arts of Pose . . . disdainful of playing to the gallery." Finally, Morley concluded that Parnell was "one of the two noblest orators of our day" (Gladstone being the other), because "His speeches, even when least exciting or rhetorical, were studded with incisive remarks singularly well compressed." He explained the "uniqueness" of Parnell as his "strategic insight" in urging political reform on agrarian principles, thereby sidestepping the religious, broadly economic, and traditional political fears, prejudices, and motives of his audience.

Parnell time and again belittled the political role of parliamentary speeches. During his first year in Parliament in 1875, he told his constituents: "We do not want speakers in the House of Commons, but men who will vote right."[32] In the judgment of his biographer, "The House of Commons seemed to him to be nothing better than a mere debating society, where Irishmen had an opportunity of airing their oratory, and were, apparently, satisfied when that was done."[33] Most significantly, the evidence is overwhelming that he never did develop any special ability as a public speaker. The evidence is too solid to be doubted, despite the high praise of his rhetoric by such astute judges as Morley and Gladstone.

In his childhood he had been a stammerer. His introversion and emotional self-questioning made him a lifelong sleepwalker to the extent that as an adult he had to tie one of his legs to his bed. As a college student only briefly in Cambridge, he disliked reading and never did learn even the rudiments of Irish history, let alone about the rest of the world. In his own defense, near the end of his life the best he could say about this was, "I have read very little, but I am smart, and can pick up information quickly." In his first public speech, which was to a small and sympathetic audience, "he broke down utterly. He faltered, he paused, went on, got confused, and pale with intense but subdued anxiety. . . ." He did not greatly improve as he got more experience. "From the beginning Parnell disliked speechifying. The process was absolutely painful to him." It was also painful for his audiences. "In fact, it was painful to listen to him. You would think he would break down every moment."[34] As his biographer concludes: "Talking was sometimes necessary to get things done (or to prevent their being done), and he was forced to put up with it. But he took no pleasure in oratory, and had not the least ambition to become a great public speaker."[35]

What role does he have, then, in a study of rhetorical influences upon British history? The reason most simply is that his influence was enormous. Gladstone summed it up in talking with his political lieutenants concerning the strategy needed to pass the Irish Home Rule Bill: "What I should like you to tell me is not what you think is the best system, but what Mr. Parnell would accept. We want to get Mr. Parnell's mind on paper."[36]

His rhetorical significance flowed from the absolute and unshakable firmness with which he maintained his position concerning Irish Home Rule. Every one, friends and opponents, knew that where he stood he would continue to stand. The Irish could rally around him as a dependable champion who would never compromise or shift. The English government knew that he could be challenged, he could be attacked, he might be defeated; but his stance would not be mollified, or compromised, or qualified, or abandoned. He was like a massive granite island in a shipping channel—too solid to be removed, so there was nothing for it but to alter course and steer around. That is why Gladstone in a final assessment accounted him "one of the most satisfactory men to do business with I have ever known."[37] He might not be accommodating but he was dependably stable; or as Gladstone phrased it: "wonderfully laconic and direct." If O'Connell can be understood by comparing him with Gandhi, Parnell's special quality was akin to that of Martin Luther; and he could say, as did the stolid German Pastor: "Here I stand. God helping me, I can do no other."

Lord Bryce, another contemporary, tried as did Morley to explain what it was that made Parnell "strangely great." His summation is more negative than positive, reflecting the puzzlement that all students of Parnell's influence must feel:

When he entered Parliament he was only thirty, with no experience of affairs and no gift of speech; but the quality that was in him of leading and ruling men, of taking the initiative, of seeing and striking at the weak point of the enemy, and fearlessly facing the brunt of an enemy's attack, made itself felt in a few months, and he rose without effort to the first place. With some intellectual limitations and some great faults, he will stand high in the long and melancholy series of Irish leaders: less lofty than Grattan, less romantic than Wolfe Tone, less attractive than O'Connell, less brilliant than any of these three, yet entitled to be remembered as one of the most remarkable characters that his country has produced in her struggle of many centuries against the larger isle.[38]

How Parnell used rhetoric as an instrument of statecraft may be illustrated by brief quotations from his speech to a mass meeting at Ennis, in Ireland, on 19 September 1880 and from his speech in the House of Commons on the Home Rule Bill on 7 June 1886. In both speeches he felt deeply the importance of the problems being discussed and he also realized that the best, perhaps the only, way to solve them was by persuasive appeal. In these speeches, accordingly, he came closer to eloquence than at any other time.

The Ennis speech dealt with the problem of farm tenantry. The problem had reached crisis proportions because of the number of tenant evictions by absentee English landlords—6,239 families had been forced from their homes in 1879 and another 10,457 in 1880. To a meeting called by the League of Tenant Farmers, Parnell spoke to the question: "Now what are you to do to a tenant who bids for a farm from which his neighbor has been evicted?" He gave his answer:

> You must show him on the roadside when you meet him, you must show him in the streets of the town, you must show him at the shop counter, you must show him in the fair and in the market-place, and even in the house of worship, by leaving him severely alone, by putting him to a moral Coventry, by isolating him from his kind as if he was a leper of old—you must show him your detestation of the crime he has committed, and you may depend upon it that there will be no man so full of avarice, so lost to shame, as to dare the public opinion of all right-thinking men and to transgress your unwritten code of laws.[39]

This solution that Parnell proposed was a far cry from rebellious uprisings and from the shootings of landlords and their agents. The peasantry saw the point of his proposal and took it up with enthusiasm. A few days later, when a landlord's agent named Captain Boycott commenced proceedings to evict tenants of the farm he managed, the community shunned him—thereby adding a new word to the English language. More importantly, they added a new mode to Irish resistance of English dominance.

Parnell returned to the Westminster Parliament to conduct a campaign of obstruction against the passage of any legislation until the Irish Land Act of 1881 was enacted. Under it tenants received the "three F's" they demanded: fair rent, free sale, and fixity of tenure. Their impoverishment nevertheless continued and that year and the next were a time of violent outbursts of Irish crime. Parnell was arrested for incitement of violence and placed in Kilmainham Jail. Then Gladstone negotiated a "treaty" with Parnell by which he and other leaders were released on the promise that they would help to maintain public order; and the government appropriated funds to pay back rental charges for some 100,000 Irish tenant farmers. Parnell did not, however, forget that his ultimate aim was Irish Home Rule.

The Home Rule Bill came up for final decision in the House of Commons in the spring of 1886. Many in England opposed it from fear that the Protestant minority in Ireland would be oppressed by the huge Catholic majority. Others feared a general outbreak of violence and the seizure or destruction of English properties. Still others believed that firm control of Ireland was essential for English security against foreign attacks. On the other hand, outbreaks of Irish violence against English rule were increasing year by year and even severe coercive measures were being ineffective. As the debate progressed, Parnell reserved his own speech for its close on 7 June. His tone was more than usually conciliatory but rose to near passion as he reminded the House of the Coercion Acts passed during the preceding five years:

> You will require all that you have had during the last five years, and more besides. What, sir, has that coercion been? You have fined the innocent for offences committed by the guilty; you have taken power to expel aliens from the country; you have revived the curfew law and the blood money of your Norman conquerors; you have gagged the press, and seized and suppressed newspapers; you have manufactured new crimes and offences, and applied fresh penalties unknown to your law for these crimes and offences. All this you have done for five years, and all this and much more you will have to do again. . . .
>
> But, sir, I refuse to believe that these evil days must come. I am convinced there are a sufficient number of wise and just members in this House to cause it to disregard appeals made to passion, and to choose the better way of founding peace and goodwill among nations.[40]

The appeal did not succeed. The bill that was advocated by Gladstone's Liberal Party was defeated in the Commons by a vote of 343 to 313. After the dissolution of Parliament, in a new election Gladstone's coalition was defeated. Irish Home Rule was once more yet further postponed.

Parnell's influence was lost because of two factors. First, he became ill. And afterwards his public reputation was shattered by a sensational trial in which he was found guilty of adultery (after which he married the woman with whom he had been living openly for ten years while her husband refused her a divorce). Not only did Parnell lose the bulk of his English friends but also for other reasons his Irish following broke asunder—with the Fenians forming a core of violence and the old religious and clannish feuds dissolving the unity that Parnell had forged. His last years were spent in mental and emotional depression, leading to his death on 6 October 1891 at the age of forty-five. Gladstone, when the news was brought to him, pronounced his epitaph: "A marvellous man, a terrible fall."[41]

"The Test of What Works"

The careers of these men are suggestive concerning what persuasive speaking means in the shaping of history. O'Connell's speeches are generally esteemed to be truly eloquent; those by Palmerston are properly termed competent; the speaking of Parnell was only one element in his general political strategy; Durham's demagoguery was effectively incitive and won him a notoriety that heightened suspicion of his abilities but also helped his appointment to key positions. Neither collectively nor individually did these speakers provide examples of artistic eloquence. Nevertheless, each of them made signally important contributions to statesmanship; and for each of them the kind of speaking that he did was the effective agency of his influence.

Effective speaking is of many kinds. It reflects, is adjusted to, and helps to shape circumstances, as well as being also reflective of persons, both of speakers and of audiences. By the test of "what works," these speakers made wise choices and performed their respective roles exceedingly well.

It is largely on this basis that the major distinction rests between the rhetorical influence of writing and speaking. Literary critics are properly concerned with the elevation of thought and of insight, with qualities of style, and with themes of eternal verities which authors develop. By no means are these factors unimportant in the evaluation of spoken discourse. But in estimating spoken discourse, they do not hold the primacy properly accorded to them in the criticism of literature. The functions of the writer and of the speaker are not the same. One difference is that the speaker must be by far "readier" (Lord Bacon's term) than a writer need be or (because of his removal from the immediate scene of confrontation) can be. Another difference is functional. The writer addresses an indefinitely extended audience, reaching readers in his own time whom he does not know and, if he is lucky or sufficiently able, readers who live in later times, under circumstances quite different from those in which and concerning which he writes. A speaker on the contrary confronts above all *immediacy*. His listeners are before him. His concern and theirs is what should be understood, what ought to be felt, and what can, or must, or might be done to alleviate the problem that they find to be disturbing. Some speeches, like Martin Luther's to the Diet of Worms, and Abraham Lincoln's at Gettysburg, achieve a timelessness because what is most appropriate for the speakers to say is precisely a statement of eternal values. But this is not the rule but the exception.

Speaking is properly assessed in terms of specific rhetorical circumstances. A particular perplexity needs to be clarified. A choice is to be made concerning an action that is to be taken. In democratic societies alternatives are weighed and the judgement of listeners is appealed to with the intention of influencing their choices. In authoritarian societies speaking serves as an appropriate agent of social control—clarifying what it is that the listeners must do and providing an impulsion for their acceptance of it. The test of the worth of a public speech is partly how well it is contrived, how skillfully it is developed, how appropriately it deals with the various contingencies that determine the audience response, and beyond these factors the quality of its conceptions and the degree of its artistry.

For such reasons the texts of even the greatest public speeches do not generally or necessarily invite or merit reading by later generations. But nevertheless the significant speeches do have a genuine value that lasts. This value is the effect that they have in shaping the course of events. An impassioned half-time speech by a football coach may appear ridiculous if its text is preserved and read in later days under circumstances remote from the gridiron contest. Yet it may have the precise effect that the coach intends, namely to inspire the players to a successful effort. And the same test is applicable to great oratorical efforts on public occasions. Does the speaking apply to the real need of the moment? Does it accomplish what the speaker aims to achieve? Does it fulfill the need to which it is addressed?

In these same terms, it is evident that the anthologist who compiles memorable speeches and the historian who assesses the worth of spoken discourse have different aims and different standards of judgment. The anthologist fails to justify his role of perpetuating the texts of speeches unless he succeeds in selecting those that do have lasting appeal. The historian's proper function is to estimate and to narrate the ways in which the course of affairs is guided in significant degree by what particular individuals say in particular situations and by how they say it. It is for this reason that a history of rhetorical influence in the shaping of public affairs differs markedly from a history of literature, both in its intent and in its character. It is for this reason that influential public speaking is distinguished not by its artistry but by its effects.

5

CHALLENGE TO THE CHURCH:
REINTERPRETATIONS OF FAITH

During this time of change, the meanings of religion came to be discussed in new ways. Legal restraints upon dissension and nonconformity were relaxed with the repeal of the Test and Corporation Act in 1828, the emancipation of Catholics in 1829, and extension of political rights to Jews in 1858–60.[1] The scope and the nature of pulpit rhetoric were deeply affected by the new science and by the egalitarian stress upon social justice. The traditional focus upon individual salvation was broadened to include concern for the reshaping of society. The validity of religion had to be reassessed in terms of the new knowledge about man and the universe. Preachers had to reexamine their own beliefs. How should they deal with these new kinds of challenges to the Church? What should they say to perplexed worshipers?

Early in the century the Congregationalist R. W. Dale could assert with confidence that "the church is a place where one day's truce ought to be allowed to the dissensions and animosities of mankind." Even for Dale this view was about to be changed. A leading historian of theological trends in the period believes that the social broadening of "the proper province" of religious concern began with support given by dissenting ministers in the campaign to repeal the Corn Laws. But at least two decades earlier Dr. Thomas Chalmers from his Presbyterian pulpit in Glasgow was steadfastly propounding "the permanent warning . . . that the greatest of all questions, both for statesmen and for churchmen, is the condition of those untaught and degraded thousands who swarm now around the social edifice, and whose brawny arms may yet grasp the pillars to shake or to destroy."[2]

"A Significant Area of Rhetorical Study"

Determination of the "proper province of religion" was the issue that dominated pulpit rhetoric during the nineteenth century. Should it be expanded from a concern with the individual's responsive relationship with God to include necessarily a responsibility for implanting spiritual values in society? What, if any, reassessment of Christian beliefs was required by the new scientific discoveries and theories? On these questions the preachers of the time diverged widely. How they responded to them provides a critical test of the nature and the effects of pulpit rhetoric during this age of transition.

The religious views of the prior age have been summarized as the conviction that "nothing will suffice the true Christian . . . but a constant sense of his own damnworthiness . . . and an implicit belief in the efficacy of an innocent victim's sacrifice in occasionally appeasing the Creator's just wrath with the corruption of his creatures. Nothing less than a whole life, incessantly dominated by the thought of getting right with God, will suffice."[3] True faith meant surrender of the individual will to the just governance of God. Salvation depended upon acceptance of the redemptive power of the crucifixion of Christ. This was the pathway available to anyone who accepted it. Such a view was individualism incarnate. What matters was the eternity of the soul; heaven was its destination; the purpose of life was to win entrance into it.

John Morley in his "Spirit of the Times" adjudged that the intellectual revolution in the sciences and humanities had shifted belief from special providence to the immutability of natural laws. He cited not only Darwin but also Buckle's *History of Civilization* and Herbert Spencer's *Social Statics* as demonstrations of belief in a patterned continuity that denied the sporadic intervention of divinity to extend special favors to those God deemed especially meritorious. This kind of thinking emphasized the importance of education in order that all might understand the true nature of the universe, further strengthened by the egalitarian view that everyone should be enabled to become all that he can be. The rapid development of schools, along with the new vitality of social philanthropy and the enlargement of knowledge, sometimes aided and sometimes obstructed religion. These were problems with which the preachers had to deal.

Among the changes that were influential were the rapid development of domestic Sunday Schools and of foreign missions. Both diverted the attention of worshipers from their own individual needs to broader and international concerns. Meanwhile, the substantial improvement in living standards that finally resulted from the Industrial Revolution drew attention from otherworldly possibilities to worldly opportunities. A dual system of morality gradually evolved: one set of beliefs for Sunday worship, another for the workplace and the market. Preachers confronted the problem of reconciling the goal of temporal well-being with the sustaining of spiritual adherence to the divine purpose.

Wingfield-Stratford viewed the religious shift with mingled approval and misgiving: "Beneath the wars and revolutions that distract attention to the surface of things, the great Emotional Revival was at work, with its enthusiasm and glowing sympathy marred by its lack of balance and all too narrow intellectual basis."[5] No more than among the political leaders was there a clear discernment by the great preachers concerning the full meaning of the fundamental changes that marked this age of transition. On the whole the preachers were neither more nor less clearsighted than the politicians. Both groups clung to the past while trying to deal with the present in terms that would lead to a better future. This was a rhetorical problem they could not be expected to solve wholly. But the fact of change they did recognize, with varied acceptance, and they devoted great abilities compounded of emotional faith and intellectual accuity in their efforts to guide the people aright.

In few other periods has rhetoric been as active in dealing with the challenge of finding a suitable way through a time of vast changes. Religious periodicals proliferated and built vast circulations.[6] Pulpit preaching reached new heights of effectiveness. The rollcall of great preachers is extensive. Among those of special note were such outstanding pulpiteers as James Fraser, Samuel Wilberforce, and E. W. Benton for the Church of England; Thomas Binney, E. F. Horton, and R. W. Dale for the Congregationalists; John Keble, E. B. Pusey, and John Henry Newman for the Catholics; Robert Hall and Charles Haddon Spurgeon for the Baptists; John Foster for the English Presbyterians; Thomas Chalmers for the Scotch Presbyterians; William Booth for the Salvation Army; Henry Drummond for the Evangelicals—and many more. An expanded list must include B. F. Westcott, A. P. Stanley, A. C. Tait, Hundley Moule, F. D. Maurice, Joseph Barber Lightfoot, H. E. Manning, H. P. Liddon, H. Scott Holland, Hugh Price Hughes, W. R. Inge, H. Scott Holland, A. M. Fairbairn, W. Boyd Carpenter, William Church, Edward Irving, F. W. Robertson and still others.

Religious rhetoric is always a vital influence. Every community had a variety of churches. Worshippers represented the whole range of society. The sheer amount of religious discourse is greater than that of any other type except conversation and schoolroom teaching. If much of it is simply repetitive, that very fact provides a part of its power. For some preachers their sermons consisted of a vital, probing, and sometimes innovative effort to deal with difficult problems; for others, their pulpit discourses were reiterative traditional appeals. Similar variations of response from the pews ranged from a regard for religion as the vital center of life to casual and habitual reception of a message that was socially approved and of only peripheral interest. The analysis of what preaching means, of how it is done, and of its effects is a significant area of rhetorical study. As is also true of speaking in Parliament, the scenes in which it occurs are restricted and contained. There are stated purposes, varied means used to try to achieve them, and some indications (such as conversions, increase or decrease of church attendance, support for missions, and joint programs of social action, among others) that indicate degrees of effectiveness.

For this brief survey of rhetorical influences in recent English history, examination will be directed to four preachers whose fame was outstanding, who exemplify central trends of this transitional time, and whose influence persists. They are R. W. Dale, who well exemplifies the religious adaptation to the social and intellectual changes of the period; John Henry Newman, who helped to guide the vital resurgence of first Episcopalianism and then Catholicism; and the two most famous independent evangelicals, Henry Drummond and Charles Haddon Spurgeon.

"The Great Discovery . . . Christ is Alive"

If R. W. Dale was not the greatest among them, he does best represent the changing nature and role of religion in coming into acceptance of social responsibilities. He spent his life in a single parish but his influence extended all through England and well beyond. With "sweet reasonableness" he influenced not only his parishioners but also leading ministers of his own and other denominations. In short, his career was pivotal.

Born on 1 December 1829, Dale spent his life largely in the great industrial city of Birmingham, where memories of Edmund Burke and the contemporary speaking of John Bright were highly regarded. Dale's family background and education gave him no special advantages. What he achieved was owing directly to his rhetorical abilities. Instead of attending one of the great universities he studied in the inconspicuous Spring Hill College that was maintained in Birmingham by the Congregationalists. His student days were not notable. After graduation he tried his hand at teaching with little success and less satisfaction. Nevertheless, his real vocation began early. He commenced as a lay-preacher in the mode of Nonconformity, and his first sermon, preached in 1845, proved to be a respectable effort for a youth of sixteen. In the fall of 1852 he was invited to become assistant pastor of the prestigious Carr's Lane Congregational Church and within a few months was promoted to co-pastor.

His faith was only in part traditional. To the 2,500 to 3,000 attendants of the church he stated his belief: "I dissent from the Church of England because I believe that the visible Church of Christ is a congregation of faithful men; but a National Church cannot be a congregation, nor can there be any security for all its members being faithful."[7] He was a "Bible preacher"; but already in that early period he departed from the common ministerial practice of citing God's authority from specific verses of the Bible. Instead he based his sermons upon entire books, which enabled him to develop broader themes and inspired him to broader views. He preached his conviction that "man is not by nature immortal; that eternal life is attainable only through the Lord Jesus Christ; and that the souls of the impenitent are annihilated."[8]

This was orthodoxy with a significant deviation. What he premised was the "destruction" of nonbelievers and sinners rather than their eternal punishment in hell. Shortly he drew further apart from traditionalism with other heretical ideas. Independence of thought was readily available to him, for by the very nature of Congregationalism, orthodoxy was not ordained. Every individual church was its own monitor. There was no general doctrinal declaration of what all must believe; there were no bishops or superintendents to discipline local deviations. Dale's mind was both brilliant and free-ranging. He formed his own judgments and stated them frankly and fearlessly. And he gradually developed convictions of his own that represented alert attention to the underlying currents of the time.

Along with abandoning hellfire, he also disavowed "original sin." Adam's fall from grace in the Garden of Eden did not, he believed, implant basic sinfulness in all humanity. Individuals instead are either "good" or "bad" depending on how they live. A basic test was how they treated one another—an idea that opened the way for the churches to become social agencies of reform.

Such views caused him to be labelled heretical. Yet so deeply were the nation's churches astir with the search for new interpretations of the faith that accorded with new knowledge and so powerful was his preaching that he was often invited as a guest preacher into the pulpits of many of England's leading metropolitan churches. In consequence, both his fame and his influence became nationwide.

In 1861 when he was just past thirty he led in a movement to unite all the separate Congregational Churches into a national Congregational Union. Its purpose, as Dale declared, was not to enforce unity of belief but to conduct annual discussions that would "mould the thought of the churches."[9] Its aim was not to establish an orthodox set of beliefs but to "spiritualize" the society. Such a need for unity was felt as keenly by Dale and many of his Congregational fellow-preachers as O'Connell felt the need to unify the Irish. Their reasoning was similar. Individual efforts are not enough. There must be a sustained assault upon public opinion to have a substantial effect.

As Dale interpreted the English scene in the wake of Lyell's geological discoveries of the age and the development of the universe and of Darwin's theory of biological evolution, there was coming to be a widespread "contemptuous rejection of the supernatural element in religion." This was the problem he discussed in his inaugural sermon upon induction as chairman of the Congregational Union. In it he announced his own discovery that "Christ is alive." As he went on to explain, this meant that the teachings of Jesus must be interpreted in terms of the spirit, the understandings, the anguish, and the troubles of the time.

Although he called it his "Great Discovery," it was not a single intellectual leap but a product of gradual growth. It represented ideas that he had been exploring in his sermons to his Carr's Lane Church. In his search, his congregation was supportive, as he gratefully attested in his sermon delivered on 26 January 1864 when he said that "there are two things that I have always admired in the people of Birmingham: in the first place, they can tolerate differences of opinion in men they can trust; and in the second place, they stand by their old friends through fire and through water."[10]

By 1866 he was deeply plunged into political activism and social controversy. To Disraeli's assertion that the franchise is a privilege, not a right, Dale hotly retorted: "Deny the people the franchise, and the right of revolution still remains." The choice was "between the hustings and the barricades."[11]

By this time he had clearly developed his conviction that the church had active social functions. In a sermon on "The Politics of the Future" that he delivered on 19 November 1867 he demanded the establishment of a national education program that would ensure "perfect freedom for every man to rise by his own intelligence and industry from the lowest to the highest positions of the state."[12] The time was ripe for such ideas. In 1870 the National Education Act was adopted. It was a crucial step, because it entailed the breaking down of the traditional view that the social classes are divided into the two segments of the rulers and the ruled. Dale's influence was not critical in winning passage for the bill; but his advocacy did critically signal the involvement of religious speakers in community affairs. His leadership was important in bringing the pulpit and the pew into direct concern with social problems.

Dale well realized that with leadership went responsibility. Social reforms are far from simplistic. Changes cut both ways. New opportunities create their own new problems. After adoption of the Electoral Reform Bill of 1867, Dale warned his listeners that: "You have achieved your own political rights; resolve to respect the rights of others." Political democracy, he realized, was far from being self-sufficient. "Suppose," he said, "that a majority of the people of England determine that every Englishman should worship in an Episcopal Church, and that every Romanist and NonConformist and Jew that refused to obey should suffer fine or imprisonment; the mere fact that a majority had passed such a tyrannical law would not make it less tyrannical."[13]

Near the end of his life in 1891 Dale led his denomination into worldwide organization. The International Council of Congregational Churches was inaugurated with Dale as its first president. Dale's mind was far more occupied with problems of effective organization than with the effect of Sunday sermons upon an assembled congregation composed of individuals who already accepted the teachings of the church. He frequently criticized scholarly Anglicans, who devoted themselves more than he felt proper to scholarship rather than to activity. He became increasingly concerned with the lack of religious conviction in the great universities; and to help turn the tide he initiated the closing down of Spring Hill College in order to use Congregational resources to open Mansfield College in Cambridge University. He founded and edited a monthly magazine, *The Congregationalist,* to uphold the principles of theological independence. He recognized that the lack of ritualism in nonconforming churches made their services too barren to be impelling, in consequence of which he advocated better architectural planning of new sanctuaries, urged use of the Book of Common Prayer in Congregational services, and encouraged a careful selection and general use of hymns in the services, commenting, "Let me write the hymns of a Church, and I care not who writes the theology."[14] His general influence was "a departure from the limits of conventional orthodoxy."[15]

He wrote and preached about the weakening effects of denominationalism on the ground that it undermined the unity of the Church "as the august society of Saints."[16] In 1889 he wrote to a Methodist friend concerning the small town of Barmouth: "We Congregationalists have a wooden church, holding perhaps 150 people; the Baptists, three years ago opened a church—stone, however—holding about as many; your people also have a church . . . . It is the same with the Presbyterians . . . . I could swear when I think of it." The spirit of separatism, he went on, was so strong that the churches "can neither combine nor confederate; how can we dream of a more general federation?"[17] His plan was that the Churches cease to be isolated and learn to be a brotherhood. Their self-centeredness so limited their social effects that they were like separate vessels, sailing each on its own way in the vast ocean of these tumultuous times and "holding out not so much as a light to each other."[18]

His achievements fell short of his aim. The unity he pleaded for as the only means of converting the whole society to Christian principles was not attainable. This was a difficulty his best rhetorical efforts could not surmount. He accomplished much, but never so much as he wished.

In his preaching Dale much resembled the speaking of his fellow townsman, John Bright: rich in intellect, broad in social sympathies, generally constructive yet not averse to sharp attacks on views and persons he felt were obstructive to needed changes. The impact that he made was more intellectual than emotional. Differing widely from the Methodists, Baptists, and Evangelicals, he sought less to deepen emotional intensity of belief than to stimulate thought about what spirituality should mean in the lives of individuals and in the laws and practices of society. By such means he became a leading architect of the new religion that was being shaped.

On 13 March 1894, still working, he died at the age of sixty-five. On his desk was the manuscript of a sermon that he was preparing, appropriately left incomplete, with its last sentence ending with the unfinished phrase: "after our mortal years are spent there is a larger, fuller, richer life in—." Perhaps he was in doubt, as so many of his contemporaries were, about how to conclude. Of what would eternity consist? His abiding interest lay more immediately with the question of how our worldly lives should be lived.

"A Faith That Needs No Change"

Even if the various denominations could not unite, they were at least coming more closely together in their theological understanding and aims. The General Baptists were coming to be virtually Unitarian—a tendency that Robert Hall furiously attacked on behalf of the Particular Baptists. The English Presbyterians, though definitely not their Scottish brethren, were also embracing Unitarian monotheism. The interdenominational Evangelicals generally opted for philosophical freedom on the ground that the "old verities are capable of new statement"—with one of their spokesmen, Edward Irving, drawing such crowds in London during the mid-1820s to the mid-thirties that De Quincey called him "the greatest orator of our time." The Quakers and the Unitarians felt no difficulty in embracing the new sociological trend of religion.

On the other side of the social-versus individual emphasis were the Catholics, the Methodists, and the most prominent Evangelicals. Catholicism was rising to new heights of emotional commitment in the Oxford Movement led by Keble, Newman, and Pusey. Methodism was holding strictly to its separation from other denominations and was also splitting apart. The divisive tendency led to a Conference of Expulsion in 1849, which resulted not only in dividing that church into the Methodist New Connexion, the Bible Christians, and the Wesleyan Methodist Association, but also in an annual loss of some 10,000 to 15,000 members—with the consequence that "The central years of the nineteenth century form one of the darkest periods in the history of Wesleyan Methodism."[19]

A different trend of development in Protestant preaching than that urged by Dale was led by two vastly influential independent preachers, Henry Drummond and Charles Haddon Spurgeon. Both of them transcended denominationalism. Spurgeon had been accepted into the Baptist Church at the age of sixteen; but he always insisted that he was not a Baptist but a Christian, for which reason he "could scarcely belong to any sect."[20] Drummond was drawn to evangelism in 1873, when he was twenty-two, by the nondenominational American, Dwight L. Moody, and plunged immediately into a campaign of daily speaking—sometimes two or three times a day—to audiences sometimes small and sometimes numbering two or three thousands, about half of whom never had been church members.[21] Both men devoted their superb rhetorical gifts to the enhancement of emotional individual faith, while ardently contesting against the antisupernatural humanism that was threatening to undermine religion.

Charles Haddon Spurgeon, an enormously popular pulpit orator, was accounted by many to be the greatest preacher of the century. During the many years of his preaching in The Tabernacle in London on Sundays and Thursdays, he spoke directly to many thousands of listeners but reached a vast number more through print. As his biographer says: "Great as was the influence of Mr. Spurgeon's preaching, it may be questioned whether the influence of his printed sermons was not greater." The publication of his *Tabernacle Sermons* grew to sixty-three volumes, which were supplemented with a dozen more composed of selected sermons on special topics.[22] He leaped into fame in his early youth and maintains long after his death an influence that is worldwide.

The theme in all his preaching was sharply focused. He believed strongly that, "The chief desire among Christians is to gain an assurance of God's love."[23] Nevertheless, his central theme was God's wrathful justice. As a critic reviewing his 1855 volume of sermons found, "The burden of all is, 'Flee from the wrath to come; lay hold on eternal life.' The order is intentional, for the supreme thought in the preacher's mind is the imminent peril of his hearers."[24] He portrayed vividly the horrors of hellfire, contrasted with the bliss of salvation. Intellectualism he disdained. He only briefly attended college, and he did not send his sons to college. He read widely and gained extensive knowledge; but what he valued was not learning but intensity of faith. He mind was saturated with the Old Testament and his preaching resembled that of the old prophets. He did not seek to "prove" the truths of Christianity but rather to sweep his hearers and readers into unquestioning acceptance. For this kind of preaching he had no equal—at least not after the time of George Whitefield.

As his biography in the Tyndale series sums up his career: "Once in a century there is given to us the balanced man of genius, the brilliant man who is a whole man, and then the world wonders."[25] His "wholeness," however is open to question. As a rhetorician, he was an anomaly—one who refused to "adjust" to his audience; who deliberately went counter to the trends of his time; who repudiated rationality; and who was undeviatingly traditional in his orthodoxy. His one significant deviation from the views of his predecessors was his constant emphasis upon the Holy Ghost, the spiritual power of divinity, along with the redemptive power of Christ. He held fast to the Christian theme of the absolute need for individuals to be "right with God." He paid little heed to the scientific discoveries and theories of his time; nor did he join in the rising demands for the moral rejuvenation of society. With what his biographer calls "childlike simplicity," he focused his attention upon the need of the individual, the creature, to live strictly in accordance with the will of the Creator. His great power stemmed from his earnestness in this conviction, along with his almost magical eloquence that reached into the depths of the feelings of those whom he addressed.

When critics accused him of egoistic arrogance, he rested his defense upon his popularity. "Do you see those bookshelves? They contain hundreds, nay thousands, of my sermons, translated into every language under heaven. Well, now, add to this that ever since I was twenty years old there never has been built a place large enough to hold the numbers of people who wished to hear me preach, and, upon my honour, when I think of it, I wonder that I am not more conceited than I am."[26]

In his own time he was truly a sensation; what he contributed of lasting merit is still being weighed. Elliott-Binns in his review of religious change during the century accounts Spurgeon one of the six greatest preachers of the time, but neither the best nor the most influential of them. His highest ranking comes from those who believe that traditional orthodoxy is what needs to be sustained.

Spurgeon was born on 19 June 1834 into a family of sturdy faith. Both his father and his grandfather (by whom he was raised from the age of eighteen months) were lay preachers to independent congregations. His basic education came from reading the religious books in his grandfather's library—among which

Bunyan's *Pilgrim's Progress* impressed him so deeply that he kept it at hand all his life and reread it at least a hundred times. Near the age of sixteen he entered All Saints Agricultural College and from there went on for two more years in Newmarket College in Cambridge. As a student he excelled in mathematics and languages, along with religious studies and the applied sciences. He briefly tried school teaching, but quickly left it in agreement with Goldsmith's view that to teach is worse punishment than to be hanged. In later life he insisted that "I had no college education," and he accounted this one of his advantages. In his maturity he travelled throughout England and into Europe; but mostly he stayed at home. His reading in the Bible and religious books was his principal education; and his enjoyment in wandering the country fields was his chief relaxation. His abiding interests were otherworldly, not worldly.

He took to preaching naturally—playing at preaching as a small child and even preaching a sermon (to a single old man) when he was six. Then he went through a five-year period of doubt in his early teens, which time and again he recounted in different forms in his later sermons. How he lost his own faith and then found it again became standard fare in his preaching, as he intimated to his listeners that their problems of attaining belief were no greater than that of the world-renowned preacher who was addressing them. He savored of these excursions in autobiography and it is easy to grasp his own pleasure as he recounted them. One instance out of the multiple examples that he provided will illustrate the conversational ease of his style, the directness of his person-to-person mode of address, and the unostentatious vividness with which he described the Christian's narrow escape from slipping into hell. The passage that follows is Simon-pure Spurgeon: in substance and in manner. It was the kind of preaching that won him his astounding success:

> I have never been thoroughly an unbeliever but once, and that was not before I knew the need of a Savior, but after it. It was just when I wanted Christ and panted after Him, that, suddenly the thought crossed my mind—which I abhorred, but could not conquer—that there was no God, no Christ, no heaven, no hell; that all my prayers were but a farce, and that I might as well have whistled to the winds or spoken to the howling waves. Ah! I remember how my ship drifted through the sea of fire, loosened from the anchor of my faith which I had received from my fathers. I no longer moored myself hard by the shores of Revelation. I said to reason, 'Be thou my captain'; I said to my own brain, Be thou my rudder'; and I started on my mad voyage. Thank God it is all over now; but I will tell you its history. It was one hurried sailing over the tempestuous ocean of free thought. I went on, and as I went, the skies began to darken; but to make up for the deficiency, the waters were gleaming with corruscations of brilliancy. I saw sparks flying upward that pleased me, and I felt, 'If this be free thought, it is a happy thing.' My thoughts seemed gems, and I scattered stars with both my hands; but anon, instead of these corruscations of glory, I saw grim fiends, fierce and horrible, start up from the waters; and as they dashed on, they gnashed their teeth, and grinned upon

me; they seized the prow of my ship, and dragged me on, while I, in part, gloried in the rapidity of my motion, but yet shuddered at the terrific rate with which I passed the landmarks of my faith. I went to the very verge of the dreary realms of unbelief. I went to the very bottom of the sea of infidelity. As I hurried forward at an awful speed, I began to doubt if there was a world. I doubted everything, until at last the devil defeated himself by making me doubt my own existence. I thought I was floating in the nothingness of vacuity; then, startled with the thought, and feeling that I was substantial flesh and blood after all, I saw that God was, and Christ was, and heaven was, and hell was, and that all these things were absolute truths. The very extravagence of doubt showed me its absurdity, and then came a Voice which said, 'And can this doubt be true?' Then I awoke from the death dreams, which, God knows, might have damned my soul and ruined my body if I had not awakened. When I arose, faith took the helm; from that moment I doubted not. Faith steered me back; faith cried, 'Away!' I cast my anchor on Calvary. I lifted my eyes to God, and here I am, alive, and out of hell. Therefore I speak what I do know. I have sailed the perilous voyage; I have come safe to land. Ask me to be an infidel! No. I have tried it; it was sweet at first, but bitter afterwards. Now, lashed to God's Gospel, more firmly than ever, standing as on a rock of adamant, I defy the arguments of hell to move me, for I know whom I have believed, and I am persuaded that he is able to keep that which I have committed unto him. [27]

There is no need to specify dates for Spurgeon's particular sermons. They are all of a piece. For him there was no change, no adjustment, no transition. His religious experience was marked not by breadth but by depth. He did not argue with the new science, he ignored it. He was not drawn into controversy about the social implications of religion. He had one theme: the need of everyone to be right with God. He had no urge to analyze or explore the majesty of God—he felt it. As an academic theologian wrote in trying to explain him: "What he saw, he saw as clear as sunlight, and what he did not see with perfect clearness, he did not see at all . . . . He was really the master of two languages: the language of a theological past, and the nontheological language of the nineteenth century." [28] His guidance came from the Bible, from *Pilgrim's Progress,* and from his own experience. His message he delivered with pungent homeliness, enlivened with touches of humor, and enforced with warning and with hope.

His sermons were carefully crafted to seem spontaneous and utterly natural. They were replete with anecdotes, as when he said: "There is a man sitting there who is a shoemaker; he keeps his shop open on Sundays; it was open last Sabbath morning. He took ninepence and there was fourpence profit on it; his soul is sold to Satan for fourpence." He was always alert to his audience and frequently interjected references to individual listeners. In one sermon, he broke off his discourse when he saw a young woman sitting in front looking dejected. "I think our sister is dead," he said, pointing to her. Then, when she sat up looking more alert, he assured the congregation that she was "washed into heaven on a wave of joy." [29]

His sermon preparation was careful but not prolonged. His Sunday morning sermon was typically prepared in the evening before with notes jotted on a sheet of paper. His evening discourses he worked out during the same afternoon. "He went to the pulpit with the assurance that he would be able to clothe his ideas appropriately at the moment, and many of his illustrations came to him during the delivery of the sermon."[30] His printed sermons needed little or no revision and were drafted to fit the requirements of print—all precisely twelve pages in length. During his last illness, as he lay near death, he was asked if he could put into a few words the essence of his faith. He answered, "it is all in four words— 'Jesus died for me.'" The end came on 26 April 1891; he was only fifty-seven years old. In his own words: "The vista of a prayerful life will never close, but continue throughout eternity." He left behind as legacies the Tabernacle and an orphanage that he had built with his own funds. But what he chiefly left was his assurance in a faith that needs no change.

"Shy about Speaking . . . Bursting Suddenly into Fame"

The short life of Henry Drummond (he died at the age of forty-five) was in its general pattern remarkably similar to that of Charles Haddon Spurgeon. Yet in significant ways they were virtual contrasts. They were contemporaries, with Spurgeon dying six years before Drummond's death, and they both won global fame as evangelical supradenominational preachers whose rhetorical influence was extended by print far beyond the immediate reach of their voices; yet they conducted their common evangelical missions as strangers to one another. Except for their deep devotion to the conversion of nonbelievers to complete acceptance of the need and the reward of subjecting their lives to the governance of God, they were in basic ways essentially unlike. Together they represent the obverse sides of the religion of the times: Spurgeon emphasizing individual salvation; Drummond adding the duty of Christianizing society—Spurgeon ignoring the "new science," Drummond adapting his theology to it.

Henry Drummond was a Scot, born into a family of agricultural nurserymen on 17 August 1851 in the city of Stirling. His father was a good businessman of sound and sincere religious belief, yet who never "opened his lips in public on religion"[31] until after his fiftieth year, after which time he helped to develop the Sunday School program, the Y.M.C.A., and a broad program of civic philanthropy. Drummond was reared to accept Christianity unquestioningly and as he later stated he never felt any special experience of conversion. His youth was an untroubled experience of pleasure in athletic games, roaming the fields, fishing, and reading in the Beadle series of novels about Indian warfare in the American West. He was sent to Edinburgh University where he was a moderately good student, "more prominent in the playground than in class," and more interested in the courses in general science than in religious instruction. Under the guidance of an excellent English teacher, he gained special skill in reading aloud and in written composition. He helped to found a debating society and became its best speaker—on such subjects as the bad influence of the Irish Catholic Church and the need to educate women. His special interest was science, especially geology, and his first published essay was on the great age of the earth as traced in its rocks. He was unnaturally small for his age—though during his college years he grew rapidly to above-average height; and he was shy about speaking in public. His voice was inadequate for large audiences and he remained all his life most comfortable with audiences not exceeding five hundred. He never won a college degree, failing in two efforts to pass the required examinations. In short, he grew to maturity undistinguished except that his buoyant personality, restrained by shyness, and his good-humored interest in pleasing his companions made him popular among his fellows.[32]

Yet, at the early age of twenty-two this shy and undistinguished youth surprised both himself and his friends by bursting suddenly into fame. Almost overnight he emerged as a great evangelist, convinced himself and able to convince multiple thousands of others of "the recoverableness of man from the depths of sin." His rhetorical influence stemmed from his complete belief in the revolutionary power of belief in Christ to change the nature of believers; from his confident teaching that geological and biological "natural law" was an added proof of the divine superintendence over the universe; his insistence that religious faith has to be expressed through programs for improving society; and his rationality (even when his facts were wrong and his logic weak) in arguing that the truths of religion were fully supported by the expanding vision of the new science. Unlike Spurgeon, he avoided any reference to his own religious yearnings or growth. His emphasis always was on the needs of his listeners; and "in the prime of his teaching he sought to win the reason of men for religion."[33] He felt himself to be primarily a "teacher," and indeed his immediate vocation was that of lecturer on geology, first at Edinburgh University then at Glasgow.

In many respects his differences from Spurgeon are striking. He travelled widely—in Ireland, Germany, America, Australia, and Africa. His reading was more in science than in theology and he considered Darwin's *The Origin of Species* the most important contribution to theology. The whole of life, he felt, was a demonstration of the divine plan, with the soul of man manifesting the peak of evolution. In his youth he believed in the literal truth of every biblical verse but later came to interpret the Bible broadly and in its general import as man's best moral and spiritual guide.

At the age of twenty he published an essay on "Spiritual Diagnosis," in which he developed his lifelong conviction that the conversion of individuals must be by "person-to-person" discussion. As he wrote in this essay: "We know well enough how to move the masses, how to draw a crowd around us, how . . . to flash and storm in passion, how to work in the appeal at the right moment, how to play upon all the figures of Rhetoric in succession . . . . Everyone knows this, or can know it easily, but to draw souls one by one and take from them the secret of their lives, to talk them clear out of themselves, . . . *this* is the spiritual diagnosis which is so difficult to acquire and so hard to practise.[34] In accordance with this conviction he studied mesmerism and practiced hypnotism on individuals—as later he did virtually with great crowds.

The transforming influence upon Drummond was the religious revival accomplished in England, Ireland, and Scotland in 1873–74 by the American evangelists, Dwight L. Moody and his hymnalist companion, Ira D. Sankey. Drummond attended the first meetings they held in Edinburgh and was deeply impressed by Moody's practice of following the mass meetings by inviting the new converts into small discussion meetings with leaders who talked with them about their own particular spiritual struggles. Drummond was selected by Moody as one of these leaders and quickly proved to be the best among them. Since his teaching duties were restricted to the winter months from November to March, Drummond had the other six months to devote wholly to this work.

Drummond's first mission was to Elgin, where there was "nothing remarkable" in his speaking; but he was deeply impressed by the success of the project of changing the lives of the converts through individual talks with them. During the remainder of the revival campaign he devoted every day to meetings with such groups and gradually overcame his shy unwillingness to address large audiences. In Dublin, on 8 November 1873 he was induced to speak to an audience of some three thousand, and a minister in attendance testified that "there are nowhere more striking instances of the grace of God." Still he clung to his belief that direct talk with individuals is the essential mode for genuine conversion.

After the departure of Moody and Sankey, Drummond returned to the university, where his fellow students found him unaffected by the fame his successes had brought him. As a biographer who was a fellow student wrote: "We younger men were a little afraid of him . . . . But we found him unaggressive, treating us as equals . . . entering into our fun." In the evening meetings that they held, they found the secret of his power: "that he was interested in us . . . . We could tell him, as we could not tell others, the worst about ourselves . . . . His sunniness brought hope with it to everybody about him . . . ."[35]

During the next decade Drummond continued quietly at the University until in 1883 he published a book that brought him instantly into worldwide fame—*Natural Law in the Spiritual World*, which was his "reconciliation" of the Bible with science. For him "the demonstration of the uniformity of nature," far from undermining the immediacy of God, proved it.

The sense of lawlessness which pervades the spiritual world at present reacts in many subtle and injurious ways upon the personal experience of Christians. They gather the idea that things are managed differently there from anywhere else—less strictly, less consistently; that blessings or punishments are dispensed arbitrarily . . . . And science could make no truer contribution to Christianity than to enforce upon us all . . . the force of causation in spiritual life.

The great failure of science, he went on, is its failure

to discover any clue to the ultimate mystery of origins . . . . Science has not found a substitute for God . . . . If there are answers to these questions, and there ought to be, theology holds them . . . . In its investigation of these questions, science has made a discovery. It has seen plainly that atheism is unscientific . . . . And science has supplied theology with a theory which the intellect can accept, and which for the devout mind leaves everything more worthy of worship than before.[36]

After the appearance of this book, Drummond was promoted by the Free University of Glasgow to Professor of Theology. It also brought him an enlarged audience for his preaching. He plunged into efforts to create a "social gospel" for the improvement of the lot of the unemployed and he entered actively into political campaigns on behalf of Liberal candidates for Parliament. His interests took him to Africa, concerning which he wrote another book, Tropical Africa, which also won wide attention to the spiritual and material needs of that continent. He organized the Holiday Mission to send students during their vacations as missionaries to Africa and the South Seas. Regularly he spoke to Sunday meetings in Edinburgh that he addressed hesitantly and without eloquence but with considerable effect from the nature of his ideas.

His great fame as a preacher commenced in 1887 when he went to America and delivered a series of sermons in churches, Chautauquas, and colleges. The effects were enormous—not only on his hearers but upon Drummond as well. He discovered his great power to move people in the mass. He was invited to Australia, where his preaching was similarly powerful and popular. Then he wrote another book, The Ascent of Man, on the theme of "the progress of spirit." Evolution operated not, he explained, through "survival of the fittest" but through spiritual power that led to social cooperation for betterment of living conditions. This was followed by a small volume drawn from his sermons entitled The Greatest Thing in the World—which is the renovative power of belief in Christ: a book that virtually took the Christian world by storm, surpassing the popular appeal of all the others.

As a rhetorical influence, Drummond's personality and his speaking were almost irresistible. But since he was reluctant to address huge crowds and since he continued in his role as professor and student of the scientific reinforcement of religion, his influence stemmed far more from his writings than from his speaking. Even more than Dale, he guided the churches to a new vision of the world—an acceptance of science and an acceptance of social responsibility. His influence was crucial in adjusting the churches to the new age. His appeal was greatest among educated people, who felt a great spiritual hunger that could be satisfied not only through individual salvation but through the recognition of scientific knowledge and through service to social needs. His immediate influence was far less than that of Spurgeon—but deeper and more lasting as a guide through the troubled anxieties of the modern age.

"The Reasonableness of Supernatural Beliefs"

A rhetorical influence of a different kind was exerted by John Henry Newman. He is remembered as an intellectual Anglican who converted to Catholicism in mid-career; as an educator who argued that a university must include theology in its curriculum in pursuit of its proper aim of developing understanding; and as a preacher and lecturer whose speeches survive as literature. He understood the tenor of his own time and he dealt with its problems in terms of fundamental and timeless principles. His chosen mode for presenting his ideas was through spoken discourse (though like the American Ralph Waldo Emerson his "lectures" are read as "essays"). Newman was far from being "oratorical" or even in the ordinary sense "eloquent," yet it was his power as a speaker that made his ideas influential. An observer of his early preaching in Oxford both describes and explains his effectiveness:

> The centre from which his power went forth was the pulpit of St. Mary's, with those wonderful afternoon sermons, Sunday after Sunday, month by month, year by year. . . .
>   The service was very simple—no pomp, no ritualism. . . . About the service, the most remarkable thing was the beauty, the intonation, of Mr. Newman's voice as he read the Lessons. . . . When he began to preach, a stranger was not likely to be much struck. . . . Here was no vehemence, no declamation, no show of elaborated argument. . . . The delivery had a peculiarity which it took a new hearer some time to get over. Each separate sentence, or at least each short paragraph, was spoken rapidly, but with great clearness of intonation; and then at its close there was a pause, lasting for nearly half a minute; then another rapidly but clearly spoken sentence, followed by another pause. It took some time to get over this, but, that once done, the wonderful charm began to dawn on you. . . . He laid his finger— how gently, yet how powerfully!—on some inner place in the hearer's heart, and told him things about himself he had never known till then.

The impression that Newman made, according to this observer, was that he transcended time and place: "The look and bearing of the preacher were as one who dwelt apart, who, though he knew his age well, did not dwell in it." The year was 1838; Newman had been preaching in St. Mary's for twelve years; and he was about to leave—not only Oxford but also his Anglican faith. As this same observer wrote of his leaving, the whole broad community felt "the aching blank, the awful pause, which fell on Oxford when that voice had ceased, and we knew that we should hear it no more."[37]

During Newman's pastorate there the Church of St. Mary's was crowded with two or three times the total population of the parish. "There was scarcely a man of note in the University, old or young, who did not during the last two or three year's of Newman's incumbency, habitually attend the service and listen to his sermons."[38] Newman preached as though engaged with his congregation in a searching conversation. "Truth is wrought out," he believed, "by many minds working freely together."[39] All his life he was "extremely shy," with a tendency to "shrink within himself," and the abrupt pauses in his speech reflected his "near escape of being a stutterer."[40] It was the rhetorician Richard Whately who, Newman testified, "first gave me heart to look about . . . taught me to think correctly, and . . . to rely on myself."[41]

J. A. Froude, the historian, as a student at Oxford was dazzled by Newman: "The simplest word which dropped from him was treasured as if it had been an intellectual diamond." In trying to explain Newman's appeal, Froude wrote: "He told us what he believed to be true. He did not know where it would carry him. No one who has ever risen to any great height in this world refuses to move till he knows where he is going. He is impelled in each step which he takes by a force within himself. He satisfies himself only that the step is a right one, and he leaves the rest to Providence." With this analysis Newman himself wholly agreed. It was in this period in his life in 1838 that he wrote his great hymn, Lead, Kindly Light, in which he averred that, "I do not ask to see the distant scene, one step enough for me." Froude went on with his description of what made Newman outstanding: "Newman's mind was world-wide. He was interested in everything which was going on in science, in politics, in literature."[42]

Newman was born on 21 February 1801 as the eldest son of a prosperous banker. Growing up with a sunny disposition, in good health, respectably ensconsed in the Church of England and educated privately, he was sheltered from vexing problems. He read widely and had no liking for sports, yet he was sufficiently popular among his fellows that they turned to him as arbiter in their disputes. At the age of fifteen he underwent a quiet conversion that assured him of "eternal glory." He entered Trinity College in Oxford the following year with the intention of becoming a barrister; but after he failed the examinations, taken while he was ill and exhausted, he acceded in his father's judgment that he should prepare for the ministry. Despite his failure in the law exam, his abilities were so well recognized that he was appointed as a Fellow of Oriel College, "the great object of the ambition of half the Bachelors of Oxford." In 1826 he was appointed curate of St. Mary's and commenced a series of thoughtful sermons on "the reasonableness of religion."

His mind was skeptical, more interested in questions than certain of answers. The greatest difficulty in the world, he said, was to believe in God. All through his life he continued to pose such problems of faith that Huxley declared he could compose a dictionary of infidelity with quotations from Newman's works. His serious concern with man's nature and destiny reached a new height in January 1828 with the death of a sister and his own severe illness. As he wrote to another sister, "I never felt so intensely the transitory nature of the world."

This quality of his mind fitted him well to deal with the particular problems of his time. Despite his own declaration that he was "out of joint with his time," precisely the opposite is true. He was well equipped both intellectually and temperamentally for the vital role—"the formation of educated Christian minds capable of resisting the increasing tide of infidel thought"[43]—which he took to be his life mission. In a letter to his mother written 13 March 1829, he deplored "the poor intellectual endowments" of spokesmen for the Church and analyzed the problem he meant to deal with:

> We live in a novel era—one in which there is an advance toward universal education. Men have hitherto depended on others, and especially on the clergy, for religious truth; now each man attempts to judge for himself. Now, without meaning of course that Christianity is in itself opposed to free inquiry, still I think it is *in fact* at the present time opposed to the particular form which that liberty of thought has now assumed. Christianity is of faith, modesty, lowliness, subordination; but the spirit at work against it is one of latitudinarianism, indifferentism, and schism, a spirit which tends to overthrow doctrine, as if [it were] the fruit of bigotry and discipline—as if the instrument of priestcraft. All parties seem to acknowledge that the stream of opinion is setting against the Church.[44]

Newman's rhetorical efforts to deal with the spread of skeptical secularism divide naturally into three periods. Each of them really dealt with the same theme, though in different ways. As he wrote in his last years, "From the time I began to occupy my mind with theological subjects I have been troubled at the prospect, which I considered to lie before us, of an intellectual movement against religion. . . . This grave apprehension led me to consider the evidences, as they are called, of Religion generally, and the intellectual theory on which they are based." As he pursued this self-set task, he gave small heed to orthodoxy, dogma, or denominationalism, instead letting his own thoughts take him wherever they led. As he said in defense of his method: "In literal warfare, weapons are tested before they are brought into use, and men are not called traitors who test them."[45]

His three great testing periods were from 1826 to 1838 in his preaching in St. Mary's; the William Street lectures in 1850 in which he discussed his disillusionment with the Church of England; and his University lectures from 1854 to 1858 when he followed his failure as a university administrator with his explanation of what he believed education should be like. Between times he lived largely in seclusion until appointed near the end of his life a Cardinal of the Church of Rome.

The St. Mary's sermons, already noted, dealt primarily with the reasonableness of supernatural beliefs. The existence of God, he felt, had no need to be "proved." His sermons were less rational or emotional than mystical: what he sought was to make the divine presence too real to be doubted. Such preaching, along with that by John Keble and E. B. Pusey, developed the Oxford Movement that for its inspiration drew heavily from the ritualism of the Medieval Church.

After this trend of thinking led him to leave the Anglican for the Roman Catholic Church, he reluctantly accepted the urging of friends to give a series of lectures on "The Difficulties of Anglicans" in the William Street Oratory in London. The first seven lectures in the series dealt with the weaknesses of the Anglican Church and the last five with the validity of Roman Catholicism. In these lectures Newman was untypically controversial, arguing that the Anglicans "had reared a goodly house, but their foundations were falling in." He saw the Church as cut off from its origins, with "no relationship to the Church in other lands," and as "nothing more or less than an establishment, a department of government. . . ."[46] In contrast he found security in the continuity of the Church of Rome from its founding by St. Peter.

But what chiefly concerned him was not the relative merits of the two churches but the argument of the atheists that "The Creator of the World is either wanting in love or power—therefore He is not God, or there is no God." What saddened Newman was that "Christianity does not touch this argument."[47] Much as he tried, neither could he. More than most people he felt strongly the inadequacy of religious explanation of the multiple evils of life; but he rested in acceptance if not in contentment upon the view set forth in his hymn: to see but a little way and to leave the rest to the wisdom of God. Even an Anglican minister, listening to these lectures and rejecting their arguments, was deeply impressed by his ability to "persuade without irritating" while being "perfectly free from any dictatorial note."[48] Even irreligious listeners or readers of the published lectures had to be aware that Newman shared many of their own questions and doubts and agreed with their insistence that answers are lacking or incomplete. The difference is that he could no more avoid belief than they could avoid unbelief. In 1864 he published his Apologia Pro Vita Sua, "a book too personal to be published," in which he sought not to deny or evade the doubts that challenged religion but to make vivid the point that at least for him religion was far too real and imminent to require either proof or explanation.

In 1851 Newman was appointed rector of a nonexistent Catholic University that the Church planned to be established in Dublin. To build support for it Newman gave a series of five lectures to an audience of about 400 on the need to teach religion as a counterweight to science in order that students may have a complete and balanced understanding of values as well as of facts. He was well pleased with the reactions to his lectures; but the aim to establish a university failed from lack of adequate planning. Another and perhaps greater reason was that Newman failed to win approval for his special view of the nature of education. From the start he found that he was in a "hornet's nest."[49] The Catholic bishops whose support was essential considered him to be "too intellectual," with too much awareness of the uncertainties hedging church dogmas; and the secular intellectuals did not accept his insistence that theology deserved the same attention in the curriculum that was given to science.

Newman resigned as rector and returned to England convinced that "the most vital question of the hour for the interests of the Church" was: "how a thoroughly liberal education could be possible for Catholics, with their tenacity to tradition and strict views as to the rights of ecclesiastical authority."[50] The question had the much broader implication of whether true education is possible for minds predisposed to supernaturalism. Newman viewed the question also from its contrary aspect—whether true education is possible for minds predisposed to reject the reality of divinity. It was to this problem that he devoted his most serious thought for substantially the remainder of his life (as he had also in the main from the early years in St. Mary's). He developed his defense of religion as essential for genuine intellectualism in a series of lectures spread over 1854 through 1858 that were published as *The Idea of a University.*

Huxley had not yet invented the term "agnostic," but it was precisely against this form of skepticism that Newman argued. How he dealt with the problem illustrates his general appeal to common sense and experience. He encapsulated the case against theology as follows:

You may have opinions in religion; you may have theories; you may have arguments; you may have probabilities; you may have anything but demonstration, and, therefore, you cannot have science. . . .

On the other hand, there is at present no real science of the weather because you cannot get hold of facts and truths on which it depends; there is no science of the coming and going of epidemics; no science of the breaking out and cessation of wars; no science of popular likings and dislikings, or of the fashions. It is not that these subject matters are themselves incapable of science, but that, under existing circumstances, we are incapable of subjecting them to it. And so, in like manner . . . as it would be absurd to dogmatise about the weather, . . . so it is absurd for men in our present state to teach anything positively about the next world, that there is a heaven, or a hell, or a last judgment, or that the soul is immortal, or that there is a God. . . . Truth has been sought in the wrong direction, and the attainable has been put aside for the visionary.[51]

So much for the case against the teaching of religion. Then comes his reply:

Some persons will say that I am thinking of confining, distorting, and stunting the growth of the intellect by ecclesiastical supervision. I have no such thought. Nor have I any thought of a compromise, as if religion must give up something, and science something. I wish the intellect to range with the utmost freedom, and religion to enjoy an equal freedom; but what I am stipulating is that they should be found in one and the same place, and exemplified in the same persons. . . .

I want the intellectual layman to be religious, and the devout ecclesiastic to be intellectual.[52]

Newman's rhetorical problem was too difficult for him to solve—perhaps too difficult for anyone. His insistence that religion and science be accorded an equal status brought storms of protest from both sides. Much as his lectures were admired, they did not convince. As he wrote sadly in a diary that he kept in his latter years under date of 8 January 1860: "I have no friend at Rome, I have laboured in England, to be misrepresented, backbitten and scorned. I have laboured in Ireland, with a door ever shut in my face." There was, however, one strange exception in his list of his own failures: "Those very books and labours of mine, which Catholics did not understand, Protestants did."[53]

Not until the closing years of his life, after the publication of his *Apologia,* was his early popularity restored. In 1878 Trinity College made him an honorary fellow; and the following year a new Pope, Leo XIII, made him a Cardinal. These honors were applauded by the English public and came to him barely in time, for he died on 11 August 1890. Shortly afterward a movement was started to declare him "venerable," the first step toward naming him a saint. In retrospect few consider him saintly; but, if not revered, he is widely admired as a sincere advocate of the view that the "theories" of religion merit fully as serious attention as do the "theories" of science. His rhetorical influence was far less widespread than that of Spurgeon and Drummond but even more than Dale's it was vital in intellectual circles and it has grown as that of the others has declined.

"It Is Preachers Who Form the Cutting Edge"

As the nineteenth century merged into the twentieth, the problems that concerned Dale, Spurgeon, Drummond, and Newman continued to be reexamined and some new ones came also to demand urgent attention. The devastating nature of war as it was reshaped by science and technology made more urgent the question of pacifism. The expanding view of the universe—ranging from the infinitely large to the infinitely small, all apparently regulated by natural cause-and-effect—sharpened inquiry as to the true nature of God. The paradox of tremendously accelerated production accompanied by unemployment, widespread starvation, and miserable living conditions for many accentuated the urgency of directing spiritual energy to the cause of social betterment. Theologians such as Sören Kierkegaard, Karl Barth, Emil Brunner, Dietrich Bonhoeffer, and Paul Tillich, along with many others have raised new questions about the nature and the value of religion.

Questions for which new answers are being sought were considered by a group of British theologians who met together for several years to discuss problems that are difficult to solve but are too important to be avoided. As they considered such matters as the nature of God and the meaning of prayer, they agreed that "this is an age of clerical despondency," and that "after the first World War, we were all debunking the nineteenth century, after the second we are deferring to it, and even yearning nostalgically after it . . . [where] all that we now lack seems present in abundance: not only peace, prosperity, plenty, and freedom, but faith, purpose, and buoyancy."[54] In successive papers they presented what seemed to them to be the most vital questions with which religion must deal in terms of current understanding:

How may theology be reconciled with philosophy? "The philosopher's job is to inquire. The philosophical theologian has only pretended to inquire. His conclusions were prescribed from the outset."[55]

How does theology relate to science? "What is true cannot be whittled down to What is useful or What works?"[56]

Does divinity transcend human understanding? "This is an odd question because if we have experience of something, we know that it is sufficiently in being for us to experience it."[57]

What justification is there for evil? "Since life for me is not all that it could be, since in some way or other I am bound to be frustrated and incapable of articulating my full potency, ... it is inevitable that I should feel deep resentment against the almighty Father . . . who . . . is ultimately responsible for all the ills from which I suffer."[58]

What should Christians think of other religions? "if we are asked to accept a revelation, it is much easier if it has no worthy rivals. . . . But there are other living faiths apart from Christianity . . . to talk their language is in part to appeal to tests of truth which they themselves will at least recognize as relevant."[59]

Still other questions that are longstanding were also discussed by this same group. What they made clear was that for theologians as for preachers there are contrary routes toward answers: the seeking of new understandings in new ways or turning back to the comforting domain of old certainties.[60] Both methods were evident in the multiplicity of pulpits from which the religious message was being preached. Along with the probing for new answers and the defense of old ones, there also developed in this period of the radio and later television new means of preaching to vast audiences and concurrently to individual worshippers who recieve these messages privately in their own homes. Preaching has by no means become less important as the new intellectualism has challenged its old teachings and altered its old methods. Theologians ask questions and answer them; but it is preachers who form the cutting edge that brings the issue to listeners. In our day as in past centuries they are purveyors of faith and shapers of lives and as such they have enormous influence.

6
THE CENTRAL TRIAD:
VICTORIA, DISRAELI, AND GLADSTONE

The issues that dominated public attention as the century advanced were clear. Most basically, should government be determined by property or by people? The Reform Bill of 1832 gave only a half-hearted, partial answer, notable as it was for initiating a new way. Should the rural or the urban interests govern? Urbanism for the first time was beginning to predominate. As late as the 1770s the second largest English City (after London) was not in the British Isles, but was the colonial metropolis of Philadelphia.[1] For the first time the long tradition of dominance by landholders—from the nobility down through the country gentry and the small-plot farmers—came under challenge.[2] Cities in England became centers of influence. The shift to a factory economy brought new wealth and influence to manufacturers. And despite the misery of the workers, their need for employment created an intertwining of the basic interests of the employers and the employed. The defeat of protectionism when the Corn Laws were repealed gave support to the laissez-faire principle because it showed that wages did not necessarily decline when prices did.

In foreign affairs, too, a new viewpoint became prominent. When Englishmen looked abroad they were repelled by the widespread revolutionism in Europe and the Americas and concerned about the expansionist ambitions of Russia. As the competitive struggle among nations for raw resources and new markets heightened, free trade seemed to offer better opportunities than colonization; but by mid-century the old dreams of Empire became vivid again.

Amid such basic changes, the Tory and Whig parties dissolved, broken by internal dissensions. The Conservative and Liberal parties succeeded them—new alliances with new leaders supporting new policies and programs.[3] All these changes had to be talked out. Leaders had to make up their own minds—no easy task—and then had to coalesce a following.

The leaders who won the greatest prominence were a strong-minded girl-queen and two orator-statemen, Disraeli and Gladstone, who differed sharply between themselves even while being manifestly superior to their associates. Notably the age was not named for these party leaders. It took its name and its distinguishing quality from a personage who was far from being a public speaker but who did much to shape the tone and establish the circumstances that dominated the rhetorical occasion—the plump, stolid, and determined Queen Victoria who came to the throne as a mere girl of eighteen in 1837 and reigned for sixty-four years until her death in 1901. In their several roles these three each in a different way formed the central caste of characters in the multifaceted drama of the Victorian Age.

"Excited Expectations . . . Against Needless Changes"

The Victorian period was far from being revolutionary. It was a time of vast and rapid growth during which excited expectations were looking ahead: technologically, with the coming of the railway, the telegraph, the steamship and later the telephone; socially, with new demands for the perennially poor, for workers, and for women; philosophically, with new scientific knowledge that altered man's view of himself and of society; and politically, with the traditional faith in hierarchy challenged by the new egalitarianism. These changes were basic both in depth and in breadth. But they had little in common with the revolutionism that shook up Germany, France, Italy, and Eastern Europe.

Disraeli and Gladstone confronted one another with sharp words that emphasized their personal animosity, with elaborate maneuvering for partisan advantage, and with contrasting programs for which they did their utmost to win public support. Yet the general tenor of each was toward a middle-grounded stability. Their views of the future were different but they agreed largely in their attachment to the English past. What Disraeli said about it during the 1874 electoral campaign was selected by an able historian as representative of his general political stance: "The proper leaders of our people are the gentlemen of England. . . . If it be true that we are on the eve of troublous times, if it be indeed necessary that changes should take place in this country, let them be effected by those who ought to be the leaders in all political and social change."[4] So much for the conservative view. But the liberalism of Gladstone was similarly based. Just four years later in the 1878 campaign to unseat Disraeli Gladstone's assertion of his "fond attachment" to the "nobleness of the inheritance that has descended upon us" was selected by another sound historian as the ultimate statement of the Liberal Party philosophy.[5] With this judgment Lord John Morley agreed in his monumental biography of Gladstone, concluding that: "However we may choose to trace the sources and relations of Mr. Gladstone's general ideas upon the political problems of his time, what he said of himself was at least true of its dawn and noon. 'I am for old customs and traditions,' he wrote, 'against needless change.'"[6] Both Disraeli the Conservative and Gladstone the Liberal were in accord on the basic premise that traditional England had been too successful and was still too valuable to be put aside. What they disagreed about was the nature and the degree of the alterations that changing conditions prescribed.

Victorianism was by far too complex to be neatly characterized. Multiple volumes have been written about it and more will be because there are many perspectives from which it may be viewed.

In a rhetorical examination, certain characteristics do stand out clearly. Disraeli and Gladstone intensely disliked one another. Queen Victoria disliked Gladstone and she enjoyed the wit and the flattery of Disraeli. Disraeli used the queen and the institution of the monarchy with great skill to help accomplish his purposes. Gladstone greatly respected the royal person and the royal prerogatives even while finding the queen an impediment to his programs. The careers of these three were closely intertwined. However much they differed, they were an impressive trio, each strong in their quite different abilities. And in their own ways they were all three effective wielders of influence. Far from being mere observant bystanders, they were shapers of the changes that came to be.

"She Influenced What Should and Could Be Discussed"

The role of Queen Victoria in an account of British public address was not that she gave speeches but that she greatly influenced what should and could be discussed. She set the tone for the discussion and she affected considerably what the national audience expected from it. She set the stamp of her personality upon the time. This was true despite the fact that hers was a very ordinary personality. It was her very ordinariness, lighted with the aura of royalty, that powered the great effects. What the queen wanted, and how the queen felt, represented the general public sentiment.

At the time of Victoria's birth in 1819 the English monarchy was in dismal disarray. George III had fathered fifteen children, seven of them sons. But they were generally dissolute and they produced no heirs. When the fourth son, the Duke of Kent, was fifty-one he was persuaded much against his own wishes to abandon his mistress of twenty-eight years in order to marry the dowager of Leiningen, a widow with two children, whom he had seen only once. His reason for agreeing to this marriage was simply to induce Parliament to increase his allotment and to pay his enormous debts. He had to borrow money for his honeymoon and when his bride became pregnant he borrowed again to enable him to bring his family to England so that the child would be English-born.

This baby born on 24 May 1819 was a "pretty little Princess, as plump as a partridge." Her uncle, reigning as William IV, disliked her father, despised the Duke's Whiggish associations, and resented the fact that it was his niece who would succeed to the throne. The accession occurred on 20 June 1837.

Queen Victoria was neither brilliant nor studious. Neither during her growing up nor during her long reign did she learn much about the problems that beset her subjects. As one of her biographers concludes: "One of the very few valid criticisms of Queen Victoria is that she was not sufficiently concerned with improvement of the conditions in which a great mass of her subjects passed their lives. She lived through an age of profound social change, but neither public health, nor housing, nor the education of her people, nor their representation, engaged much of her attention."[7] What she did attend to was the magnification of the glory of the throne and of the greatness of the nation. Never socially at ease in company or in public, she remained isolated. On ceremonial occasions she rode through cheering crowds with an impassive expression and only an occasional small gesture. Her attachment was not to the people but to her throne. She was a devoted wife, a domineering mother, and a resolute queen. Her popularity derived principally from the first and the last of these factors.

Victoria's monarchism was strengthened by her love-match marriage to her cousin, Prince Albert of Saxe-Coburg and Gotha, a handsome lad whose Prussianism fitted with and fortified her antidemocratic views. When they married on 10 February 1840, Victoria's chief emotion was fear—her dread of "the possibility of having a large family of children." Their first months together were stormy. Victoria had never been taught to control her temper and she was used to having her own way. Albert complained that "she will not hear me out but flies into a rage and overwhelms me with reproaches." This comment was made to their German adviser, Baron Stockmar, who served as an intermediary between the two, and it was to Stockmar that Victoria made her reply, "Dearest Angel Albert, God only knows how I love him." In Albert's view, "the difficulty of filling my place with proper dignity is that I am only the husband, and not the master in the house."[8]

Gradually they learned how to live together, cherishing one another and sternly dominating their children. After Albert's death, the widowed queen sincerely, publicly, and persistently idealized his memory. Among the social gentry of the time adultery was commonplace and undisguised; but the queen's constancy was praised and admired even when it was not imitated. What Dr. Johnson had said during the reign of Victoria's grandfather—that "Hypocrisy is the tribute that vice pays to virtue"—even more surely marked the language and the conduct of the Victorian socialites. There was a need to assert virtue if not to practice it.

This was the queen whose determined exaltation of royalty won back for the crown much of the splendor and some of the power it had lost during the last years of George III and during the innocuous reigns of George IV and William IV. Her stolid dignity on public occasions, her example of duty, morality, and religious faith, and her display of poised self-confidence won for her great popularity and an influence that surmounted constitutional restrictions. During the midyears of her reign Disraeli, with his talent for creating fiction, vested her with magical qualities and called her a Faery Queen who exemplified the innate greatness of her people.[9] With persistent flattery and gallantry he not only won her favor and friendship but also greatly enhanced her popularity.[10] To one of Disraeli's biographers, this image-building of the queen "was his most notable achievement as a statesman, for it popularized the monarchy in Great Britain and gave the English throne a prestige throughout the world which it has never lost."[11]

In contrast to the cordial relationship Disraeli established with the queen, both Victoria and Albert disliked Gladstone and made no effort to conceal their feelings. Her preference for Disraeli between the two is somewhat strange since Disraeli was cynical, skeptical, and eccentric in his ideas, dress, and manners; whereas Gladstone, much like the queen and her consort, was strictly orthodox in religion, staid to the point of dullness in his social behavior, and always studiously correct in his dealings with her. Yet the relations of these two are best indicated in a memorandum that Gladstone wrote following his last audience with her on 2 August 1886: "I respect her for her scrupulous avoidance of anything which could have seemed to indicate a desire on her part to claim anything in common with me."[12] In a very different vein were Disraeli's comments about his conversations with her during his prime ministry: "She opened her mind and heart to me. . . . Free from all shyness, she spoke with great animation and happy expression; showed not only perception, but discrimination of character, and was most interesting and amusing."[13] Disraeli's interpretaton of her was overly generous. But what matters is that he won the queen's support while Gladstone had to contend with her animosity. What matters even more is that Disraeli impressed upon the public his own view of her as a transcendent personality.

Almost despite herself Queen Victoria became a symbol around which her people rallied. With the creation of a party government that was based on broad representation, the throne was reduced to being a passive mouthpiece of the prime ministers. But this did not derogate from the queen's influence. On the contrary, her lack of authority and consequent lack of responsibility combined with Disraeli's idealized portrayal brought her a unique and overriding popularity. She was viewed as being separated from and therefore above political controversies. She represented the resurgence of empire. She came to be a "kind of universal mother, a Pan-Brittanic Madonna. To the colonies and dependencies beyond the seas she embodied the Empire in the most convenient, because the most inoffensive form."[14] Rudyard Kipling's *Barrack Room Ballads* well represented the feelings of the British public, that they were "aserving of Her Majesty the Queen." The very loss of the constitutional power of the throne made possible the transition to a new kind of power, one of centralizing and unifying the loyalty of the people. Despite the disruptive problems of the Victorian Age, an energizing power of patriotism, an overwhelming pride in being English, and an expression of these sentiments in an attachment to the person of the queen sufficed to hold the society together.

This was precisely the point that was emphasized during the celebration of the sixtieth anniversary of Victoria's coronation in the Diamond Jubilee that was held in the summer of 1897. Sir William Harcourt defined it in his speech to the House of Commons on 21 June:

> It has been asked what has been the office which the Queen has performed? That office has been the supreme tie which bound together various classes and diverse races in these vast dominions, which has held them in one united whole by a sovereign partaking the spirit of the people, which has gathered them in growing affection round her throne.[15]

The role of Victoria is further clarified by comparison with that of the first Elizabeth, her greatest predecessor queen. Elizabeth I yielded only a little of her constitutional authority while impressing her personality on her time. Victoria, by contrast, tried hard to enlarge the power of the throne and failed to do so; yet in the very process she gained greater influence as a symbol than she could have had as a ruler. Both queens won tremendous popularity. Both made the monarchy a force for national unity that no bitterness of contention—which was notable in both their reigns—could destroy. It was within this curbing influence of the "tie that binds" that the sharp confrontations between Disraeli and Gladstone took place.

"A Master of Fiction, a Dazzling Personality . . . Young England"

In the view of Asa Briggs, the culminating step in the achievement of democracy in England was the Reform Bill of 1867 that was brought to passage by the leadership of Benjamin Disraeli. As Briggs saw it, Disraeli accomplished what his Liberal opponent, Gladstone, could not, by Disraeli's skillful utilization of Machiavellian tactics. In a deeply divided House of Commons in which no party held a majority, Disraeli had to seek votes by combining appeals to his own reluctant Conservatives, to the Radicals who believed that the measure did not go nearly far enough, and to the Liberals who were disenchanted with Gladstone and had no other leader whom they trusted. As Briggs interpreted Disraeli's methods, he introduced provisions "which few of his opponents accepted," and thereby "confused his enemies in their purposes and made them fight not against him but among one another." As for the effects of the bill, Briggs quotes the conclusion stated by Walter Bagehot in his work on the British Constitution:

> A political country is like an American forest: you have only to cut down the old trees, and immediately new trees come up to replace them; the seeds were waiting in the ground, and they began to grow as soon as the withdrawal of the old ones brought in light and air.[16]

Benjamin Disraeli was unique and unparalleled among British statesmen. Above all he was a master of fiction—not so much a statesman who tried also to be a novelist as a novelist who succeeded in becoming a statesman. He was not above substituting fiction for fact. As one instance, he invented for himself a line of forebears that, as he claimed, for two hundred years had been in the aristocracy. Even in his parliamentary speeches, according to a friendly interpretation, he displayed "imaginativeness and an exceptional alertness to the power of symbolic acts and phrases."[17] "Dizzy" was his nickname and "Dazzle" was his quality. With sarcasm and ridicule and also by wit and by charm, "he excited the interest of the nation, quickened their imagination, and inspired their affection."[18] Both his personality and his career were extraordinary.

It is remarkable that in such a period he could rise to national leadership. His antecedents were Jewish. His grandfather, who came to England from Italy, was named Israeli. His father who was bookish, ambitious to be a writer, and a successful compiler of literary trivia, changed the name to D'Israeli. Young Benjamin was baptized into the Church of England but never took religion seriously. He was a careless student and left school early. The change of his name to Disraeli was made by his father for him when he was placed in school, presumably to make it seem less foreign. As a mere youth he tried his hand at both business and the editing of journals and failed utterly in both attempts. Then, before he was twenty-one, he commenced the writing of novels and in this he became an instant and a lasting success.

He was openly disdainful of public speaking. In his first novel, the auto-biographical *Vivian Grey*, he has one of his characters say, "Nothing is more undignified than to make a speech. It is from the first an acknowledgement that you are under the necessity of explaining, or conciliating, or convincing, or confuting; in short, that you are not omnipotent, but opposed." Nevertheless, he also credits his hero (himself) with having "a tongue which was born to guide human beings." This was a bit of insight that proved to be prophetic.

Even so, when he developed political ambitions he had to try five times before he won election to Parliament. And when he got there, his first five years of membership were undistinguished. In this period his chief political assets appeared to be ambition and an egoistic self-confidence. Even in 1834 while he was still trying to win an election, when he was asked courteously by Lord Melbourne, then Home Secretary, what he wanted to be, he shocked the austere party leader by retorting, "I want to be Prime Minister."[19] But he was also intelligent enough and purposive enough to realize that he had to plan and to work for success. The problem was that he did not know in what direction to go. He flirted for a time with radicalism, then chose the Tory Party. To his associates he was very much a man of mystery. As an outsider, he seemed more Jewish than Anglican, son of a dilletante father who was a dabbler on the fringes of literature, and an ambitious newcomer who had neither popularity nor the support of powerful interests. His intelligence, dexterity, and creative imagination did not seem to be sufficient counterweights. "Only supreme confidence in himself could have overcome the obstacles which confronted him."[20]

His career started slowly. He first stood for election in June 1832, while the Reform Bill was changing the nature of politics. That same fall he made his second attempt, urging the voters to forget the Whigs and the Tories, terming them "two names with one meaning . . . and unite in forming a great national party." In both these campaigns he ended at the bottom of the poll. When he tried again with a different constituency, the outlook was so hopeless that he quickly withdrew. Through it all he insisted that he represented "the people." But he did not look like it. He dressed flamboyantly in black velvet with lace at the collar and wore a bright multicolored waistcoat. The eccentricity of his attire was accentuated by his pale complexion, his flowing black hair, and his wearing large rings on his fingers and a chain draped around his neck.

He continued all his life to cultivate an eccentric appearance. Even in Parliament during the height of his career when he was leader of the Opposition he customarily sat slouched in his front row seat with his head bent low and his hat pulled down over his eyes, as though he was totally ignoring the ministerial speeches, when in fact he was alert to interject a challenge or a retort. Always introspective and eager to understand himself, he kept a diary in which an entry for the autumn of 1833, while he was still seeking his first electoral victory, is revealing. "Nature," he wrote, "has given me an awful ambition and fiery passions." Then he added: "I wish to be idle and enjoy myself. . . . I am only truly great in action. If ever I am placed in a truly eminent position I shall prove this. I could rule the House of Commons, although there would be a great prejudice against me at first."[21]

In the general election of 1835 he stood once more for election, this time as a Tory; but although the eminent Duke of Wellington gave him support, once again he came out at the bottom of the poll. He refused to be discouraged. He knew by that time that he had to keep trying. Politics had an allure for him that he could not resist. This was partly because of the excitement he found in it. In his letters and in his novels, "Disraeli conveys the drama and the excitement of parliamentary life—not to mention the comedy—in a way that no one else has quite achieved: the intrigues, the manoeuvres, the calculations, the rumours, the fluctuations of fortune, the agony of being out, and the triumph of being in. Politics was the very fibre of his being."[22]

But he was also developing convictions that he was determined to espouse. What he believed in most lastingly was the need "to uphold the aristocratic settlement of this country." As he saw it, "It is our Institutions that have made us free, and can alone keep us so." What he feared was the new industrialism, the extension of the franchise, and the loosening of restrictions on Catholics and Dissenters. What he believed needed support included the influence of the monarchy, of the House of Lords, of the established church, and of the landed interests. These views were deep-seated and they remained his lifelong guides. But when he explained them to the voters during the electoral campaign in 1835, he described himself as less ideological than pragmatic.

The truth is, gentlemen, a statesman is the creature of his age, the child of circumstances, the creation of his time. A statesman is essentially a practical character. . . . The fact is, the conduct and the opinions of public men at different periods of their career must not be too curiously contrasted in a free and aspiring country. The people have their passions, and it is even the duty of public men occasionally to adopt sentiments with which they are not sympathetic, because the people must have leaders. Then the opinions and prejudices of the Crown must necessarily influence a rising statesman. . . . All this, however, produces ultimate benefit; all these influences tend to form that eminently practical character for which our countrymen are celebrated. I laugh, therefore, at the objection against a man, that at a former period of his career he advocated a policy different to his present one. All I seek to ascertain is whether his present policy be just, necessary, expedient; whether at the present moment he is prepared to serve the country according to its present necessities. [23]

Pragmatic though he meant to be, cautious practicality was not his nature. During the campaign all unknown as he was he undertook to depict Daniel O'Connell as a traitor while that Irish statesman was at the height of his fame. O'Connell's response was contemptuous dismissal: "He is a liar in action and in words. His life is a living lie. He is a disgrace to his species." [24] If there was a lesson here to be learned, Disraeli did not learn it. After his election to parliament on 15 November 1837 Disraeli not only ignored the tradition that a new member should remain quiet but he boldly used the occasion for another attack upon O'Connell. The speech was a total disaster. He prepared the speech carefully but unwisely, loading it with what he thought to be impressive diction. The members had no stomach for this pretense of his literary superiority. A veritable uproar of jeers, laughter, and hisses kept him from being heard. Greville noted in his diary that it was an "Exhibition . . . beginning with florid assurance, speedily degenerating into ludicrous absurdity, and being at last put down with inextinguishable bursts of laughter." [25] Another member called it "such a mixture of insolence and folly as I never heard in my life before." [26] Above the hubbub Disraeli shouted his last words: "I will sit down now, but the time will come when you will hear me."

During the next several years his political philosophy matured through his association with a Cambridge group calling itself "Young England" that met to discuss current problems with a romantic yearning for the olden times when the country gentry were prominent, before there were factory workers and labor unions, and when the peasant farm tenants touched their caps and addressed their betters as sir. What Young England stood for Disraeli summarized in his preface to an 1870 edition of his collected novels:

To change back the oligarchy into a generous aristocracy round a real throne; to infuse life and vigor into the Crown, as the trainer of the nation . . . to establish a commercial code on the principles successfully negotiated by Lord

Bolingbroke at Utrecht . . . to govern Ireland according to the policy of Charles I, and not of Oliver Cromwell; to emancipate the political constituency of 1832 from its sectarian bondage and contracted sympathies; to elevate the physical as well as the moral condition of the people by establishing that labour required regulation as much as property; and all this rather by the use of ancient forms and the restoration of the past than by political revolutions founded on abstract ideas.

In Disraeli's subsequent parliamentary speeches, which were generally advocating "the ascendancy of the landed interest as the dominant group in society,"[27] he did not attempt to conciliate his opponents but to overpower them. In a typical outburst during the session of 1845 he ridiculed the speeches of the ministers as they appeared in the parliamentary journal: "What dreary pages of interminable talk, what predictions falsified, what pledges broken, what calculations that have gone wrong, what budgets that have blown up! And all this, too, not relieved by a single original thought, a single generous impulse, or a single happy expression! Why *Hansard*, instead of being the Delphi of Downing Street is but the Dunciad of politics."[28] His conclusion was in the heavy sarcasm that had become his trademark: "Let us tell the persons in high places that cunning is not caution, and that habitual perfidy is not high policy of State."

It was that session of 1845 that repealed the Corn Laws. Changes had come fast and Disraeli rightly sensed that the people wanted a respite. In the debate he savagely denounced the Peelites as "political pedlars that bought their party in the cheapest market and sold it in the dearest." He went on: "I know, Sir, that all confidence in public men is lost. But, Sir, I have faith in the primitive and enduring elements of the English character. . . . Then, when their spirits are softened by misfortune, they will recur to those principles that made England great, and which in our belief will only keep England great."[29]

As Monypenny and Buckle observed, "The House had now begun to await Disraeli's risings on the tiptoe of expectation."[30] His speeches made him the focal point of political attention. A journalist writing in the 23 March 1845 issue of the *Weekly Chronicle* described the effect:

For him to rise late, in a stormy debate, cool even to iciness, amidst the fever-heat of party atmosphere around, was suddenly to arrest all passions, all excitement, all murmurs of conversation, and convert them into one absorbing feeling of curiosity and expectation. They knew not on whom to fix their watch—whether on the speaker, that they might not lose the slightest gesture of his by-play, or whether they should concentrate their attention on his distinguished victim, whom he had taught them almost to regard with levity.

Disraeli's eloquence poured forth in a series of Phillipics against which the ministry could not stand. When Peel defended his policies as being not expedient but for the long-term good of the nation, Disraeli poured scorn upon such an aim: "What an advantage to a country to be governed by a Minister who thinks only of posterity! The right hon. gentleman has before assured us that he and his colleagues are only thinking of the future. Who can doubt it? Look at them. Throw your eyes on the Treasury bench. See stamped on every ingenuous front 'the last infirmity of a noble mind.' They are all of them, as Spenser says, 'imps of fame.' "[31]

Peel resigned. Lord John Russell came in as prime minister and at last Disraeli had a cabinet position. When the new Parliament met on 19 January 1847 he took his position on the front bench where he was to continue to sit in office or in opposition for the next thirty years. Responsibility brought him a new sobriety. He abandoned his flashily colored garb and dressed thereafter in sober black. His speeches became calmer—and duller. But his devotion to Young England did not cool. Throughout the remainder of his career he represented a point of view that many in England wanted to support: that changes were coming too fast; that the trend toward democracy should be slowed; that the greatness of the traditional constitution was too precious to allow it to be lightly altered.

Nevertheless, as has been noted, it was Disraeli who accomplished adoption of the Reform Bill of 1867 by which the suffrage was greatly broadened. As a pragmatist he realized that such a reform had to come. As a partisan he wanted his own party to bring it in in order to "dish the Whigs." In every sense, it was a personal triumph. "Every quality of a great leader was his at command; he could ridicule, conciliate, exasperate, soothe. He spoke more than three hundred times. . . . It was an astounding performance."[32] To this judgment by Pearson it should be added that he had an additional advantage in seeking support from natural opponents of such legislation, because he himself had opposed it in prior years. When Lord Russell had been ready to proceed with such a bill in 1850 while war with Russia was becoming likely, Disraeli objected to shifting the "depository of power" on the ground that it would be unsettling at a time when national unity was essential. "I thought that we were going to make war upon the Emperor of Russia," he told the House. "I find we are only going to make war upon ourselves."[33] As late as 1865 he was still arguing urgently against extending the suffrage, saying that "the suffrage should remain a privilege, and not a right; a privilege to be gained by virtue, by intelligence, by industry, by integrity. . . . And I think if you quit that ground, if you come to admit that a man has a right to vote . . . you would change the character of the Constitution." His principal appeal was to past experience: "you must remember that this peculiar country . . . is not governed by force; it is not governed by standing armies; it is governed by a most singular series of traditionary influences, which generation after generation cherishes because they know that they embalm custom and represent law."[34]

With such a background of reluctance, when electoral reform became inevitable, Disraeli was able to declare his own sponsorship for it and to carry with him enough conservative votes to secure its passage. The speech he made on the second reading of the bill was hailed by his followers as "one of the best you ever made; and, after our troubles, it has come like the warm weather after frost and snow."[35] What he said was temperate, pragmatic, and proved to be convincing: "We are prepared, as I think I have shown, to act in all sincerity upon this measure. . . . Act with us, I say, cordially and candidly; you will find on our side complete reciprocity of feeling." His shift of stance was timely, it was expedient, and it worked. A great step toward democracy was taken, led by the one who had most opposed it.

For a volume of his speeches on parliamentary reform published by Longmans in 1867 Disraeli prepared an "Advertisement" in which he claimed that his views on the subject had been always consistent. It was a claim he continued to make. To a party convention in Manchester in 1872 he made a speech lasting three hours and a quarter, reviewing the general political trends of the time. He was then sixty-eight years of age and his health was frail. To maintain his strength, during the course of the speech he consumed two full bottles of white brandy, which his audience took to be water. He contended that the continuing prosperity of England during the two preceding centuries had been due to the power of the throne, "something in this country round which all classes and all parties could rally." In the speech he ridiculed the notion of "some philosophers" that the House of Lords should be replaced by an assembly of ex-governors of colonies. For himself, he said,

> I am inclined to believe that an English gentleman—born to business, managing his own estate, administering the affairs of his county, mixing with all classes of his fellowmen, now in the hunting field, now in the railway direction, unaffected, unostentatious, proud of his ancestors, if they have contributed to the greatness of our common country—is, on the whole, more likely to form a senator agreeable to English opinion and English taste than any substitute that has yet been proposed.[36]

How should Disraeli be assessed? He was a master of persuasive style. He was a master of political timing. He was an alien to English society who through sheer superior ability rose to mastery over it. He changed course dramatically—from opposing empire to extending and magnifying it; from arguing against democratic extension to accomplishing a major step toward it; from being great in opposition to being also great in administration. Some have regarded him as a meteor-like phenomenon, distinguished by "his marvellous rise from the midst of a then despised race to the summit of power, by his mysterious and romantic personality, by the high and imperial patriotism of his ideas, and by that imaginative quality in him which fired the imagination of others."[37] Another study of his career credited his success primarily to his persuasive abilities: "Where Disraeli excelled was in the art of presentation. . . . He knew how much depends upon impression, style, colour; and how small a part [is] played in politics by logic, cool reason, calm appraisal of alternatives. . . . There is a champagne-like sparkle about him which has scarcely ever been equalled and never surpassed among statesmen."[38] Inevitably in any evaluation of him he must be compared with Gladstone, for the two were tightly intertwined. In the view of an able student of the time:

> Not since Pitt and Fox faced each other across the floor of the House had there been so Homeric a conflict of personality in Parliament as that presented by Gladstone and Disraeli. They were flint and steel to each other's genius, the one all moral fervour, to whom politics was an article of religion, the other a romantic artist, to whom they were the material of a diverting tale. Gladstone always seemed to be hurrying with a message from Mt. Sinai and meeting Disraeli coming from the feet of Scheherazade. The gravity of the one and the levity of the other left them no common ground of intercourse. To the great sceptic, Gladstone's seriousness was an incomparable jest; to the great Churchman, Disraeli's cynicism was an outrage on all the sanctities of life.[39]

What must further be said of Disraeli is that he truly represented a faith and a feeling that are deeply lodged in the English character[40]—an abiding respect for the national traditions even while they are being basically revised. This was the foundation for his career. In one sense he represented the sharp break with the traditions that he generally upheld—that is, he showed by example that the upward path to success was available even to one who stood outside and apart from the Establishment.

The success that he attained was considerable, especially considered in terms of the odds against it, but it was far from complete. Of his thirty-five years in public life, only eleven were spent in the cabinet, and in only five of these years did he exercise real power. Much that he stood for—the extension of empire, the retention of aristocratic dominance—has eroded away. His penchant for wit and ridicule, his air of cynical skepticism, and his claim of personal superiority caused his opponents to dislike him and even his friends to doubt his sincerity. Yet as the decades pass, his reputation continues to grow. What is clear is that he was a dazzling personality who did much to influence the direction of affairs and also the tone and the temper of his time. In both his person and his political effects, he remained Young England to the end.

"Somber Earnestness, Moral, Dutiful, Sincere"

William Ewart Gladstone entered Parliament at the age of twenty-three in 1852 with his character, his personality, and his general views already well formed. He remained in the forefront of English public affairs until his retirement in 1894 at the age of eighty-three. He has been accounted the most voluminous speaker in British history. In 366 Hansard volumes, reports of his speeches fill some fifteen thousand columns of fine print. Outside of Parliament, on the hustings and on public occasions, he spoke almost as much. If it be true, as Ben Jonson asserted, that "speech most shows the man," all that Gladstone was he profusely revealed.

Earnestness was his trademark. Witticisms and mere rhetorical glitter he disdained. To an unfriendly critic, he "contained within himself the peculiar qualities of an age that exhibited self-righteousness, moral indignation, democratic enthusiasm and religious emotionalism. . . . What disabled Gladstone as a human being, but contributed greatly to his personal majesty and public achievement, was a total lack of humour. . . . He loved disputation and would argue about anything. . . . But like all men of his type he was a complete egotist."[41] In these respects, he was the obverse of Disraeli—even in his egotism, which in Disraeli was largely vanity and in Gladstone a sense of being an anointed spokesman for divine truth and for civic virtue and duty.

Like Disraeli, Gladstone was an "outsider"—Disraeli with his Jewish ancestry, Gladstone from being of full Scottish descent. For both, their backgrounds were handicaps. Morley, in his monumental biography of Gladstone, stresses the point as being genuinely significant:

Mr. Gladstone stands out as far the most conspicuous and powerful of all the public leaders in our history, who have sprung from the northern half of our island. When he had grown to be the most famous man in the realm of the Queen, he said, "I am not slow to claim the name of Scotsman, and even if I were, there is the fact staring me in the face." . . . It is easy to make too much of race, but when we are puzzled by Mr. Gladstone's seeming contrariness of temperament, his union of impulse with caution, of passion with circumlocation, of pride and fire with self control, of Ossian flight with a steady foothold on the solid earth, we may perhaps find a sort of explanation in thinking of him as a highlander in the custody of a lowlander.[42]

Morley was by instinct and habit of mind a rhetorical critic and it was from this stance that he wrote his two-thousand-page analysis of Gladstone's career. After noting that from the time of Socrates oratory has been disparaged as one of the black arts, Morley describes a week of campaigning in the Midlothian constituency, in bleak winter weather at the end of November 1879, when Gladstone was in his seventieth year. Cold winds blew over snow-clad hills, but this did not prevent the people from coming at his call. Seats were available for some six thousand listeners, but forty to fifty thousand came daily from the surrounding area, hoping to hear him. During the week, according to an estimate by an opponent, he spoke 85,840 words. On one day he spoke at Glasgow University for an hour and a half on the familar theme of the values of education; "and some even of those who had no direct interest in the main topics, and were not much or not at all refreshed by his treatment of them, yet confessed themselves sorry when the stream of fascinating melody ceased to flow." Another day he spoke on government finance at the Edinburgh Corn Exchange, where his auditors were "interested and delighted" even "in the midst of his most formidable statistics."

These speeches were instances in the steady flow of his campaigning in which he was "the orator of concrete detail, of inductive instances, of energetic and immediate object; the orator confidently and by sure touch startling into watchfulness the whole spirit of civic duty in a man; elastic and supple, pressing fact and figure with a fervid insistence that was known from his career and character to be neither forced nor feigned, but to be himself. In a word, it was a man—a man impressing himself upon the kindled throngs by the breadth of his survey of great affairs. . . ."[43] Morley ended his description of the Midlothian speeches by insisting that such eloquence as Gladstone exhibited must not be underestimated: "to disparage eloquence is to depreciate mankind." The alternative to "talking problems out" is "to leave sovereign mastery of the world to Machiavelli."[44]

So what, we must ask, was it that Gladstone accomplished? In a word, he made morality the test of policy. The results were manifold during the five times, totalling more than eleven years, that he served as prime minister. Through his influence Irish Catholics were relieved of having to support the Protestant Church of Ireland; the judicial system was revised with a clear channel for appeals; the military was humanized and made more efficient by ending the purchase of commissions and by the elimination of flogging; the secret ballot was adopted; a system of public education was brought into effect (though for this he deserves little direct credit); the Civil Service was reformed as part of a general program of making governmental administration both more efficient and less costly; the subordination of the throne to the parliament was systematized; controls over the colonies were loosened, on the theory that the less they were governed by London the firmer would be their loyalty to the homeland. It is an impressive catalogue.

His blind spots were also impressive. He sided with the slave-holding secessionist South in the American Civil War; he needlessly aroused the hostility of the Egyptians and their Arab allies; he had small sympathy for the Eastern European and Italian nationalist movements; he denied self-determination to the Boers in South Africa; and he was sternly coercive in Ireland before shifting to reform. His understanding was broad rather than deep; and he was inconsistent in the application of principles to action.

How much his successes depended upon his ability as a public speaker is difficult to assess fairly. The current of liberalism was strong in his time and much that was achieved under his leadership derived from this change in public sentiment. Nevertheless, it must be granted that he hastened changes that had been delayed by Peel and Palmerston. He was less an advocate of genuine democracy than was John Bright, but he won the management of affairs while Bright was restrained to the role of critic. With the extension of the suffrage

along with all the other political and intellectual renovations, it became essential in Gladstone's time, as it had not been before, for aspirants to national
leadership to be persuasive with the masses; and it remained true, as it long had
been, that ministers had to justify their proposals and conduct with persuasive
explanations through appeals to the Parliament. It can not be said that public
speaking was *the instrument* accounting for Gladstone's power; but assuredly it
was *an instrument* without which his dominant position could neither have been
won nor maintained.

As a speaker he was much less exciting than Disraeli. Disraeli's well-known
description of Gladstone-the-orator as "a sophisticated rhetorician inebriated
with the exuberance of his own verbosity and gifted with an egotistical imagination that can at all times command an interminable and inconsistent series of
arguments to malign an opponent and glorify himself"[45] came close to the
mark. Gladstone surely talked too much. For no other public speaker in the
history of Great Britain is there so extensive a remaining record of what he said.
Much of it makes dull reading. Gladstone took every care to preserve even the
most fleeting of his own remarks, even his schoolboy effusions, and even many
casual comments throughout his long life. Most of them deserve to be forgotten.
And mostly they have been. After his death, when a publisher undertook to
bring out a multivolumed edition of his speeches, the project was quietly
dropped when it turned out that the first volume attracted few readers. Lord
Morley, admitting this, pointed out that in this respect Gladstone was not
exceptional. The greatest of orators are remembered not for their typical but for
their greatest utterances. Such a precautionary reminder is worth noting as a
proper limitation of the claim that rhetorical skills do have historical significance:

> With all admiration for the effulgent catalogue of British orators, and not
> forgetting Pitt on the slave trade, or Fox on the Westminster scrutiny, or
> Sheridan on the begums of Oude, or Plunkett on the Catholic question, or
> Grattan, or Canning, or Brougham, we may perhaps ask whether all the
> passages that have arrived at this degree of fame and grandeur, with the
> exception of Burke, may not be comprised in an extremely slender volume.
> The statesman who makes or dominates a crisis, who has to rouse and mould
> the mind of senate or nation, has something else to think about than the
> production of literary masterpieces. The great political speech, which for that
> matter is a sort of drama, is not made by passages for elegant extract or
> anthologies, but by personality, movement, climax, spectacle, and the action
> of the time.[46]

What Morley added is especially significant. No speech ever has significance
except in terms of the broad set of circumstances that led to its being made,
influenced its character, and were also modified by it. In Morley's words: "To
think of the campaign without the scene, is as one who should read a play by

candle-light among the ghosts of an empty theatre. When the climax came, it was found that Mr. Gladstone's tremendous projectiles had pounded the ministerial citadel to the ground, and that he had a nation at his back."[47] This was indeed persuasive success.

What made Gladstone effective was not what he said or how he said it at particular times or on particular topics but the general sense of his solid dependability. Men listened to Disraeli with delighted anticipation of exciting sallies that he would conjure from the richness of his imagination. They listened to Gladstone with the confidence that what he said would be practically attainable, desirable, or even necessary to be done, and that it was morally right. The qualities that made Gladstone the natural leader of Victorian England were summarized by Wingfield-Stratford in an excellent overview of Gladstone's leadership as being his will rather than his understanding; and his being genuinely representative (rather than being innovative) of the England of his time.[48] In short, he told the people what they wanted to hear and asked them to do what they felt, however reluctantly, that they ought to be doing.

His background and upbringing prepared him well for his representative character. Born in Liverpool, the son of a successful merchant, of Scottish parentage, on 29 December 1809, he was five years younger than Disraeli. Unlike Disraeli, Gladstone was advantaged by traditional education for leadership, spending six years at Eton and three more in Christ Church, Oxford. All through his schooling he was a dutiful but not brilliant student, popular among his fellows, and outstanding in the debating clubs. Never enthralled by knowledge for its own sake, he was ambitious to prepare himself for political leadership. He was devoutly religious in the orthodoxy of the Church of England; and consistently from early youth he viewed politics not as "the art of the possible" but as a championship of moral and religious values. He was a very "proper" youth and as such as soon as he was old enough he was offered a "safe" seat in the Commons by the Duke of Newcastle. Like Disraeli he hastened toward fame by rising quickly for his maiden speech. Also like Disraeli, the topic he chose to address was controversial and touched the sensibilities of important members of the House. But unlike Disraeli he carefully avoided arousing resentments and was listened to attentively. For fifty minutes in a conciliatory mode he denounced the mistreatment of slaves on West Indian Plantations, some of them owned by members of Parliament; but the most that he asked by way of reform was that the owners ensure "the inestimable benefits of our religion to the slaves." The leaders of the House praised his moderation and skill in debate; and very soon Gladstone was a frequent and respected participant in the discussions. These qualities of his youth were hallmarks of his whole career.

In the judgment of one of his biographers, he "could sway masses of opinion as no one before or since."[49] Another found the Midlothian campaign speeches to be epochal in that they denied "all the aristocratic traditions" by their appeal to the moral sense of the populace.[50] Still others point out that "On the hustings as in the House of Commons, it was Gladstone's personality that translated even the most detailed content into human terms."[51] Typically he spoke extemporaneously, from carefully prepared notes. Morley collected the opinions of contemporaries concerning the nature and effects of his speaking manner:

> His countenance, they say, is mild and pleasant, and has a high intellectual expression. His eyes are clear and quick. . . . Mr. Gladstone's gesture is varied, but not violent. When he rises, he generally puts both hands behind his back. . . . His pale complexion, slightly tinged with olive, and dark hair, cut rather close to his head, with an eye of remarkable depth, still more impress you with the abstracted character of his disposition. The expression of his face would be sombre were it not for the striking eye, which has a remarkable fascination. His triumphs as a debater are achieved not by the aid of the passions, . . . not of prejudice and fallacy, . . . not with imagination and high seductive colouring, . . . but—of pure reason. He prevails by that subdued earnestness which results from deep religious feelings, and is not fitted for the more usual and more stormy functions of a public speaker.[52]

Wherever one opens editions of his speeches, the general tone and persuasive pattern are much the same. It has been said of him that he spoke with the self-righteous assurance, but not with the fierceness, of olden day prophets. One of his speeches, delivered at the age of seventy in the city of Edinburgh in 1879 in which he denounced the colonial mode of "denying to others the rights we claim for ourselves," will suffice to illustrate the quality that he sought to infuse into the conduct of affairs:

> I am sustained and encouraged, and I may almost say driven on in public life, by the sentiment believed and entertained by me most sincerely, whether erroneously or not, that the principles at issue are much broader than those of ordinary contention. . . . I humbly ask for confidence when I state my own belief that the objects we have in view at the present time are objects connected with the welfare of mankind upon the widest scale. . . . Whatever we may say amidst the din of preparation for warfare in time of peace—amidst all this there is yet going on a profound mysterious movement, that, whether we will or not, is bringing the nations of the civilized world, as well as the uncivilized, morally as well as physically nearer to one another, and making them more and more responsible before God for one another's welfare. . . . I do most heartily thank you for having given me the credit of being actuated by the desire to consider in public transactions the wider interests of mankind, and I venture to assure you that so far as my objects and intentions are concerned, objects of that nature, and nothing meaner or narrower, will ever be taken as the pole-star of my life.[53]

There is nothing in this, nor generally in his speaking, that resembles the sparkle so characteristic of Disraeli. All is somber earnestness—moral, dutiful, and sincere. It was the quality upon which his leadership was based. It built for him a solid foundation of public confidence. And it was sensibly balanced between faith and fear—faith that the good could prevail along with fear that it might not. When at the age of seventy-six he contemplated retirement from public life, he wrote to a protesting friend that he dreaded especially just one tendency in the affairs of the nation—"that is to say, taking into the hands of the state the business of the individual man." Even so, he trusted in "the sense of justice which abides tenaciously in the masses" to prevent any crisis of "convulsive action."[54] When, finally, he actually did retire—at the age of eighty-six, it was with a sense of deep regret: "it seems as if I must, God knows how reluctantly, lay burdens upon others."[55] He had borne them longer than most, if not always brilliantly, at least always with grace.

The last words concerning him may well be words that he spoke about himself during the Midlothian campaign in 1879 when he said of his own speeches what may appropriately be said of public speaking in general—that they might not change opinions significantly "at the moment in the place—though I believe they have a good deal of silent and slower effect on the tone of the public mind generally." Typically British in its understatement, this is a judgment about Gladstone and about public speaking as a force in history that will stand.

7
AFTER THE WATERSHED:
DREAMING ABOUT DEMOCRACY

The confusion in the Victorian mind about what democracy was and was not, about its values and its flaws, was well represented in the public speaking of the time. A perceptive French scholar, Hippolyte Taine, who visited England in 1862 was particularly alert to the state of mind of the people. He cited as typical what a prosperous industrialist said to him: "It is not our aim to overthrow the aristocracy: we are ready to leave the government and high offices in their hands. For we believe, we men of the middle class, that the conduct of national business calls for special men, men born and bred to the work for generations. . . ." As more months passed, Taine formed his conclusion: "I believe that I am beginning to form some idea of the nature of the English mind, so different from a French one. . . . The inside of an Englishman's head can be fairly compared to a Murray's Guide: a great many facts, but few ideas."[1] The English mind was more complex than he understood. Part of it was filled with perplexed dreaming about the emergent democracy that was still unformed and difficult to envision.

The new Reform Bill of 1867 did not bring democracy to England. But the watershed had been crossed; after it there was no turning back. The leaders who stimulated a talking out of the problems included such intellectuals as Charles Kingsley, William Morris, and Thomas Henry Huxley; and such statesmen as Lord Randolph Churchill, the Marquis of Salisbury, and Joseph Chamberlain. A major historian gives all of them the back of his hand: "The race of giants, who had rendered the first half of Queen Victoria's reign so memorable, had passed or was passing: . . . a younger generation succeeded them; . . . it is obvious that giants were much fewer, and on the whole of less stature."[2] Perhaps so; but as social critics, as responsible men who sought to understand the age, and as innovative thinkers, they too had contributions to make.

As is common in human affairs, the out-of-office ivory tower "thinkers" were unrestrained in their notions as to how the society should be reshaped; whereas the political leaders, being dependent upon consensus for their authority, were constrained to deal with practicalities. The tendency of the intellectuals was represented fairly enough in a letter that Huxley wrote to Charles Darwin: "I will stop at no point as long as clear reasoning will carry me further."[3] And, in contrast, Salisbury, representing pragmatic political sense, said that "We must work at less speed and at a lower temperature than our opponents. Our bills must be tentative and cautious, not sweeping and dramatic."[4]

The intellectuals merit consideration because even impractical dreams both reveal half-realized wants and help to stimulate efforts to make them attainable. One significant effect that they had was to extend greatly the realm of the discussable. Thereby they stimulated other minds to search for ways more practical than they could conceive for clarifying understandings and for improving the way of life. Even errors, when presented ingeniously and enthusiastically, can prod more practical minds toward progressive improvements.

"The First of Scientific Orators"

Among the intellectuals, Thomas Henry Huxley was by far the most practical-minded, being neither a "dreamer" nor a "doer" but primarily an "explainer." He was born on 4 May 1825 the son of a school teacher but he was self-educated through his own reading until in his late teens he attended a medical school. After graduation he served as surgeon on a south seas voyage, during which time, remarkably like Charles Darwin, he made a close study of biology and zoology and wrote important papers for the Royal Society that made him a promising scientist by the age of twenty-six. When Darwin's *The Origin of Species* appeared in 1859, Huxley found its theory of evolution convincing and became the leading exponent for it in a series of essays and lectures on "Man's Place in Nature." This "monkey damnification" of humanity brought bitter denunciations upon him. Undaunted, he proceeded to a careful study of fishes and reptiles and in 1867 delivered a series of lectures at the College of Surgeons in which he demonstrated the fundamental likeness of these two genera to birds. By 1892 he felt able to assert flatly that "The doctrine of evolution is no speculation."

By that time he had won a firm position in society by activities of a very different sort. Between 1862 and 1884 he served on some ten Royal Commissions; for nine years during that time he was secretary to the Royal Society, and then he served as its president. For two years from 1870 to 1872 he was a member of the London School Board, established as a result of the monumental Education Act of 1870. In this position he exerted lasting influence in shifting education from memorization to exploratory learning. During his later years he wrote and lectured on philosophy and religion, insisting that science teaches "the great truth which is embodied in the Christian conception of entire surrender to the will of God."[5] He insisted also that "atheism is on purely philosophical grounds untenable"; but he likewise concluded that "There is no evidence of the existence of such a being as the God of the theologians."[6] To define his position he invented the term "agnosticism," which ever since has had the enormous rhetorical effect of making dubious uncertainty intellectually respectable. His justification for it was his belief in "the passionless impersonality of the unknown and unknowable, which science shows everywhere underlying the thin veil of phenomena."[7]

How much the general intellectual understanding changed during these years and how much Huxley contributed to directing the nature of that change becomes evident in reading the volume of his *Lay Sermons,* published in 1870, his *American Addresses* of 1877, and his *Science and Culture* lecture of 1880. There is truth in the assertion that "in public debates with the most formidable antagonists of his time he demonstrated his confidence, his good humor, his mastery of all relevant facts, his power of marshalling argument, his complete lucidity."[8] More even than Darwin he won acceptance for the theory of biological evolution, and much more significantly he taught the meaning of science and the necessity of adjusting our minds to it. His life abundantly refutes the absurd claim of Taine that the English mind contained facts but not ideas.

With a crusading determination to educate the public, Huxley did not sidestep controversy; on the contrary, he charged against foes of true science when he feared they were having an effect. His most dramatic conflict was with the bishop of Oxford when he responded to the scornful question, "Is it on your grandfather's or on your grandmother's side that the ape ancestry comes in?" by taking advantage of the public attention that ensued to present an enlightening explanation of the evolution theory.

As a lecturer, Huxley's chief merit was lucidity. He knew not only his subject but also his audience and was able to explain the most complicated set of data in familiar terms. One of his most daring lectures was given first in Edinburgh in 1868, and afterward, as was his custom, was repeated to other audiences. The title was "On the Physical Basis of Life"; and his theme was that all forms of life are similarly rooted in protoplasm. "And out of these same forms . . . the vegetable world builds up all the protoplasm which keeps the animal world agoing." In the same year he delivered to workingmen in Norwich his most famous lecture, "On a Piece of Chalk," in which he demonstrated the antiquity of the world and of primitive (and afterward gradually more complex) life forms by showing what may be seen in a common piece of such limestone as forms the white cliffs of Dover.

One of Huxley's most influential lectures was the one he presented on 1 October 1880 at the opening of Sir Josiah Mason's Science College in Birmingham. Huxley's purpose was the bold one of seeking to change the nature of education. "Practical men," he said, had held the view that "science is speculative rubbish; that theory and practice have nothing to do with one another; and that the scientific habit of mind is an impediment, rather than an aid, in the conduct of ordinary affairs." He placed this view in the past tense, he said, because he was confident it was passing away. The continuing problem was the dominance of letters (literature and language), both ancient and modern, as the essential center of education. As for himself, "I hold very strongly to two convictions. The first is that neither the discipline nor the subject-matter of classical education is of such direct value to the student of physical science as to justify the expenditure of valuable time upon either; and the second is, that for the purpose of attaining real culture, an exclusively scientific education is at least as effectual as an exclusively literary education." In addition to the physical sciences, Huxley called also for the study of sociology. Since the government was now subject to broad male suffrage, "every man who does his duty must exercise political functions." A drastic change was needed because "The purely classical education . . . gives no inkling of all this."

This challenge by Huxley was answered two years later in August 1882 by Matthew Arnold, the most prestigious advocate of the classics and like Huxley an academic lecturer. At Cambridge University Arnold spoke on "Literature and Science," a lecture he afterward repeated in his tour across America. In it he answered Huxley's charge "that the notions of our forefathers about the beginning and the end of the world were all wrong, and that nature is the expression of a definite order with which nothing interferes." In Arnold's view, such study as Huxley urged would give students nothing but knowledge—whereas, "art, and poetry, and eloquence have in fact not only the power of refreshing and delighting us . . . —they have a fortifying, and elevating, and quickening, and suggestive power, capable of wonderfully helping us to relate the results of modern science to our need for conduct, our need for beauty." As Arnold concluded, "there will be crowded into education other matters besides, far too many . . . but letters will not in the end lose their leading place."

What is of major significance is that the realm of the discussable had much more than broadened, it had assumed a different character. Authority—both that of superiors and of tradition—was giving way to reason and experience. New topics were talked about, and they were discussed in a new way—not in the spirit of "Listen to what I say," but in the mode of egalitarian sharing: "Let us reason together." Huxley was a prime example of this new spirit; and so to a lesser degree was the classicist Matthew Arnold. The people were coming to a new understanding not only of expanding knowledge but of what it meant to them. It is as a significant contributor to this change that Thomas Henry Huxley merits a notable place as a shaper of rhetorical influence. He was indeed as the *Pall Mall Gazette* asserted in its 24 October 1888 issue "the first of scientific orators."

"The New Outreach of Discussion"

William Morris entered upon lecturing only late in his life and then no more than incidentally. His many interests included painting, interior decoration, the printing of handsomely bound books, and the writing of poetry and romantic novels. Born to wealth and educated at both Cambridge and Oxford, he had all the advantages life could supply. With enormous energy and endless yearning for the betterment of man and of society, he sought for a model of the ideal environment, first in his highly selective interpretation of the Middle Ages and afterward at the age of fifty in socialism. It was in this last stage of his life that he took up lecturing to spread the ideas of Karl Marx. He joined the Social Democratic Federation but soon left it to found his own Socialist League.

Always an individualist, Morris did not believe in seeking social and economic reform through Parliament but through the arousal of public awareness. He began his new career of lecturing by presenting such radical ideas that he was several times arrested. To win for his ideas a wide audience, which the newspapers denied him, he wrote a Utopian book, *News from Nowhere*, in which he pictured what life could be: "an England devoid of railways and factories, with the large cities broken up into small towns, nature restored to its proper place in the English landscape, everybody beautiful, simple, and kind, with no private property and all labor done joyfully and voluntarily."

In a lecture on "How I Became a Socialist," delivered repeatedly in 1894, Morris explained the need for his kind of leadership, for "civilization has reduced the workman to such a skinny and pitiful existence that he scarcely knows how to frame a desire for any life much better than that which he endures perforce." As for the practicalities, Morris largely ignored the problems of bringing about the enormity of the social transformation that he desired. A student of the social issues with which he dealt concluded that "Morris takes the usual refuge of assuming that people will become morally good when conditions are changed."[9]

Scarcely more practical, though far more active as a public speaker, and with social concerns contrasting with those of Morris, was the reverend Charles Kingsley, an Anglican preacher and novelist who devoted his maturity to supporting the cause of Christian Socialism. He was far more conventional in his interests, ideas, and conduct than was William Morris. In 1859 he became chaplain to Queen Victoria, through the 1860s he was professor of modern history at Cambridge and for the two years before his death in 1875 he was a canon of Westminster. Like the Church of England in which he preached, his basic ideas were conservative. The people, he felt, needed the guidance of peers and churchmen. The social reforms that most appealed to him included the establishment of cooperatives and improvement of the sanitary system. He strongly rejected the medievalist nostalgia of the Oxford Movement and of William Morris.[10]

As a young preacher, he was deeply disturbed by the poverty and misery of the early Industrial Revolution, and he was scandalized by the adulteries and selfishness of the upper classes. He was drawn to Christian Socialism by the influence of Thomas Carlyle and the founder of the movement, Frederick Denison Maurice. The mainspring of the movement was the generous spirit of sharing, inspired by the teachings of Christ. Like Morris, Kingsley pleaded for a turning away from factories back to home handicrafts. His preaching was more ardent than intellectually acute. In the pulpit he made a handsome figure with his swarthy complexion, dark hair, and flashing eyes, while he poured scorn and indignation on all that was impure and ignoble. As a novelist, a poet, and a writer for children he won a fame that gave special weight to his preaching and lectures. In 1864 he precipitated a sensation in London intellectual circles by charging John Henry Newman with hypocrisy in his conversion to Catholicism—to which Newman delivered a searing response and one of his best statements of the values of Catholicism as he knew them.

Kingsley, like Morris, was no more than a minor figure in the development of British public address. Their inclusion in the history of public speaking is largely to illustrate the new outreach of public discussion to encompass the feelings and sentiments that accompanied the birth pangs of English democracy. Confusion concerning what democracy meant and implied was inevitable. Strange dreams stirred, while practical programs and policies were developing. Like Huxley, Kingsley and Morris were intellectuals and spoke primarily to their own kind. Huxley was able to shift currents of thought; Morris and Kingsley were also influential, but mostly through their writings. As lecturers, they represented an aberrant fringe. But this, too, helps us to understand the time. The public was not ready to welcome ideas as radical as theirs.

"The Dream of Democracy Became an Empirical Reality"

Not dreamers but eminently practical politicians were three leaders who guided policies as the Victorian period was ending. Robert Cecil, Marquis of Salisbury who in three terms held the prime ministry longer than either of his more famous predecessors was regarded by the public as "a comfortable bearded symbol of continuity."[11] Randolph Churchill, easily the liveliest speaker of his time, strengthened the Conservatives by attracting to their fold the prosperous white-collar urbanites.[12] Joseph Chamberlain, the first middle-class politician to achieve the prime ministry—a wealthy industrialist whose theme was national greatness—became "the first professional politician . . . who pursued one idea, the extension of democracy and the betterment of the working class"[13]—to which it must be added that he was also almost the last of the great imperialists. It was during their time of leadership and to a significant degree through their influence that the dream of democracy became an empirical reality.

What was happening was not only a shift of sentiment from faith in aristocracy to egalitarianism but also a reconstruction of government to provide aid for the disadvantaged and to ensure the authority of the general electorate. Such a shift increased the importance of public speaking as an essential political instrument. Randolph Churchill stated the case well in a speech he made in Blackpool on 24 January 1884:

I know this, if I know anything at all, that if once the people of this country as a whole can be induced to interest themselves in any matter, to take it up, to make it their own, to settle it one way or another, the people will not go wrong. Governments will go wrong. Parliaments will go wrong, classes will go wrong, London society and the Pall-Mall clubs always go wrong; but the people do not go wrong.[14]

The significance in this statement is its qualifying phrase, "if the people can be induced." These leaders well understood that people must be "induced." They must be influenced. And what influences them is less a matter of fact than of how the facts are interpreted. The new democratic kind of leadership that derives directly from popular support necessarily requires effective persuasion.

And, each in his own way, these three were masterful speakers. Salisbury spoke like a superior who could safely be trusted. As his daughter assessed his means of asserting leadership: "The crispness of his style, his gift for lucid statement, served to gain and hold the attention of minds unexercised in elaborate vocabularies; his claim to come to close quarters with facts; the impression of solidity induced by his independence of other men's opinions— were all qualities to attract unsophisticated audiences."[15] As the most famous son of Randolph Churchill wrote of the father he scarcely ever knew, it was "his skill in debate and political tactics" that "carried him beyond all his rivals."[16] As for Joseph Chamberlain—not Churchill's rival but an ally—he was "the best debater without exception,"[17] with "a keen eye for all the weak points of an opponent's case and a flow of clear and easy language."[18] The first two for several years pursued power as partisan fellows, until their competing ambitions split them apart.

The Marquis of Salisbury was "an aristocratic survival into an age of democratic politics, a great landowner at a time of rapid urbanization, aloof, even neurotic by temperament, an intellectual at the head of an unintellectual party. . . . In both home and foreign policies he pictured himself in charge of a long rearguard action. He was too shrewd to resist change totally, but he tried to slow it down."[19] He accepted democracy because he had to, but he didn't like it. Nor did he pretend to. In 1889 he stated his pessimistic interpretation of the new political scene as characterized by: "No common principles, no respect for common institutions or traditions . . . To loot somebody or something is the common object under a thick varnish of pious phrases."[20] He was recognized as one of the last of the oligarchs and he drew his support mainly from the social groups that expected he would be as conservative in his acts as he was in his words.

To his political critics, Salisbury was a selfish obstructionist of progress. Chamberlain made the strongest case against him during the campaign of 1883, describing him as the spokesman for aristocrats who "toil not and neither do they spin," and whose family fortunes originated "in times gone by for the services which courtiers rendered kings." Salisbury's own best defense of his rearguard policies was presented in his last public speech, delivered to his supporters in the Primrose League in the great Albert Hall in London on 7 May 1902. Looking more like a prosperous middle-class businessman than a landed aristocrat, he was tall, corpulent, slightly stooped, with a heavy beard topped by fiercely bent eyebrows and dressed, as always, in a careless and shabbily unkempt costume. He was within sixteen months of his death, was seventy-three years old, and his enthusiastically cheering admirers had come to render him their grateful farewell. He opened with a gracious tribute to his erstwhile friend and later rival, Randolph Churchill, praising him for his judgment, vigor, and enormous skill in helping to form the program Salisbury had carried through. Then he offered his own interpretation of his own career:

> During the last 17 years we have passed through a troublous time of political experience. We have had to meet great dangers, to solve difficult and subtle questions. . . . We must not expect that the ashes of past conflicts shall be extinguished at once; we must not imagine that the necessity for our exertions will be soon dispensed with; but we must see that in these 17 years we have had a tremendous recognition of the effect of patriotic combination . . . and that by its force we have, if not absolutely dissipated, to a large extent conjured the most formidable dangers that threatened us 17 years ago. . . . We did not at all give way or quail before the dangerous indications of that time. . . . We can recognize that . . . the power, the prestige, the influence, aye, and the magic effect of our Empire is more potent, more efficient, more admirable than it was when that period began.[21]

Neither in his bearing nor in his words was there even a suggestion of eloquence. On the contrary, he seemed to disdain it as a plain man speaking plain words. This was precisely the source of his authority: "a comfortable bearded symbol of continuity." He assured his listeners that the Boer War had been properly fought, then discussed the new trend within the colonies:

> We have no power by legislation to affect the flow of opinion and of affection which has arisen so largely between the mother country and her daughter States. . . . All kinds of difficulties are there before us. . . . There is no danger that appears to me more serious for the time that lies before us than an attempt to force the various parts of the Empire into a mutual arrangement and subordination for which they were not ready. . . . If we will be patient and careful, there is a tremendous destiny before us; if we are hasty, there may be the reverse of such a destiny; there may be a breaking apart.

As leaders must, he was seeking to define the situation in terms designed to make his own interpretation imperative for his listeners. It was not domestic but foreign problems that appeared to him most pressing. Shortly before this speech he had forecast "some great change in public affairs." And he had interpreted the change as posing a disastrous threat of major warfare: "The large aggregation of human forces which lie around our Empire seems to draw more closely together, and to assume almost unconsciously a more and more aggressive aspect."[22] The two factors to which he wished to draw particular attention he joined together in his closing words to the Primrose Club: namely, that "terrible difficulties have arisen . . . a state of things perfectly new to the world"; and that how they were to be dealt with "must be in such a country as ours largely affected by the trend of popular opinion."

The tone of his last speech was heavily foreboding. The era into which he had grown to maturity had already passed away. The future that he foresaw he feared. New combinations of forces in Europe were posing new threats to English security; and the coming of democracy had changed the very basis of judgment concerning how the threat should be met. The burden for England that he anticipated—"the liability of having to defend the frontiers of Germany and Austria against Russia"—turned out to be wrong, at least for the two generations that would have to fight World Wars I and II. But he was right in warning of the "terrible difficulties" comprised of new European combinations having a "more aggressive aspect" that threatened the stability of the empire. And he was right in his final recognition, that formed the concluding paragraph of his speech, that if the leaders successfully induce popular opinion to meet the challenge of "their high destiny, their mission will be remembered as the greatest blessing which the Empire of England has been able to obtain."

"The Free Lance of Tory Democracy"

What to do about the force of public opinion but newly buttressed by the extended franchise was the preoccupation of Salisbury's associate-turned-rival, Lord Randolph Churchill. The problem to be dealt with was clear: "The vote was no doubt in the hands of the poor man, but it was an instrument he had not the knowledge and perhaps hardly the will to use effectively." The new necessity facing the aspiring political leader was "to engender in him the team spirit, to make him desire the triumph of his political colour as he did that of his football team, to get him wild with enthusiasm about a few selected catchwords or formulas."[23] This was the "inducement" of which Churchill spoke. It was a new and distasteful demand upon leaders reared in the aristocratic traditions; but he mastered it.

Like Salisbury, Churchill feared the new forces that were taking form across the Channel. He gave pungent expression to this fear in a speech to the Lords in 1885: "Are we being swept along a turbulent and irresistible torrent which is bearing us towards some political Niagara, in which every mortal thing we know will be twisted and smashed beyond all recognition? Or are we, on the other hand, gliding passively along a quiet river of human progress that will lead us to some undiscovered ocean of almost superhuman development?" Which alternative would prevail, he felt, must not be left wholly for the popular vote to determine. As he wrote in the May 1883 issue of the *Fortnightly Review,* the power of veto must be retained by the House of Lords to ensure the safety provided by a conservative monitor.

His brief life of forty-six years (1849–1895) was conspicuously stormy. Born in Blenheim Palace and educated at Eton and at Merton College, Oxford, he had all the advantages of social status and was elected as a matter of course to Parliament at the age of twenty-five. For a time he devoted himself quietly to the development of his own conception of "Tory democracy," then some five years after his election he commenced a series of furious attacks against the moribund leadership of the Conservative Party. He organized a clique known as the Fourth Party and with equal vigor denounced both the Conservatives and the Gladstone Liberals. He became known as "the free lance of Tory democracy," refusing to be bound by party discipline on either domestic or foreign policy issues. In general, his influence was directed toward influencing the Conservatives to compete against the Liberals for progressive leadership. But on whatever issues arose his stand was independent. He accepted the post of House of Commons leader under the Salisbury ministry, then abruptly resigned, apparently to maintain his independence of judgment. He is remembered in part for his marriage to an American, Jenny Jerome, from which union came his son, Winston Churchill. He deserves to be remembered also as a brilliant and audacious platform speaker, a keen debater, and a leader who spoke his own mind with a freshness and individuality that induced the London *Times* to print the full texts of most of his speeches during the heyday of his career.

Lord Rosebery describes his speaking during 1880–86 as "almost unbroken triumph."[24] In the opinion of his son, "In 1884 and 1885 he equalled, if he did not surpass, Mr. Gladstone himself in the interest and enthusiasm which his personality aroused."[25] He took his speeches seriously. For a major address he would shut himself up for two days, write the speech, and largely memorize it. Then he would deliver it with such freshness and apparent spontaneity that it appeared to be a creation of the moment.

How he set about "inducing" support is well illustrated by "the single speech which characterized all his qualities,"[26] which he delivered in Blackpool on 24 January 1884.[27] Although the topic announced was the rather dull one of "Financial Reform," he roamed freely across a wide spectrum of subjects and his tone was far from dull.

In his opening sentences he attacked Gladstone's Irish Home Rule bill, which he described as "the mixture of treachery and incapacity which poisoned the councils of Mr. Gladstone's administration." He leaped almost at once to emotional attack: "It is a monstrous and dangerous coalition we have to face; it strikes at the vitals of the empire. The union of England, Scotland, and Ireland is the nerve-centre of the wide-spread dominions of the Queen. If you sever it, the empire is dead; if you injure it, the empire is paralyzed." Moreover, he went on, "It is not only in Ireland that your imperial interests are imperilled." He proceeded to denounce Gladstone's intervention in the Egyptian War—assertedly to protect the Suez Canal—as "a bondholders war. . . . The Suez Canal will always take care of itself. The whole world, the East and the West, are equally and mutually interested in the freedom of the Suez Canal. . . . It was bonds and bondholders and no other power which diverted Mr. Gladstone. . . . England has never before interfered with the internal affairs of other nations on account of bonds or debts which might be owing to her people. . . . The Southern States of America . . . Honduras, Costa Rica, and Venezuela . . . Turkey . . . repudiated. The Government of England took no action."

Then he aimed his persuasion directly against the seat of power. "I want the people to look into this question of our business in Egypt; because I know that until the people look into it, and settle and solve it for themselves, no good will be done." Governments do go wrong, he went on, and made his charge concrete: "Mr. Gladstone intervened" and "from that disastrous day till now he has wandered amid the ruins, purposeless and bewildered, has made no effort to reconstruct Egyptian society, no effort to relieve from their burdens the Egyptian people; but . . . by the guiltiness of his intervention he has added misery to misery, woe to woe, till he has transformed the fair land of Egypt into a perfect hell upon earth. The people of England would say that such a state of things must cease."

He turned then to "look for a few moments at our own domestic affairs," which he found to be in woeful disarray. The ministers blamed their failures on "the villainy of the Tory party" and "the baseness of the House of Lords." But, "if for a passing moment, by the exertion of some supernatural power, they could be clothed in the garb of truth, they would be the first to acknowledge that their own prodigious imbecility was alone to blame for the catastrophe." For the problems he blamed the ministerial policy of free trade—as truly guilty "as if I found a man standing over a corpse and plunging his knife into it"—and the refusal of the ministers to agree to a land tenure program that would keep laborers on the farms.

From policies he shifted to personalities. "The Prime Minister [Gladstone] is the greatest living master of the art of personal political advertisement. . . . People used to say that Lord Beaconsfield [Disraeli] was theatrical; but Lord Beaconsfield was a perfect child in this matter; . . . he never dreamt of such grand and theatrical representations as those with which Mr. Gladstone and his starring company astonish the British public week by week." These were the men who "use their eloquence for no nobler purpose than to lash into frenzy the needy and the discontented; . . . who, to gain a few votes either in Parliament or in a borough, ally themselves equally with the atheist or with the rebel, and who lightly arouse and lightly spring from one delirium of the multitude to another in order to maintain themselves at a giddy and perilous height."

It is obvious that such speaking was inflated by exaggerations and violations of restrained taste. The violence of Churchill's language echoes the tone of that early "Tory Radical," Richard Oastler. And the reasons motivating both men were similar. When the politician has to reach out to a large national audience that is largely uninformed and indifferent, sensationalism is the natural mode for catching public attention. This style of speaking was one of the concomitants of the coming of democracy. But it was not the only one; and it was not necessary. In a far soberer, far more rational guise another leader of the same period, Mr. Joseph Chamberlain of Birminghan, was making his own very different way to political success.

"Precedents He Set Were the Most Potent Influence"

Joseph Chamberlain expressed his own faith in democracy and his view of how it should operate in one of his speeches in Birmingham in 1886:

> I think a democratic government should be the strongest government, from a military and Imperial point of view, in the world, for it has the people behind it. . . . The problem is to give the democracy the whole power, but to induce them to do no more in the way of using it than to decide on the general principles which they wish to see carried out and the men by whom they are to be carried out.[28]

Here again is the critical term, "to induce"—along with the cautious aim of holding the electorate at a safe arm's length from actual operations of the government. In his younger days Chamberlain called himself a socialist; and all his life what drove him was his "intense desire to remedy the grosser forms of social misery."[29] As he saw it, such miseries are the direct result of social institutions and therefore must be dealt with by political measures. "What folly it is," he told his Birmingham constituency, "to talk about the moral and intellectual elevation of the masses when conditions of life are such as to render elevation impossible!"[30]

The son of a wealthy father, in early life Chamberlain became a successful manufacturer, and he entered political life with no aim but to contribute to the improvement of society. "He pursued one idea, the extension of democracy, and the betterment of the working classes." But in order to do so, he became "the first professional politician," by bringing to politics something of the system and the discipline of business. "The precedents he set throughout his career were the most potent influence in establishing the conventions of British democracy. . . . Modern forms of party discipline, electioneering, party conferences, propaganda, and a lot else, owe as much to him as to any other."[31]

His political career was launched when he was named a member of the first city school board, after the adoption of the Education Act of 1870. Three years later, when he was elected mayor of Birmingham, he learned that what the people most needed—better housing, cheaper public utilities, improved sanitation, jobs, slum clearance, roads and parks—only government could provide. He entered politics under the influence of Gladstone to attempt to infuse morality into public affairs. But when he found that generalized moral sentiments were of far less consequence than specific pragmatic programs, he organized his own party following. For this role of party leader he did not appear to be well qualified. As an astute critic of his career concluded: "He could not see things from any viewpoint but his own, and he lacked imagination and elasticity to adapt his manner to the psychology of others. He preferred to antagonize and defeat his opponents rather than win them over by conciliation."[32]

Even while Chamberlain was taking the lead in making democratic government effective, he was neither an advocate of egalitarianism nor pleased with its effects. As late as 1894 when he was about to take office in the ministry headed by the Marquis of Salisbury, he wrote a play, "The New Radicals," in which he avowed his uneasiness:

> As I grow older, my doubts increase. Of course there has been great indirect progress, but with it there has disappeared much that was lovable in the past and that made men happier and better. Faith, reverence, self-sacrifice were potent factors in the lives of men; and science and democracy and the struggle for existence seem to me to leave something wanting. . . .
>
> The House of Commons is not what it was when I entered it. There were giants in those days. . . .
>
> The new democracy resents pre-eminence of talents and everything else. The ideal is a dead level of commonplace and mediocrity. This is the age of small men and small things. . . . now the men who are called leaders are only straws blown in front of every gust of popular opinion. . . .
>
> Your orators mould themselves on the eloquence of the parish vestry or even the public house, and they gain the suffrage of the mob by barefaced appeals to their cupidity and their passions.

This same regret for the passing away of the old order—much resembling Disraeli's nostalgic vision of Young England—Chamberlain also expressed in his political speeches. To an audience in Leeds on 25 February in that same year, he frankly avowed his malaise: "When I first went into the House of Commons, when we spoke of the opinions of the House . . . we meant 'the common sense of the most,' but now we mean the decision of the majority, the party majority of the day. We meant then that in the process of free discussion, and as a result of mutual concession, legislation assumed a form which, if indeed it were not universally accepted, at all events met the strongest objections of its opponents. Now everything of the sort . . . is in the process of disappearance."[33]

Such sentiments seem curiously paradoxical, for Chamberlain was a chief deviser and implementer of the modern party system that unites members under a leader who serves as their spokesman with an enforced discipline that requires unit voting. "Mutual concession" was neither his ideal nor his mode. From his first public speeches in his teens to the civic gatherings to which he poured out his socialist sympathies on through the whole of his increasingly conservative career, he sounded more like an aristocrat than a populist. "An orator of a practical but consummate type, cool and hard-hitting, his spare figure, incisive features, and single eye-glass soon made him a favorite subject for the caricaturist; and in later life his aggressiveness made his actions and speeches the object of more controversy than was the lot of any other politician of his time."[34]

Basically he clung to the old idea that the best government is that administered by the best people. As he put it in a memorandum he wrote in 1905: "In my experience the ordinary voter never cares for details. He seizes upon a principle or a large issue, and is quite willing to delegate to his representative all questions of detail and method."[35] Yet he had full confidence in what he could do with a popular audience. As he confided to a friend about himself and his colleague Arthur Balfour: "Arthur and I can win together, for each has the qualities the other lacks; Arthur can manage the House of Commons, and I think I can manage the electors."[36] It was an astute conclusion. Balfour, a nephew of Lord Salisbury, had dabbled only languidly in politics until in the late eighties, when, according to the *Times,* "his skill in oratorical fence, and his trenchant powers of reasoning have brought him into the very front rank of contemporary statesmen." But even then, as Chamberlain's son Austen observed, Balfour was ineffective as a campaigner: "He has no comprehension of the habits or thoughts of his countrymen and no idea of how things strike them."[37] Chamberlain on the contrary was relatively ineffective in winning adherents in the Commons because his acidulous tone and apparent disdain for opponents denied him personal popularity.

In his speaking to the public, however, the effect was quite different. His sympathy with the problems of the people was apparent and his patrician tone seemingly enhanced confidence in his ability to lead. In general, Chamberlain made no concessions to popularity. He remained icily true to himself whether in Parliament or on the hustings. How he appeared to the House has been well described by one of his biographers: "Cool as a cucumber himself, he excites turmoil in others, the upright figure, the aggressive face, the mocking lips, the keen challenging eyes, the defiant nose, the eyeglass coolly placed in position, the clear-cut phrases, the many-toned voice have been conspicuous in numberless debates when passions ran high in St. Stephen's."[38] Curiously, these same qualities made him effective with the public. In the opinion of the historian Wingfield-Stratford:

> To strike a greatest common measure between the wills of millions of poor and uneducated men . . . and to get this average or general will translated into action [was the achievement of Chamberlain, who] was destined to wield an influence in English politics comparable to that of Gladstone himself. . . . In

one respect the two men were strikingly similar. To an even greater extent than of Gladstone, we think of Chamberlain as a force, a torrential energy. He never displayed the least trace of Mr. Balfour's intellectual detachment or Disraeli's philosophic grasp. What manner of man he was his face reveals with extraordinary clearness—the head like a spear, the keen-cut features, the tight lips, the aggressive nose—one of those men who, whether for good or ill, are destined by sheer force of will to play the leading part on whatever stage they happen to figure.[39]

During Chamberlain's years in Parliament he was generally under attack from all sides for taking mid-positions on issues that aroused passionate feelings. On the issue of Irish Home Rule he sided half-heartedly with Parnell but was determined to block Irish independence from fear that Ireland might become a base useful to future enemies of England. His stand for free trade antagonized protection-seeking English manufacturers, while his limitation of such trade advantages to the colonies was denounced by global free traders. He was condemned as a racist for insistence on English control over such "inferior" populations as those in India and Africa; and was also criticized for his effort to replace dominance with partnership in relations with the English-settled colonies. Concerning South Africa, where 430,000 English competed for supremacy with 410,000 Dutch, his maneuvering precipitated the Boer War—called "Mr. Chamberlain's War." In the midst of it Queen Victoria died, further dimming the luster of imperialism. What Chamberlain thought about it he told the public of Johannesburg after the war ended: "You are destined to become a powerful element . . . in a group of free nations gathered round the motherland. I think that is an inspiring thought. The day of small kingdoms with their petty jealousies has passed. The future is with the great empires, and there is no greater empire than the British Empire."[40]

For an important speech that both illustrates his persuasive methods and summarizes much of what he chiefly stood for he went to his home base of Birmingham to set forth his stand on various major issues on 15 May 1903. He was on friendly ground and the response to his speech was enthusiastically supportive. His mode of emphasizing the necessity for a mid-position and his skill in doing so are well illustrated in what he said about South Africa. A few paragraphs will suffice, for he was adroit in focusing attention on essential points:

> . . . my whole mind was turned toward the problems connected with the birth of a new nation in South Africa, and, above all, the question of how it was possible to reconcile the two races who were bound to live together as neighbors, and who, I hope, will live together as friends. . . . Who would wish that the traditions of either should be forgotten, that their peculiarities should disappear? And yet we have to make of them a united nation. . . .
>
> Upon that Imperial policy and what you do in the next few years depends that enormous issue whether this great Empire of ours is to stand together, one

free nation, if necessary, against all the world, or whether it is to fall apart into separate States, each selfishly seeking its own interest alone, losing sight of the commonweal, and losing also all the advantages which union alone can give.[41]

Chamberlain turned to the question of empire, reminding his hearers of that time not long before when imperialism had lost its attraction, demonstrating the emotional appeal to patriotism that formed a strong base for his leadership:

It has had a hard life of it. This feeling of Imperial patriotism was checked for a generation by the apathy and the indifference which were the characteristics of our former relations with our colonies. It was discouraged by our apparent acceptance of the doctrine of Little Englanders, of the provincial spirit which taught us to consider ourselves alone and to regard with indifference all that concerned those, however loyal they might be, who left these shores in order to go to our colonies abroad. But it was never extinguished. The embers were still alight. And when in the late war this old country of ours showed that it was still possessed by the spirit of our ancestors, showed that it was still prepared to count no sacrifice that was necessary in order to maintain the honour and the interests of the Empire that was committed to its charge, then you found a response from your brethren, your children across the seas, a response such as has not been known before, that astonished the world by a proof, an undeniable proof, of affection and regard. . . .
    Remember, we are a kingdom, an old country. We proceed here upon settled lines. We have our quarrels and our disputes and we pass legislation that may be good or bad, but which, at any rate, can be altered; but we go toward an object which is sufficiently defined. We know that whatever changes there may be, whatever meandering of the current, at all events the main stream ultimately reaches its appointed destination. That is the result of centuries of constitutional progress and freedom, but the Empire is not old. The Empire is new, the Empire is in its infancy. Now is the time when we can mould that Empire and when we and those who live with us can decide its future destinies.

Speaking of this kind echoed across the decades, reflecting the sentiments, if not quite the eloquence, of the two greatest imperialists, Lord Chatham and Winston Churchill. Chamberlain's style and mode of speaking—unbending, unsmiling, austere—was more aristocratic than democratic; yet he represented the new era in that he went before the people not to tell them what was done but to explain, to justify, to ask for their assent. "Come, let us reason together" was his mode. He exemplified it well:

Just let us consider what that Empire is. I am not going to speak tonight of those millions, hundred of millions, of our Indian and native fellow-subjects for whom we have become responsible. It is upon us that the obligation lies to give them good government. . . . I want you to look forward. I want you to consider the infinite importance of this not only to yourselves but to your descendents. . . . Think what it means to your power and influence as a country; think what it means to your position among the nations of the world; think what it means to your trade and commerce. . . . I say it is the business of British statesmen to do everything they can, even at some present sacrifice, to keep the trade of the colonies with Great Britain. . . . That is the critical issue. . . . There is still time to consolidate the Empire. We also have our chance, and it depends upon what we do now whether this great idea is to find fruition or whether we will for ever and ever dismiss it from our consideration and accept our fate as one of the dying Empires of the world.

In his conclusion he stressed the responsibility that had come to rest upon the general population by the acceptance of democracy. It was the burden formerly carried by leaders, which was now theirs to bear:

I leave the matter in your hands. I desire that a discussion on this subject should be opened. The time has not yet come to settle it; but it seems to me that for good or for evil this is an issue much greater in its consequences than any of our local disputes. Make a mistake in legislation, yet it can be corrected; make a mistake in your Imperial policy, it is irretrievable. You have an opportunity; you will never have it again.

The closing stages of Chamberlain's career were marred by his greatest failure. Still in the name of empire, he split the Conservative party in 1903 by advocating a protective tariff from which only the colonies and dominions would be exempt. This again was a "middle course" that invited attack from both sides. Even Chamberlain's own brother Arthur would not go along with it. "I don't think they will vote for Protection," he said, "because I can't think they would be so silly as to ask the government to tax the food they eat, the clothes they wear and the commodities they use, on the promise of the politicians that their wages will rise."[42]

Joseph Chamberlain's political career was near its end. In 1906, soon after his seventieth birthday, he suffered a paralytic stroke and never made a public speech again. The last speech he did make, on 9 July 1906, closed with words descriptive of the new spirit of democracy, which had come to be dominant in England at last: "I trust in the good sense, the intelligence and the patriotism of the majority, the vast majority, of my countrymen."

8
TORCHBEARERS OF A NEW REVOLUTION: PEACEFUL BUT RADICAL CHANGE

The decade between the death of Queen Victoria and the outbreak of the First World War is commonly known as the Edwardian Era, named for one of the most popular monarchs of his time or of the long stretch of English history. Edward VII loved luxury, enjoyed lavish living, and exuded zest in his performance from early youth of the many ceremonial duties the members of the royal family were called upon to perform. He travelled extensively as the Prince of Wales both throughout the dominions and to many foreign countries, winning admiration as a splendid and warm-hearted personage and as a supporter of international friendship. His marriage to Princess Alexandria of Denmark was popular and he won still deeper affection from the British people by his ardent sponsorship of programs for the poor as well as for his exuberant pleasure in public ceremonies, in sports, and in ostentatious luxury. During his reign the British Empire was at its zenith. The British pound was the global standard for currency exchange. The middle class was expanding and was enjoying general prosperity. More than in most times, everything looked good.

It was only beneath the surface that grievous ills roiled and only among the large segment of the poor that discontent was angry and widespread. Some few intellectuals understood and vigorously stated the need for basic reforms. H. G. Wells in his novel *The Wife of Sir Isaac Harman* itemized some of the problems: "the crazy makeshift of our legal and political systems, the staggering accidents of economic relationship, the festering disorder of contemporary philosophy and religious teaching." These were the kinds of problems that intellectuals viewed with deep concern and in consequence "the relations between the established order and the intelligentsia was one of antagonism and suspicion."[1]

Political leaders were also aware of problems that bore heavily upon the lower classes, such as unemployment, underemployment, inadequate pay, poor working conditions especially in the mines and factories, and both bad and insufficient housing. The intellectuals, not being bound to confront legislative and fiscal limitations, took a much broader view and denounced the whole structure of the society as being irrational and unjust. Both groups had spokesmen of great power who were eager as well as able to take their case to the public. Consequently, despite the surface glitter of the Edwardian Era, the period was marked by a heightened degree of anger and bitterness in its public debate.

"The Middle Class . . . the Population That Mattered"

Representative of these two groups—of the ideologists and the politicians—were such parliamentarians as Herbert Asquith, David Lloyd George, and the young Winston Churchill; and such diverse intellectuals as Sidney and Beatrice Webb, George Bernard Shaw, Hilaire Belloc, G. K. Chesterton, and Bertrand Russell. Much as they differed among themselves, they were all concerned in their several ways with "the development of a situation heading straight to misery and ruin without precedent"—climaxed by World War I—"in the midst of a world where the happy, abundant life of the people [as seen from the perspective of the middle class] flowed on unconcerned, and all thoughts were turned toward the approaching holidays and the glories of triumphant summer days."[2]

The political leaders were no longer discussing whether democracy was good or bad; it had become a fact with which they simply had to deal. The intellectual radicals were not "dreamers of impossible Utopias" like Morris and Kingsley but took themselves very seriously as architects of social changes that were not only urgently needed but were also—at least in their view—eminently practical. The two groups together—but not in harmony, for they were by far too individualistic to cooperate as partners—constituted the "torchbearers of a new revolution" that sought to make democracy socially and economically and even philosophically operative. Apart from this common aim they had little in common.

Herbert Henry Asquith was a middle-class pragmatist who verged toward intellectualism. He loved poetry and cared about ideas as well as about programs. He lacked the sparkle that makes for popularity; but in parliamentary debates he handled facts and statistics with such solid effectiveness that he was nicknamed "The Sledge Hammer." The young Winston Churchill did associate with such intellectuals as the sociologist William Beveridge and with Sidney and Beatrice Webb, who convinced him that government is responsible not only for maintaining social order but also for enhancing social welfare, thereby making him an advocate for such reforms as unemployment insurance and government employment offices. David Lloyd George, by far the most incitive speaker among them, had a gift for imaginative appeal unmatched between the times of Lord Chatham and the "great period" in Churchill's life during World War II. Lloyd George's was "the voice and magnetic personality to sweep an audience into an emotional frenzy."[3]

All of the intellectuals were more noted as writers than as public speakers; but they all had a keen sense of audience, they were propagandists of ideas, and they were as skilled in spoken as in written words. Their concern was for the whole of humanity; but their appeal was not to the mass but to what Lloyd George called "the worst section of the middle class—that which thinks itself aristocratic."[4] While they felt themselves to be ultrademocratic, they were in fact—in attitude, in tone, and in self-regard—patrician, not representing the great public but dedicated to telling it what was good for it. Their underlying concern was less with bread-and-butter practicalities than with the ultimate question on which the practicalities rest of whether "it was possible for mankind to level up its mental capacities to the demands of the environment that its own conquest of matter created."[5]

The rhetorical problem that both the intellectuals and the politicians had to solve was how to arouse interest and concern about social problems in the audience that the new democracy had made dominant: the middle class. This was the population that mattered since it was the part that carried elections; and it voted in terms of its own interests and according to such information as it had. What it saw and what it felt was the surface appearance—of peace and prosperity. What the "torchbearers" had to do was to enlighten its understanding and to arouse its feelings concerning the very real and very imminent dangers posed by the unseen and therefore unrecognized subterranean desperation. It was a time when persuasive discourse made a significant difference because it was a period of unusual intellectual instability: "a time balanced uneasily between two great periods of change. On the one hand is a past still showing faint survivals of vitality; on the other is the future but hardly coming to birth."[6] This is how it was discerned by the intellectuals. The political leaders focused their attention upon immediate problems; for these were the ones they had to try to solve.

"Way of Discussing Did Make a Difference"

One perspective from which to gain an overview of the three political leaders whose persuasive effectiveness had a shaping influence on events of this time is provided by the sharply definitive, brief essays concerning them written by John Maynard Keynes, who knew them well.[7] As he freely admitted, his account was prejudiced rather than well balanced, which very fact reflects the strength of contemporary feelings about them.

In his view Lloyd George was a "chameleon," "rooted in nothing," "void and without content," who "lives and feeds on his immediate surroundings; he is an instrument and a player at the same time which plays on the company and is played on by them too . . . a prism . . . which collects light and distorts it . . .," purposeless, irresponsible, without "fundamental beliefs and principles." Then along with such condemnations, Keynes confesses: "But it is not appropriate to apply to him the ordinary standards. How can I convey to the reader, who does not know him, any just impression of this extraordinary figure of our time, this syren, this goat-footed bard, this half-human visitor to our age from the hag-ridden magic and enchanted woods of Celtic antiquity?" So much for Lloyd George: "intellectually the subtlest," with an "incurable love of a deal." We must keep in mind that this sweeping disparagement was colored by Keynes's despair at the inadequacies of the Peace of Paris after World War I, that Lloyd George had helped to forge.

In contrast, Keynes's evaluation of Asquith was equally sweepingly favorable. Asquith, he says, was liberal with a conservative temperament: "perfect for carrying into execution those Radical projects of his generation which were well judged." To him was owing "not the invention of any part of that programme, but the wisdom of its selection and execution." His intellect combined "lucidity, critical sharpness, a copious and accurate memory . . . with an absence of originality and creative power." He "was built for the purpose of dealing with the given facts of the outside world." He had "no intellectual fancies to lead him astray; no balloons of his own making to lift his feet off the ground." For the role he played of "selecting and judging" of what most needed to be done, "there has been no man in this century by any means his equal." Not a deviser but an administrator of essential reforms, "He was the solid core around which that brilliant circle revolved."

Keynes's essay on Winston Churchill is the longest of the three yet the least definitive, which is significant in terms of the date, 1929, at which it was written. By that time Churchill had strongly impressed upon the English mind a sense of his greatness, but also uncertainty as to what it was he sought to achieve. How the "early" Churchill appeared is summed up in Keynes's admiring conclusion: "gratitude" for "so much eloquence and feeling of things that are part of the lives of all of us. . . . Admiration for his energies of mind and his intense absorption of intellectual interest and elemental emotion in what is for the moment the matter in hand—which is his best quality. A little envy, perhaps, for his undoubting conviction that frontiers, races, patriotisms, even wars if need be, are the ultimate verities for mankind. . . ." The essay concerns only Churchill's commentary on World War I in which he "does not dissemble his own delight in the intense experiences of conducting warfare on the grand scale," nor "does he conceal its awfulness. . . ." Perhaps most significantly, Churchill felt that the professional soldiers were "generally wrong," and the professional politicians were "generally right" on how the campaigns should be conducted. Equally perceptive is Keynes's observation that Churchill "does not lose himself in details. He deals in the big with the essential problems. . . ."

As the careers and the speeches of these men are examined, other perspectives from which to evaluate them round out a more balanced portrayal of what they sought to accomplish and of how they went about it. All three were persuasive speakers of great power—each in a quite different way. If in their persons the time of giants had not yet come again, at least it was coming close. The problems they dealt with were momentous; and their way of discussing them did make a difference in giving new form to the British scene.

"Eloquence . . . Far Beyond Facts and Ideas"

As Keynes's essay indicates, many doubted the statesmanship of David Lloyd George but few questioned the fact of his charismatic persuasiveness. The effects he produced are the more remarkable in that he came into British public life under the grave handicap of being an outsider. What the English thought about the Welsh was capsulized in their nursery rimes: "Patty was a Welshman, Patty was a thief." English derogation of Wales was such that Welsh Anglican bishoprics were held by Englishmen, most of whom seldom or never so much as visited them. Middle-school education was actually more advanced and universal in Wales than in England; but in 1846 a Royal Commission on Welsh education blamed the "backwardness" of the people on their use of the Welsh language and recommended its replacement with English. The result, ironically, was not the Anglicanization of the people but on the contrary a great surge of resentful and defensive emphasis on the values of Welsh culture.

It was during this period of resurgent Welsh pride that David Lloyd George was born on 17 January 1863. His father was a poor schoolteacher living temporarily in Manchester, and when he died, the infant David, just seventeen months old, was placed in the care of his uncle in Wales, a home-craftsman, with a small income but a deep religious faith and an intense interest in books and in politics. This uncle presided over a village debating society and encouraged his young charge to read, to think independently, and to discuss social issues. The results were that young David became Unitarian in religion— revering Christ as a social reformer rather than as a redeemer—and that he determined to become a man of great consequence. When in later life he was asked when he first came to think of himself as a genius he replied that it was at the age of eleven while reading Euclid's geometry. In order to rise in the world, he determined to become a lawyer, and his uncle obligingly apprenticed him to a law firm. Such was the background of the man who came to belong to "the company of the great, and even very great, British statesmen."[8]

Actually, legal studies bored him and he quickly turned his attention to politics. In 1880 when he was seventeen he first attracted the attention of the Liberal Party local leaders by a series of articles he wrote for a local newspaper in which he said England needed leaders who "really hated oppression."[9] His mind was already well matured. As his best biographer attests—in contradiction of Keynes's charge that he was "unprincipled"—"Historians have tended to interpret Lloyd George's career as a progression from narrow Welsh nationalism to world statesmanship. The interpretation is false. He *started* with a broad outlook, and with a number of basic ideas which remained remarkably constant throughout a long life."[10]

One of his ideas was to make his convictions operative by persuasive speech. He made his first speech to a municipal debating society in January 1882 and a few months later, he made to the same audience another that the local newspaper said would have been entitled to praise if delivered in the House of Commons. Lloyd George was keeping a diary in which he faithfully recorded "my thirst for renown." He was admitted to the bar and quickly made a reputation as an able pleader and a barrister of independent mind and utterly without fear of the presiding judges. When a county court judge reproved him for making an "insulting and ungentlemanly" reference to judges and demanded to be told whom he meant, the young lawyer replied gravely, "I refer to you in particular, sir."

In 1889 he stood as a candidate for Parliament and made a speech at Cardiff that stated eloquently the theme that was to dominate his life: "There is a momentous time coming. The dark continent of wrong is being explored, and there is a missionary spirit abroad for its reclamation to the realm of right. A holy war has been proclaimed against 'man's inhumanity to man.'" When the votes were counted the County of Carnarvon sent to Parliament "one who would leave a more decisive mark upon the British State than any man since Cromwell."[11]

His reputation as a public speaker was already established. He was invited to speak in the London Metropolitan Tabernacle, where he was well received, and then at the Free Trade Hall on 4 June 1890 in Manchester. This speech—denouncing the trade in liquor, which "reeks with human misery, vice and squalor, destitution, crime and death"—had a tremendous effect. Lloyd George described it in a letter to his wife:

> The hall was packed with an audience numbering several thousands. . . . Immediately I got up the audience cheered again and again. . . . This set me up. . . . I spoke for half an hour amid continued and long continued cheers. . . . I never saw a people more profoundly impressed. . . . During my closing sentences a hush fell over the whole place. I spoke fiercely—feeling myself mind you intensely every word I uttered and charging my sentences with all the intensity of my heart. . . . when I sat down there came a sight which I shall never forget—the whole dense and immense audience seemed for a moment stunned but recovering they sprang up as one man and flung hats handkerchiefs sticks . . . anything they could get hold of. I trembled like a leaf with passion for a long while. I was overwhelmed with congratulations.[12]

After that, as he told his wife, he was invited to "go to all sorts of places." He proved to be equally effective both on the public platform, speaking to masses of generally uninformed listeners, and in the House of Commons, where he traded arguments with sharp and well-filled minds. His first speech in the Commons was made just a week after his great success in Manchester and consisted of a daringly sharp attack against Randolph Churchill and Joseph Chamberlain, the two most prominent members. Its audacity attracted attention and its ability won admiration. To his wife he wrote that he was "overwhelmed with congratulations" and he was so encouraged that he plunged regularly into the debates. On 13 August on his own motion to delete from the ministerial budget a small sum to be given to the Prince of Prussia, he grandly told the members: "I think it absolutely monstrous that we should be paying these sums . . . when there is so much suffering. . . . thousands of hard-working, thrifty people are living a life of hopeless, ceaseless toil."

Both his impassioned, sarcastic, denunciatory style and his lifelong theme of championing the poor were already firmly established. Both may be illustrated from a speech he gave in the town of Rhyl on 10 November 1891. His purpose was to demonstrate how little the Church of England served the real needs of the people and his method was to ridicule the bishops who claimed to be "the successors of Peter, the plain, bluff, honest old fisherman."

> Can you picture him coming down to attend the Church Congress in a special train, with a man in buttons dancing about him . . .? Can you portray him driving up in a brougham to the door of the House of Lords, lolling on its scarlet benches . . .? Can you imagine him dwelling in a stately mansion with a host of menials ministering to his luxury? Can you fancy him drawing a salary large enough to have kept the Temple going for months? And all this with the poor rotting in misery at his very palace gates.

By 1895–96 his ideas and his abilities had made him the acknowledged chief among the disorganized Liberals in the Commons. As an editorialist in the *Daily Chronicle* wrote of him: "I should certainly say that Mr. Lloyd George has made the greatest mark of the session." In the opinion of a Tory opponent, "he had disclosed a perfect mastery of the subject, a readiness of force and resource in debate."[13] When the Boer War broke out, he not only denounced it on principle but also saw it as an opportunity for the Liberals to wrest the governing power from the Conservatives. To an Oxford audience he reviewed the cost of the war in money, in lives, and "in something infinitely more precious . . . and that is the distinction of being the hope and shield of the weak and oppressed in all lands." By the war's end he had been in Parliament for twelve years and his aim was clearly to be the leader of Great Britain.

His reputation was great both in Parliament and out; though there also were complaints that "the credit which nearly everybody, high and low, accorded to him at the time was substantially more than he deserved."[14] The negative view of him that has been cited from Keynes derived largely from the view of conservatives that he was demagogic in manner and Quixotic in his advocacy of social justice. When the Liberals came to office under the prime ministry of Asquith, Lloyd George was linked with Winston Churchill as the party's strongest supports. Both of them, but Lloyd George most effectively, "focused the opera-glasses of the rich on the miseries of the poor."[15] Together these two and Herbert Asquith did much to implant the basic program of the Welfare State. Lloyd George, acknowledged as the greatest orator in the country, was the most effective in waging the campaign. "Shame upon rich Britain," he exclaimed in a speech in Wales on 25 September 1906 "that she should tolerate so much poverty among her people! . . . There is plenty of wealth in this country to provide for all and to spare. What is wanted is a fairer distribution."[16]

In January 1909 as Chancellor of the Exchequer, Lloyd George proposed "The People's Budget," to cement the reform program. In a speech in the Limehouse district of London on 30 July 1909 he supported the proposals with an appeal to a densely packed audience of four thousand rowdy Cockneys, which opponents labelled his "Slimehouse speech," and which an admiring biographer properly claims "must stand high among the great popular orations of history."[17] To his cheering listeners he proclaimed the theme of the new revolution:

> The provision for the aged and deserving poor—it was time it was done. It is rather a shame for a rich country like ours—probably the richest country in the world, if not the richest the world has ever seen—that it should allow those who have toiled all their days to end in penury and possibly starvation. It is rather hard that an old workman should have to find his way to the gates of the tomb, bleeding and footsore, through the brambles and thorns of poverty. We cut a new path through it, an easier one, a pleasanter one, through fields of waving corn. . . .
>
> These things I am going to tell you of have only been possible up to the present through the fraud of the few and the folly of the million. In the future those landlords will have to contribute to the taxation of the country on the basis of the real value, only one half-penny in the pound! And that is what all the howling is about. . . .
>
> The landlord is a gentleman—I have not a word to say about him in his personal capacity—who does not earn his wealth. He does not even take the trouble to receive his wealth. He has a host of agents and clerks that receive it for him. He does not even take the trouble to spend his wealth. He has a host of people around him to do the actual spending for him. He never sees it till he comes to enjoy it. His sole function, his chief pride is stately consumption of wealth produced by others. . . .
>
> The landlords are receiving eight millions a year by way of royalties. What for? They never deposited the coal there. It was not they who planted these great granite rocks in Wales, who laid the foundations of the mountains. Was it the landlord? And yet he, by some Divine right, demands—for merely the right for men to risk their lives in hewing these rocks—eight millions a year! . . .
>
> No country, however, rich, can permanently afford to have quartered upon its revenue a class which declines to do the duty which it was called upon to perform. . . .
>
> Why should I put the burdens on the people? I am one of the children of the people. I was brought up amongst them. I know their trials. . . .
>
> Finally, I say to you, without you we can do nothing, with your help we can brush the Lords like chaff before us.[18]

By such advocacy Lloyd George won the necessary support. The House of Lords did veto the budget bill but it was enacted anyway. By an Act of Parliament in 1911 the power of the Lords to veto legislation was ended. Substantially the new revolution became an accomplished fact.

After the outbreak of World War I Lloyd George's duties were administrative, first to provide the sinews for waging war, afterward as Prime Minister to win it. In a long decline from the period of his persuasive effectiveness, he lived on until

26 March 1945. As a swan song in the Commons in November 1939, after the fall of Norway, he called upon Neville Chamberlain to resign and asked that Churchill not make himself "an air raid shelter" for the failing administration. But the time had well passed when oratory was an effective instrument for him. His reputation as the advocate for the poor declined as the efficacy of the welfare state came under increasing question. In retrospect his successes have lost at least some of their luster. But his place in history is secure, for in significant degree it was his persuasive eloquence that brought the new revolution into effect.

How should Lloyd George be judged as a public speaker? What makes for persuasive effectiveness includes more than just being right on the issues. In his demand for a restructuring of the state he was a spokesman for "an idea whose time had come." But so were many of his peers. What made his speaking special was the charisma that always won audiences for him and then won them to his side, an eloquence that went far beyond facts and ideas and even beyond the verbal arousal of emotions. Even for people who strongly disagreed with him, including those who feared him as an opportunistic, evil, society-wrecking influence, he still had a fascinating appeal.

Partly this stemmed from his being a Welshman, the only one in centuries to become central in English politics. Partly it was his magnificently handsome appearance and his musically attractive and appropriately tuned voice. Partly it was his air of supernal assurance, suggestive of a Celtic sprite with unearthly powers. Added to this was his skill in contrivance: his sophisticated understanding of what was impressive. It was this that led him to transmute his patronymic name of "George" into the unhyphenated dualism of Lloyd George, something unique. His first name the English spelled David but there also was the special appeal of its Welsh spelling as Dafyd. His speaking style was also contrived. He prepared his speeches carefully,[19] sometimes even writing them out and typically using detailed notes, yet he managed to make them sound spontaneous with a spur-of-the-moment immediacy. What he believed he believed with constancy and intensity; yet he was also sensitively responsive to both his immediate listeners and to the expectations of the public.

This was the combination that his adverse critics branded as opportunistic and demagogic even while he held steadfast in the course to which he was deeply committed. In his private life he was a philanderer even while being also deeply devoted to the two women whom he truly loved, for a long time simultaneously. In another paradox, he was an effective temperance advocate while also being a moderate drinker. In foreign affairs he was less farsighted and often less clear-sighted than statesmanship requires. Yet he won admiration from liberals for his opposition to the Boer War and from the nation for his conduct of World War I. There is no doubt that he had great abilities—nor that transcendent among them was his ability in persuasive speech. As was true also of Canning, Brougham, Disraeli, and Churchill, his political course was not always easily understandable. But there is no challenging the strength of his personality or the force of his rhetorical effects.

"Independence of Mind and a Jaunty Flaunting"

It was Lloyd George who won young Winston Churchill to liberalism and helped him to become effective in politics. They first met during the Boer War, on which their views were very different. Yet even then they felt the mutual attraction that drew them together in what has been called "the most fruitful and momentous association of its kind in British history." This at least was how it appeared to the biographer of Lloyd George who believes that "Churchill soon fell under Lloyd George's spell and for the rest of his life never ceased to regard the Welshman as his mentor." The Welshman was twelve years the elder and when they met was well established as a leader. The two felt an affinity from their first encounter, partly because they "recognized in each other the same quality of ruthless, unlimited, egocentric ambition." Beyond this: "Both were brilliant talkers, but Lloyd George, unlike Churchill, was also an excellent listener [who] revelled in the free trade of conversation and discussion, whereas Churchill was addicted to monologue. People would leave Churchill's presence feeling that they had encountered a man of cosmic importance, but they would leave Lloyd George feeling *themselves* more important than when they arrived."[20]

The chief caveat with Grigg's estimate must be with his claim that Churchill always felt Lloyd George to be his "mentor." Churchill never accepted the mastery of anyone. Even while he was an unwilling and rebellious student at Harrow—refusing to study and characterized by his housemaster as "so regular in his irregularity that I really don't know what to do"—even then the school doctor found him to be "the most extraordinary young man that I have ever met."[21] When Churchill first entered Parliament, Violet Asquith told her father of her impression that for the first time in her life she had met a genius. Asquith shrugged off the comment with the quip that, "Winston would certainly agree with you"; but then he added that, "he is not only remarkable but unique." Lloyd George initially reacted like an orator fearing a rival, derogating Churchill as "being just like an actor," for whom "the applause of the House is the breath of his nostrils."[22] Of course this was a mirror image of himself.

As far as it went, this perception was correct. Churchill himself in his early childhood declared it was his "only ambition to be master of the spoken word." On a youthful trip to America he met the Irish orator Bourke Cockran and undertook to model his own speaking upon Cockran's ornate style. The most exhaustive recent biography of Churchill notes that "his feeling for the English tongue was sensual, almost erotic; when he coined a phrase he would suck it, rolling it around his palate to extract its full flavor."[23] He read and reread

Macaulay and Gibbon, working to develop a style akin to theirs. He never lost his savor for the right word and the right phrase, often while preparing a speech trying them out on his secretaries and testing them with his own ear.

Public speaking did not come naturally to him. He had a speech impediment, variously described as a lisp and as a stammer, of which he long remained conscious. As his son saw it, "He had to fight every inch of his road through life; nothing came easily to him, not even oratory and writing."[24] He succeeded because he worked to develop the abilities he cherished most. He read and analyzed the speeches in the *Annual Register* and especially studied his father's phrasing, even memorizing long passages of his speeches, always intent to develop a similar style. As a result, this "most modern man" developed an old-fashioned style both in writing and in speaking. He never deviated from his purpose. Shortly after his entrance into Parliament he wrote to his mother that "With practice I shall obtain great power on a public platform. My impediment is no hindrance. My voice is sufficiently powerful, and—this is vital—my ideas and modes of thought are pleasing to men."[25]

His stature as a predominant English statesman-orator—equalling when not surpassing such others as Chatham, Burke, Fox, the younger Pitt, Disraeli, Gladstone, and Lloyd George—has led to a vast outflowing of books that undertake to explain him. Since his basic qualities were rooted in his early years, many of these books naturally concentrate upon the young Churchill. Margot Asquith (who didn't trust him) made the same mistake about him that Keynes made about Lloyd George: that he was a man of "transitory convictions." His biographers generally agree that, as one of them says, the opposite was true: "Churchill never changed at all. . . . his views once formed were immutable."[26]

His lifelong feeling was that people should be served rather than catered to. His view of democracy was that the well-being of all, which is its goal, depends upon leadership, which is the means. In explaining his first try for a seat in Parliament in July 1899 he said: "I must explain that in those days we had a real political democracy, led by a hierarchy of statesmen and not a mass distracted by newspapers."[27] A student of his career asserts that he had a "sense of destiny . . . a mystical certainty that he was marked for greatness."[28] His son adjudged that from the start of his career "he ruthlessly thrust himself forward . . . spurred by a burning sense of destiny."[29] A writer in the *Morning Post* in 1929 concluded that, "Mr. Churchill is still his own Party, and the chief of the partisans. He still sees himself as the only digit in the sum of things, all other men as mere cyphers, whose function it is to follow after and multiply his personal values a million-fold."[30] It was precisely this insistence upon following the beat of his own drum that made it necessary for him to "fight every inch of his road through life."

His many biographers are singularly in agreement on this characteristic. They find him transparent, no man of mystery. Personality qualities that bulked large were his self-regard, which made him resolutely self-reliant, combined with a tendency to deep depression, which led him to continuous self-examination; a massive courage, enabling him to stand alone; indestructable industry and energy; a personalized patriotism marked by self-identification with the long tradition of English greatness; a patrician aristocracy that condescended to the masses while he sincerely sought to serve their needs; a capacious mind that mastered history and brought it to bear upon immediate issues; boundless curiosity and eagerness to comprehend; and, bringing it all to a point, a vivid sense of imagery that he utilized with irrepressible determination to impress his own vision upon his time.

His personality traits, emerging early, were little modified by experience. Paramount among them was *cheekiness*—a combination of independence of mind and a jaunty flaunting of it. This trait he displayed in his first political speech at the age of twenty-three in 1897 when he was invited to speak to the prestigious Primrose Club for just fifteen minutes and deliberately continued for twenty-five. As he explained: "One must not yield too easily to the weaknesses of audiences. There they were, what could they do? They had asked for it and they must have it." His spirit of self-assured irreverence he displayed often, as in a comment he made in 1901 when shifting from the Tories to the Liberals: "Politics is like waking up in the morning. You never know whose head you will find on the pillow." Justifying his independence in 1904 he confessed to the House: "I did not exactly, either by my movement or my manner, invite any great continuing affection." His cheekiness readily led to the deprecation of other political leaders, as when he explained in the same speech why he had left the Tories: "They are a class of right honourable men, all good men, honest men—who are ready to make great sacrifices for their opinions, but they have no opinions. They are ready to die for the truth, if only they knew what the truth was."[31] In the view of his son, it was this spirit that made him a leader:

> He never feared taking responsibility, nor was he wont to lay the blame on others when events wore an ugly aspect. His metal was the very reverse of Asquith's. He knew that he had great aptitudes for leadership and he always grasped any opportunity to exercise it.[32]

Churchill's childhood was both privileged and lonely, exalted yet depressed by failures. He was born on 30 November 1874 in the splendid palace of Blenheim into a family that had been distinguished for generations. His father and his American mother were both ardently pursuing their chosen careers and woefully neglected him. Harrow, where he was sent for schooling, utterly failed to inspire him. When he transferred to the Royal Military College of Sandhurst, he was rated 92nd in a class of 102. Here however, his mind was awakened, for he gloried in the study of militarism.

But it was not the kind of education that would seem to fit him for the new age of democracy. As he later confessed, "I was brought up in that state of civilization when it was everywhere accepted that men are born unequal."[33] As his son wrote of him, he became "his own university." He developed a passionate love for books—the reading and later the writing of them. How he handled books never made him a scholar but greatly enlarged his mind. He liked his method and recommended it: "If you cannot read all your books, at any rate handle them, or, as it were, fondle them—peer into them, let them fall open where they will, read from the first sentence that arrests the eye, set them back on their shelves with your own hands, arrange them on your own plan so that if you do not know what is in them, you will at least know where they are. Let them be your friends; let them at any rate be your acquaintances."[34] He did not pretend to more erudition than he had.

With a restless love for adventure, he set out as a journalist to war fronts in Cuba, India, the Sudan, and to the Boer War in South Africa. His reporting won him a popularity that helped him to be elected in October 1900 to Parliament. Since he needed money—he often boasted that he did not spend what he did not earn—he set out on a lecture tour. First he traversed Great Britain, "speaking for an hour or more almost every night except Sundays, and often twice a day." His lectures, illustrated with lantern slides of battlefield scenes, were presented in the manner that remained typical throughout his life: "the slightly hunched shoulders from which the head jutted forward like the muzzle of a gun about to fire." His tour took him next to New York City, where his first speech at the Waldorf Astoria Hotel on 12 December 1900 was introduced by Mark Twain with the blunt comment: "I think England sinned when she got herself into a war in South Africa which she could have avoided, just as we have sinned in getting into a similar war in The Philippines."

Churchill was shaken by this reception; and the subsequent tour did not go well. He explained to his mother: "First of all the interest is not what Maj Pond made out and secondly there is a strong pro-Boer feeling. . . . Several times I have harangued in local theatres to almost empty benches. I have been horribly vulgarized by the odious advertisements . . . and only my cynical vein has helped me to go on." He proceeded next to Canada where his "audiences were adoring and huge." In February he sailed for home with money enough to support the start of his political career.[35] Like Twain, Matthew Arnold, Dickens, and many more, he profited from the fact that lecturing in those days was a lucrative enterprise.

When the new parliamentary session commenced on 14 February, Churchill was ready for it. He was impatient to lunge toward leadership. "New members were usually in a state of bewilderment at the strange practices, but Winston knew the protocol and language of the House by heart, from studying his father's career." He made his maiden speech on 18 February late in the evening, and such was his reputation (and that of his father) that the members were eager to hear him. "The moment he rose to speak, the word went out that 'Churchill's up' and every inch of the Chamber was occupied; even the side galleries and the bar were thronged." Churchill's speech was a defense of the Boer War, which "from beginning to end has only been a war of duty." He ended with a graceful acknowledgment that the exceptional reception accorded him was owing to "the splendid memory" of his father. In the report in the *Daily Chronicle,* Churchill was deprecated as "a medium-sized, undistinguished looking young man, with an unfortunate lisp . . . and he lacks force."[36]

It was not a promising beginning but it went much according to his own plans. Five years earlier while listening to debates in the House of Lords, Churchill had written to his mother that "It is a fine game to play—the game of politics—and it is well worth waiting for a good hand before plunging in." After his first speech to the Commons he spoke less ostentatiously, waiting for good cards to be dealt. By the end of 1901, however, he had made eleven speeches in the House while also giving some thirty political talks around the country and formal lectures in twenty towns.

His views were taking form. More and more he was associating with intellectual liberals—including Hilaire Belloc, G. B. Shaw, H. G. Wells, the Webbs, and the sociologist William Beveridge—and they helped to shape his maturing political philosophy. How he impressed them Beatrice Webb wrote in 1908: "He is brilliantly able—more than a phrase-monger."[37] Churchill's most recent biographer believes that political considerations were more important than the stimulation from these intellectuals, and concludes that "motives for the liberation of Churchill from patrician dogma were immeasurably strengthened by the charisma and leadership of his colleague Lloyd George."[38] Both influences were undoubtedly important.

The relationship of Churchill and Lloyd George has been much discussed and was undoubtedly important to both. In their first acquaintance, because of disagreements concerning the Boer War Churchill dismissed the Welshman as "a vulgar, chattering little cad."[39] Shortly afterwards the two became political allies and friends, though always with a wary alertness and jealous awareness that they were claimants for the same following. Morgan's description of their relationship seems accurate: "Churchill thought Lloyd Goerge was the greatest political genius he had ever met and became his lieutenant and henchman. . . . Lloyd George welcomed Churchill as a disciple, while knowing that his ambition equalled his own." What drew them together, Morgan went on, was similarity of personality and common views on social questions. What most sharply separated them was their contrasting views of war: Lloyd George hating it and Churchill feeling its grandeur. When World War I commenced, "In Churchill's declared liking for the war, Lloyd George saw the capacity to exploit national disaster for personal ambition. He and Churchill remained friends but Lloyd George sensed an unscrupulous side that made him keep a certain distance."[40] The wariness in their relationship is symptomatic of factors that made Churchill a "loner" throughout his career.

The "good cards" for which Churchill was waiting were dealt him when Asquith became prime minister and in April 1908 named him president of the

Board of Trade. From this time until his death his influence rose and fell in sharp contrasts; but his prominence seldom faded. During the critical debate over Lloyd George's "People's Budget" in 1909 Churchill vigorously supported it. The following year as home secretary he made his greatest contributions to the Welfare State by drawing up plans for a labor exchange and for unemployment insurance and by winning support for them. In October 1911 he became First Lord of the Admiralty, in which position he began to modernize the navy; to set up the Royal Navy Flying Corps; and to sponsor the development of an armored car that although called "Winston's Folly" became World War I's battle tank.

Both Churchill's views and his political relationships were ambiguous. "It is almost as though the radicals had felt uncomfortable with him in their midst. Henceforth he would be regarded as a conservative. . . . The awakening of the working class, which he himself had stirred, had altered the political climate. . . . Social stability was wobbly, and civility diminished."[41] It could be said that he changed his principles; or that conditions changed and he was realistic enough to change with them.

In any event the "early liberal Churchill" had played out his role. The "mature conservative Churchill" was yet to emerge. This was true not only in regard to domestic issues but to foreign relations as well. In a speech he gave on 15 August 1900 on relations between Great Britain and Germany, he said: "There is no real cause of difference between them. These two great peoples have nothing to fight about, no prize to fight for, and no place to fight." The changes that came to Churchill and to the world may be measured by contrasting the miner's rally at Swansea, where he gave this speech, with the cemetery of Flanders Field, the meeting at Munich, and the landing on the Normandy beaches. As conditions changed, so did Churchill's role as a public speaker and his mode of speech. This change belongs to another chapter.

"The 'Solid Core' of Persuasive Advocates"

Herbert Henry Asquith won the ultimate political prize of the prime ministry ahead of Lloyd George and a full three decades ahead of Winston Churchill. His mode of persuasion and his manner of speaking were far less flamboyant, less sensational than theirs. The contrast stands out starkly in the great debate on "The People's Budget." All of them knew that the barrier to be overcome was the opposition of the House of Lords. Lloyd George charged against it like a wave of cavalry, calling the upper house "the great slaughterhouse of good bills" and boasting that "we can brush the Lords like chaff before us." In similar spirit Churchill, speaking in Birmingham, declared that either amendment or rejection by the House of Lords was "out of the question—That way revolution lies." Asquith, as head of the government, avoided such provocative oratory. But he did give the speeches that mattered most, "at crucial times and in crucial places"—most notably on 10 December 1909 to an enthusiastic Albert Hall audience of ten thousand in which he quietly but firmly promised to resign if the Lords rejected the bill.[42]

Historians generally depict Asquith as the "solid core" of the brilliant persuasive advocates who brought the new revolution into effect. Asquith himself, in a little play that he wrote in March 1915, tried to explain why, by representing what "a fairly intelligent observer" might conclude about him:

> a classical example of *Luck*. You were endowed at birth with brains above the average. You had, further, some qualities of temperament which are exceptionally useful for mundane success—energy under the guise of lethargy; a faculty for working quickly, which is more effective in the long run than plodding perseverance; patience (which is one of the rarest of human qualities); a temperate but persistent ambition; a clear mind, a certain quality and lucidity of speech; intellectual, but not moral, irritability; a natural tendency to understand & appreciate the opponent's point of view; and, as time went on, & your nature matured, a growing sense of proportion, which . . . secured for you the substantial advantage of personality and authority.[43]

His self-analysis was essentially correct. He had neither the eloquence nor the charisma of Lloyd George and Winston Churchill. But he avoided their pugnacity, which in them attracted resentment and aroused opposition. After his election to Parliament in July 1886 he remained quietly in his place for nearly nine months. When he did rise to participate in the debate he was ready. Lord Haldane in his *Autobiography* termed this first speech "brilliant" and found that it "turned toward him the attention of the public as well as the Liberal leaders in the House." For the next several years Asquith spoke seldom in the House; though oftener to public audiences. Typical was his speech in October 1887 in Nottingham, where he received "tumultuous applause" for what Morley called an "eloquent and powerful" address; but it followed the safe course of simply praising Gladstone's management of the Liberal Party. In August 1892 he was rewarded for his sober dependability by being named Home Secretary, a success not to be discounted. "He was younger than his colleagues, and he was without inherited wealth or influence, he had been in the House of Commons only six years, and he had addressed it on little more than a dozen occasions."[44] What, then, was the reason for the shaping influence that he came to have?

One clear answer is trustworthiness. When Asquith, Lloyd George, and Churchill were all serving together in the cabinet of Campbell-Bannerman during the Boer War, the prime minister discussed his most intimate concerns with Asquith but not with the other two. Another was moderation—more in his style of speech than in his policies for he was as staunch an advocate for social changes leading toward the Welfare State as were his party associates, but he avoided incitements. Still another was his claim to "represent" opinion rather than to "lead" it—as when, after some seven years as prime minister, he quietly assured his quarrelsome cabinet (which included both Lloyd George and Churchill) that he would gladly resign if they did not fully trust him. Far less eloquent than either of these associates, he won his way by being more dependable. Asquith's opinion of them is reflective of his own sense of personal values. Concerning Lloyd George he wrote (on 3 March 1915) that "He is a wonderful person in some ways, but is totally devoid of either perspective or judgment"; and about a month earlier he recorded his view that Churchill "has no personal following" and his prediction that, "I think his future is one of the most puzzling enigmas in politics."[45]

Asquith's speaking reflected the qualities of his personality. As a seventeen-year-old youth in the City of London School (where a fellow student was Richard Jebb, later to write the notable book *Attic Orators*) he won the speaking prize with a eulogy marked by "resonant, elaborately constructed, yet beautifully balanced and lucid English diction." When he attended Oxford he spoke in almost every political debate in the Oxford Union and was elected to its presidency. The qualities of these early speeches were those he retained all his life. He made little effort to "adjust" to his listeners. "He was always at his best defending a well-prepared position and picking out with a deadly destructiveness the intellectual weaknesses in a hastily prepared enemy attack."[46] His speeches lacked the dash and sparkle that induce publication in newspapers or in anthologies. What they did was to represent Asquith as he was: a solidly substantial leader who proceeded in the right direction in a way that reduced tensions and won acceptance. That is what made him the "solid core." "Great speaking"—as is illustrated time and again in the history of British public address—is typically in some degree counterproductive. There is a kind of truth in Disraeli's comment in *Vivien Grey* that "to make a speech" is to admit that you "are under the necessity of explaining, or conciliating, or convincing, or confuting." A distinction always to be maintained is the one between "great" and "effective" speaking. Asquith well knew that for political leadership, effective (rather than impressive) speech is essential. Positions must be stated, clarified, and supported. And as the history of public address also illustrates, this is an ability that leaders of all kinds do possess and do use. Such a quality is not incidental; it is required.

Two comments sum up much of Asquith's special persuasive qualities. One of them was by Earl Edward Grey: "When things were going well . . . he would be careful to see that any colleague got credit. . . . On the other hand, if things were going badly he was ready to stand in front and accept all responsibility."[47] The other is a judgment that Asquith made on Campbell-Bannerman and that aptly applied also to himself: "He was to the last . . . an emollient & unifying factor in our party, & indeed in public life."[48] It is as suitable an epitaph as that which his family chose to engrave on his monument when he died in 1928: "Unmoved . . . to swerve from truth, or change his constant mind."

"Independent Rebels . . . Dedicated to Fundamental Reform"

Unlike the politicians, the intellectual rebels "had more liking for ideas than for action."[49] There were many of them in this time of revolt against Victorianism—ranging from the Webbs, Oscar Wilde, Charles Algernon, Swinburne, Thomas Hardy, George Meredith, E. M. Forster, and H. G. Wells to the more activist George Bernard Shaw, Hilaire Belloc, G. K. Chesterton, and Bertrand Russell. All were sincerely and deeply dedicated to fundamental societal reform; and all were vigorous practitioners of persuasive and propagandistic words. Among them all, Shaw, Belloc, and Chesterton, along with their writings, were also persistent, devoted, and able public speakers. What they were interested in was the sweeping question of how to make society more efficient. They had a good audience for this was also the preoccupation of the public.

The Spectator in its issue of 16 August 1902 editorialized that "At the present time, and perhaps it is the most notable social fact of this age, there is a universal outcry for efficiency in all the departments of society, in all aspects of life. We hear the outcry on all hands and from the most unexpected of persons. From the pulpit, the newspaper, the hustings, in the drawing-room, the smoking-room, the street, the same cry is heard: Give us Efficiency, or we die." The driving force behind this cry was manifold. In part it derived from the shock people felt at British military incompetence during the Boer War. In part it reflected the emphasis upon education following the adoption of the 1870 Education Act. In part it grew from the prevalence of the new industrialism.

Efficiency meant very different things to different people. To the Webbs, who organized the Fabian Society—and along with it the Coefficients Club—it meant an organized socialist state. To G. K. Chesterton and Hilaire Belloc, organizers of the Distributionist League, it meant the withering away of both the government and big business, leaving only decentralized small enterprises that would presumably ensure general equality of opportunity and wealth. There were many other ideas as well, for above all these intellectual radicals were individualistic. To John Galsworthy, who was one of them, it appeared that the typical liberal mind had become "a sour, dour, superior affair, full of kinks and ill-disposed to mankind at large."[50] The political reform movements that inaugurated the beginnings of the Welfare State created a view of the lower class that was far removed from the sympathetic but condescending attitude of earlier times. Instead, to idealists and conservatives alike, "The poor were no longer simple, dependent inferiors to be dealt with in a district-visitor manner; they were a mysterious and frightening new force."[51] The result was an ambiguous mixture of sympathy and apprehension. Concurrently many of the radical reformers who had enthusiastically welcomed the new science as an assurance of more rational social behavior became disillusioned as they found science widening the distance between social classes and increasing the horribleness of war.

What the intellectual rebels did accomplish was to create a general sense that matters were not going well for humanity and that affairs might be much better managed, if only we knew how.

What they sought to accomplish and how they used public speaking as a means of arousing interest and enlisting support may be illustrated by a speech given by H. G. Wells in the Fabian Society on 9 February 1906;[52] and by a debate between George Bernard Shaw and G. K. Chesterton before a large audience in Kingsway Hall in London on 28 October 1927.[53] All three of these speakers were so popular from their writings that what they had to say attracted unusual interest and exerted strong influence on both intellectuals and politicians.

Wells had gladly accepted Beatrice Webb's invitation in 1900 to join the Coefficients Club because it included such members as Arthur Balfour, Richard Haldane, Sir Edward Grey, Bertrand Russell and a dozen more of scarcely less repute. One of Mrs. Webb's enticements was that "he would find a great deal that was stimulating and challenging in their debates," including one coming soon between Shaw and Graham Wallas.[54] Wells became active in the club discussions and three years later also joined the Fabian Society. He always managed to be impressive, though he was "a little man of undistinguished appearance" with "the build of a teddy bear"; but "he never appeared to be fat," looking, "with his air of alertness and vitality" like "someone who was always on tip-toe, poised for a take-off."[55] With a vast self-assurance he poured forth ideas with a certainty that they were right and with a crusading urgency to have them accepted. He was positive that both individuals and society can be much better than they are and he felt a personal mission to make them so. He loved to talk and listeners found him entertaining, even while many rejected his pacifism and found his "scientism" to lack depth of understanding. Such was the man who stood before the distinguished membership of the Fabian Club to deliver a withering charge that they were haplessly ineffective:

> I came into your society very curious to know what you are up to. . . . I perceive . . . an extraordinarily inadequate and feeble organization in the midst of a world that teems with undeveloped possibilities. . . .
>
> We could be, we ought to be, pouring socialistic ideas into the student class, into the professional classes; every journalist ought to be a socialist, the clergy, the religious ministers, public officials, ought to be consciously saturated with our ideas. . . .
>
> I find in our society, cropping up sometimes in a speech of this member, and sometimes in a speech of that, a curious conceit of cunning, something like a belief that the world may be manoeuvered into socialism without knowing it.[56]

He went on to remind them of how the society got its name from Fabius Maximus, the Roman general who tried to "out wait" the enemy, avoiding battle with a hope that somehow, some time, the enemy would simply surrender. But his tactic did not win; instead it became "an enervating habit of inaction." So it was also with the Fabian Society. As Wells saw it, the members not only did little except talk to one another, they also made their membership exclusive. "Obviously, my first proposal is that we should grow." And, he went on, they could do so. "Now here, about this platform, you have . . . some admirable debaters, and one or two of the most interesting and most entertaining speakers in the world." He named two of them: Hilaire Belloc, "a terrible individualist, . . . wild and fierce"; and George Bernard Shaw, "who is not like everybody else . . . Shaw has a habit, a brilliant habit, of seeking to arrest the attention by a startling, apparent irrelevance, and he has a natural inclination to paradox." Such speakers, Wells said, must be used and must be supported. He concluded with an appeal that they organize "a vast network" of "local meetings, where inexpert speakers can find courage for discussion."

Such criticism did not endear Wells to the Fabian members, but Mrs. Webb reminded them that "he is a useful missionary to whole crowds of persons whom we could never get at. It will be sad if he turns completely sour. . . ."[57] Wells remained within the ranks. After World War I the Fabian Society lost its role to the new Labour party. But during the critical period in which the new revolution was accomplished, the Society helped to bring it about through the leadership of its prestigious members.

For the Shaw-Chesterton debate, Hilaire Belloc, serving as chairman, set the tone of "impertinent seriousness" by telling the crowded audience that: "They are about to debate. You are about to listen. I am about to sneer." What topic the two were to debate about was not specified. They were simply to say what they wished and see what happened.

Shaw, speaking first, told the audience that he and Chesterton were "two madmen" who went about in the world "uttering all sorts of extraordinary opinions for no reason whatsoever." Why, then, he asked, should anyone care what they had to say? His counsel was: "Reject all the contradictory things they say and concentrate your attention on the things on which they agree, and you may be listening to the voice of revelation." The issue that had become central in importance, he went on, was "a revolt against the mal-distribution, the obviously monstrous and anomalous mis-distribution of wealth under what we call the capitalist system."[58]

Chesterton in reply agreed that "the distribution of property in the modern world is a monstrosity and a blasphemy." Where he disagreed with Shaw was on what should be done to remedy the problem. What he flatly rejected was Shaw's view that "the means of production should be owned by the community." With a bow to Shaw's "vast superiority, to his powerful intellect," Chesterton insisted that nevertheless he himself was the one better "acquainted with the elementary facts of human life." A basic fact is that ownership of property by the government would not at all mean ownership by the people. Instead, "when you have vast systems, however just and however reasonably controlled indirectly by elaborate machinery of officials . . . you do in fact find that those who rule are the few." While Shaw, Chesterton contended, was trying to draw plans for an abstract society, what he himself advocated was fitted to the real nature of the typical man who "likes a certain amount of liberty, certain kinds of ownership, certain kinds of local affection, and won't be happy without them."

Shaw, speaking again, pointed out that Chesterton did agree that coal mines must be nationalized and therefore could not reasonably object to "the nationalization of everything else." As for the charge that his approach was too abstract, Shaw replied that "as a playwright, I think of all problems in terms of men and women." He turned to the central issue: the private ownership of property. The problem with it, Shaw argued, was that differing standards were applied. The land owner "can do exactly what he likes with the land he owns. . . . [He] can take women in child-bearing and throw them into the snow and leave them there. That has been done." On the other hand, the owner of an umbrella is not permitted to use it to batter people over the head. Land owners, he concluded, should be restricted similarly.

Chesterton replied that "Among the bewildering welter of fallacies which Mr. Shaw has given us, I prefer to deal first with the simplest. When Mr. Shaw refrains from hitting me over the head with his umbrella, the real reason is . . . that he does not own my head." As for his supporting nationalization of coal mines, the circumstances concerning it were not typical but exceptional. Since coal is in concentrated deposits, it could not be owned individually. On the contrary, farm plots could readily be owned individually. As to Shaw's charge that some landlords were unjust to their tenants, the state might behave with equal inhumanity if it owned the land. The nub of their differences, Chesterton concluded, is that "The morality he represents is the morality of negations. Just as if he says you must not drink wine at all as the only solution to a few people drinking too much."

Hilaire Belloc wound up the meeting in the same "felicitously fierce" spirit in which it had been conducted. "I am surprised," he said, "that neither of the two speakers pointed out that one of three things is going to happen. . . . This industrial civilization . . . will break down, . . . leading to a restoration of sane, ordinary human affairs. . . . Or it will break down and lead to nothing but a desert. Or it will lead the mass of men to become contented slaves, with a few rich men controlling them. Take your choice. You will all be dead before any of the three things come off."[59]

The speaking by the intellectual rebels was much in the spirit of "relevant irrelevance" that marks the Oxford Union debates. It is paralleled by the "out-of-doors" speaking that occurs in Hyde Park and on Tower Hill.[60] The mode is conversational; the tone is impudently assertive; the aim is to fix attention on long-range problems and goals rather than on immediate practicalities. The circumstances are unrestrainedly permissive for expression of the most eccentric of views, ranging from fundamentalist, to ultraconservative, to radical attacks on parliament, on royalty, on capitalism, on religion. The mood of both speakers and listeners (who frequently reverse roles in animated challenge and response) is a curious mix of belligerent arrogance and relaxed good humor. Among all the things that Great Britain stands for in the world, this highly sophisticated give-and-take of remarkably free discussion must be included. Except for India and some of the dominions (particularly Australia) it is not elsewhere to be found. It is a significant part of what Great Britain contributes to the philosophy of government.

9
SPEAKING UP FOR WOMEN:
BRIDGING THE GENDER GAP

Throughout history it has generally been taken for granted that women had no right to participate in government—with the exception of ruling queens—until the new idea of genderless equality was initiated in the French Revolution. The chief protagonist for this new view was the Marquis de Condorcet. In his epochal book, *Esquisse d'un tableau historique des progrès de l'esprit humain,* he described the evolution of humanity through nine successive stages. In the last of these, women were urged to take their proper role in a just society. And in the tenth epoch, yet to come, he argued for equality of nations and of classes and forecast the growing perfectability of human nature. Inspired by Condorcet's ideas, Mary Wollstonecraft wrote her daring book, *A Vindication of the Rights of Women,* published in 1792. This idea was submerged, however, by the unpopularity of the French Revolution.

The effective development of a movement for women's rights was delayed for another generation. When the Chartist Movement drew up its "Charter of Rights and Liberties" in 1838, it included a demand for women's suffrage. This however was omitted from the final draft as being unduly damaging to the free-trade cause. The seed, nevertheless, had been planted. During the next decade some few leading politicians supported the idea in their speeches. More significantly, a few courageous women commenced to organize and to speak in public in behalf of women's rights.

Winston Churchill, in his survey of English history, observed that "in an age of proud and domineering men . . . the women of the nineteenth century [demanded] a new status, which revolutionized the social life of the country, and even made them want to vote."[1] This new movement developed in parallel forms in the United States[2] and in Great Britain under conditions of almost unimaginable severity, and the right to vote was finally won under the stressful conditions of World War I. In England its progress was delayed by the opposition of Prime Ministers Gladstone and Asquith. It was effectively fueled by the organized efforts and courageous public speaking of Lydia Becker, Dame Millicent Garrett Fawcett, and, most sensationally, by the aggressive leadership of Emmeline Pankhurst, her daughters Christabel and Sylvia, and their associate, Annie Kenney. The struggle was epochal, its leaders were eloquent, and the campaign was marred by bitterness.

174

"Theories and Projects of the Most Absurd Speculation"

From our current perspective, the difficulties encountered by the women defy ready comprehension. The assumption of feminine inferiority was not only virtually unchallenged. It was considered too obvious even to be discussed. John Milton's *Paradise Lost* presented the view that was wholly orthodox. In his account, woman, created from Adam's rib, was less than he made in the image of God. She was "inferiour, in the mind and inward Faculties." She was more a handicap than a helpmeet, for she was sufficiently seductive that after the Satanic Tempter had induced her to disobey God's will she was able to persuade her husband to join in this sin. Adam, after their ejection from the Garden of Eden, lamented that

> Thus it shall befall
> Him who to worth in woman overtrusting
> Lets her Will rule.

Eve completely agreed, averring submissively to him:

> My author and disposer, what thou bid'st
> Unargued I obey; so God ordains.
> God is thy law, thou mine; to know no more
> Is woman's happiest knowledge, and her praise.

The very subject of women's equality and women's rights was undiscussable. If some few women objected, they had no means for effective protest. The comment by Dr. Samuel Johnson, that no more could it be expected that a woman should preach—or speak in public—than that a dog could walk on its hind legs, represented the common view. Women had no need for voices of their own. It was taken for granted that their interests were "included" in those of their fathers and husbands as James Mill phrased it in an article in the 1824 edition of the *Encyclopedia Britannica*. Although women were clearly abjectly subjected to the control of men and were often ruthlessly exploited, they could not speak for themselves and few men felt induced to speak up for them.

The prevalent attitude is well illustrated in a speech given in the House of Commons by England's outstanding liberal, Charles James Fox, on 26 May 1797. Fox was speaking on one of the earliest efforts to broaden the male suffrage. After conceding that no such reform could be carried, Fox made it clear that he, like the other members, was strongly opposed to women's suffrage, since their uneducated votes would smother the reasoned and informed judgment of the men. Further clarifying his views, Fox said:

> In all the theories and projects of the most absurd speculation, it has never been suggested that it would be advisable to extend the elective franchise to the female sex; and yet, justly respecting, as we must do, the mental powers,

the acquirements, the discrimination, and the talents of the women of England, in the present improved state of society—knowing the opportunities they have for acquiring knowledge—that they have interests as dear and important as our own, it must be the genuine feeling of every gentleman who hears me, that all the superior classes of the female sex of England must be more capable of exercising the elective franchise with deliberation and propriety, than the uninformed individuals of the lowest class of men to whom the advocates of universal suffrage would extend it. And yet, why has it never been imagined that the right of election should be extended to women? Why! but because by the law of nations, and perhaps also by the law of nature, that sex is dependent upon ours; and because, therefore, their voices would be governed by the relation in which they stand in society. Therefore it is, Sir, that . . . it has never been in the contemplation of the most absurd theorists to extend the elective franchise to the other sex.[3]

"A Pity She Couldn't Have Been a Lad"

It was in 1832 during the agitation for the Reform Bill that the women's rights movement began to take form. That year, in Yorkshire, Mary Smith petitioned Parliament for the right of unmarried women to vote. Lord Grey considered including votes for women in his plan to extend the suffrage, but he dropped the idea as being too provocative. Instead his bill for the first time in English history explicitly denied women the vote. By this time the subject was emerging into infrequent and limited discussion. As has been noted, the People's Charter at first contained an appeal for women's right to vote before it was eliminated from the final draft. The Anti-Corn Law League did not favor votes for women but did establish women's auxiliaries in which women were encouraged to speak on behalf of free trade for grains. Richard Cobden ardently supported female suffrage, and Benjamin Disraeli gave it friendly mention.

During the next two decades the women's rights movement greatly expanded. Its strongest base was in Manchester, which was the center for English liberalism. It was Manchester that despite its dependence on Southern American cotton nurtured a warm spirit for the abolition of slavery. It was there that the abolitionist preacher, Henry Ward Beecher, came to ask for support for the American federal government. It was there that Lydia Becker founded her weekly Women's Suffrage Journal. And it was there that Emmeline Goulden, whose father was on the committee that welcomed Beecher, grew up to propagate the idea that women are people. How movements commence is difficult to trace, but at least one significant source was the Goulden household.

Emmeline Goulden, born in 1858, was just old enough to start school when one evening her parents came into her bedroom to say goodnight; and her father, thinking her asleep, said sadly to her mother "What a pity she couldn't have been a lad!"

This remained one of the memories that incited her to a lifelong crusade to win equal rights for women. Another was the insistence of her mother that she must help to make their home comfortable for her father and brothers. Why, she asked herself, should her life be devoted to service for men? This feeling was sparked into open rebelliousness when her parents seriously discussed school and career plans for her brothers, while merely counselling her to neatness, decorum, and skill in housewifery.

The whole family knew that she was the brightest of them all. It was she whom her father chose to read aloud selections from the newspaper while the family was having breakfast. Her brothers called her "the dictionary" because of her mastery of words. Even so, nothing disturbed the tacit assumption of her inferiority. After all, she was "just a girl."[4]

Being "just a girl" signified a much lower status than it had in the years prior to the Industrial Revolution. In rural areas in earlier times women were virtual partners of their husbands, not only in field work but also in the cottage industries. Shakespeare represents his heroines as free-minded and outspoken. In the seventeenth century Aphra Behn was a popular poet, playwright, and novelist. In the early eighteenth century Mary Wortley Montague was well-known and highly regarded for her reports and views on foreign and domestic political affairs. In the latter part of that century, Frances Burney's *Evelina* was popular and Mrs. Hannah More was esteemed along with other Bluestocking intellectuals. But "by the eighteen-fifties nearly all the personal rights of women had been whittled away."[5] Legally, economically, and morally their subjection was taken for granted. The double code not only granted sexual liberty to men while denying it to women but extended throughout most aspects of life.

In the following years, firm steps toward feminine assertion were taken. In 1851 in Sheffield a local Women's Political Association was formed. Other suffragette societies were organized in London, Manchester, Bristol, Edinburgh, and Birmingham. In 1867 Miss Lydia Becker founded a National Association for Women's Suffrage and under its guidance over four thousand separate claims for the right to vote were sent to Parliament by women ratepayers in Manchester. Meanwhile, a broad-based women's rights group organized in Kensington to campaign for John Stuart Mill's election to Parliament. Mill published a book, *The Subjection of Women*, which he had written seven years earlier. After his election, Mill presented in the Commons a petition drawn up by his supporters calling for voting rights for women. In its support he delivered a moving speech in which he said:

> I know there is an obscure feeling as if women had no right to care about anything, except how they may be the most useful and devoted servants of some man. . . . This false claim to confiscate the whole existence of one half the species for the supposed convenience of the other appears to me, independently of its injustice, particularly silly. . . . Is it good for a man to live in complete communion of thoughts and feelings with one who is studiously kept inferior to himself?[6]

Miss Becker organized a drive to encourage property-owning women to assert and exercise the right to vote under the terms of the 1832 Reform Bill. The courts decided against their claims. The public was not much interested. The youthful Winston Churchill stated the view held by the vast majority when he asserted that to claim political and legal equality for women "is contrary to natural law and the practice of civilized states." He went on in similar vein, saying "that no necessity has been shown—that only the most undesirable class of women are eager for the right—that those women who discharge their duty to the state—viz marrying and giving birth to children, are adequately represented by their husbands." He ended by warning that if such rights were granted "every kind of hysterical fad would gain strength."[7]

This attitude was so deeply embedded in the culture that it was held by most women as well as by most men. The generality of women had neither the desire, the expectation, nor the opportunity to speak for themselves. They were expected to keep themselves and their families religious—but on biblical authority they were strictly subject to the will of their husbands in every respect. They might exercise such influence as they could inside their own homes. But they were not expected to communicate their views in public either by writing or by speaking.

One woman who did speak out was Millicent Garrett, who was born in 1847 in Suffolk. At the age of twenty she married Professor Henry Fawcett, a remarkable man who although blind won election to Parliament and afterward became postmaster-general. Encouraged by him she began immediately after their marriage to take an active role in behalf of women's rights. Her first public speech was made in 1867 to a meeting advocating women's suffrage, which led to denunciation of her and a fellow speaker by a member in the House of Commons as "two ladies, wives of members of this House, who had disgraced themselves by speaking in public." For a full half-century Mrs. Fawcett spoke and worked tirelessly for the cause. She was also passionately patriotic, with the result that she desisted from her campaign during the Boer War and the First World War, to the dismay of the more militant groups. After the extension of the vote to women in 1918, she converted her National Union of Women Suffrage Societies into the National Union for Equal Citizenship and retired from public life. She recorded these long years of struggle in two books, *The Women's Victory and After* in 1919, and *What I Remember* in 1924. In reward for her wartime services she was named a Dame of the British empire. She died in 1929 at the age of eighty-two, honored by many and criticized by many more for her devotion to persuasion through moderation and appeal to reason rather than making passionate demands. Her speeches were not notable; but the fact that she did speak in public, frequently and regularly, was an important aid to the cause.

Other efforts, particularly those by Lydia Becker, had partial success. In 1869 the courts concluded that women ratepayers could vote in municipal elections. The 1870 Education Act made women eligible for membership on local boards of education, and some were elected. In that same year a bill presented in the Commons by Jacob Bright to permit women to vote in parliamentary elections passed to a second reading. Ten years later the Isle of Man did grant to propertied women the right to vote. A sustained effort was made to include votes for women in the broadly inclusive electoral reform bill of 1884, but Prime Minister Gladstone firmly rejected it. Instead he urged public-spirited women to join women's alliances through which they would support the election of Conservative male candidates.

"Not a Question of Whether Women Are Angels"

The rhetorical problems that women had to overcome in order to improve their lot were numerous, complex, and difficult to deal with. They were unorganized. They lacked money with which to organize, for even if they brought wealth to their marriage, their husbands controlled it. They were restricted from travel and from attendance at meetings by their husbands' disapproval, by social convention, and by household responsibilities. Their right even to communicate publicly was sharply limited. Under such circumstances they could not readily establish common goals—such as the "Declaration of Principles" that was adopted by the Womens Rights Convention in 1848 at Seneca, New York. Nor did English women have even the restricted opportunities to develop new ideas that were more available in the tradition-breaking American society.

They needed leaders with skill in speech to plead their cause. But they were not allowed to attend the universities. Even their grammar school education was shaped for household duties. And they were excluded from membership in community discussion and debating clubs. They were in fact custodians of the language since it was under their tutelage and example that children learned to speak, to listen, to converse, and to form their ideas of the nature and value of communication. But how they used their own language was curbed by a strong cultural aversion to a man being "hen-pecked."

A view into the social and psychological attitudes that supported the legal restraints on women's human rights is provided in a speech by Henry Labouchere, a leading member of the Liberal Party, in the 1884 debate on Gladstone's franchise bill in the House of Commons:

There are a great many things which I am ready to admit that women can do better than men, and there are other things which I think men can do better than women. Each have their separate functions and the question is whether the function of electoral power is a function which women can reasonably discharge. I do not think it is. As yet I understand that no country has really given women the vote; and were it not that . . . a very large majority of women would vote for the Conservatives, I should be surprised at their making this desperate leap in the dark. Some honorable members on this side of the House have told us that women are better than men. That is the language of poetry. . . . It is not a question of whether women are angels or not, but whether they will make good electors. . . . We learn that, by the operation of nature, more women are born into the world than men, that women live longer than men, and that a considerable number of men leave the kingdom as soldiers and sailors, while women remain at home. . . . And what would be the consequence? They would look to the interests of women; they would band themselves together. . . . Instead of being on an equality with them, we would put ourselves under petticoat government.[8]

Throughout the society the rights of women seldom came under discussion. For a matter to be discussed, various opinions about it have to be held and stated. But few men or even women questioned the status relationship that was taken for granted. Even the Fabian Society, co-founded by the very intelligent and determined Beatrice Webb, did not include the subject on its agenda. So complete a radical as Annie Besant lectured fiercely, frequently, and effectively on behalf of such a diversity of subjects as atheism, revolutionary socialism, her Theosophical Society, home rule for India, and reforms of the education and marriage laws, but not explicitly for equal rights for women.

Restrictions of long standing come to be taken for granted. The social culture carefully maintained the age-old subordination of girls. In much earlier times even the convent schools for girls were closed in 1546 by edict of King Henry VIII. When a bit later grammar schools were established, they were restricted to boys. Some few families kept tutors in their homes for their daughters. But even these girls were taught to regard themselves as "just silly women"—much as in later times women were taught that it was their husbands who "worked" and that their own day-long drudgery at home chores amounted to being "just a house-wife." Neither in history nor in literature—and surely not in church—could the women find precedents for the equality of status that some among them were beginning to seek.

Historians of the women's rights movement have found it difficult to state the enormity of the problems that had to be solved. "Women were fighting to throw off legal disabilities that hindered their full command over their own persons, limited their share in societal resources, including employment and protection from illness and poverty, and blocked their role in societal decision making," one of them wrote. "They were also fighting for the right to be treated as adult persons worthy of consideration and respect, rather than as children or idiots vulnerable to any abuse."[9] The women who led in the movement were far from being united because they gave priority to divergent goals. For some, economic issues were predominant. For others, the right to vote was paramount. Still others sought to end the double moral standard that made wives sexually subordinate to their husbands, that punished prostitutes but not their customers, and that condoned promiscuity for men while denying it to women.

During the closing years of the nineteenth century women won some of their battles, including the right to enter universities, to own property, and to become doctors and lawyers (but only as solicitors, not as barristers). They also won the right to vote in local elections. Such partial successes made their persuasive problems even more difficult. The more they gained, the sturdier became the opposition to their getting still more. Most women as well as most men feared that if the protected status of women was destroyed for the sake of equality, the basic structure of society would be disrupted with consequent disabilities for men, women, and children. Family life would be weakened. Women, confronting harder challenges outside the shelter of their homes, would suffer in physical and emotional health. The home would cease to be a foundation for discipline and stability. Too much would be lost in contrast to whatever might be gained.

Even the frontline suffragettes who were most ardent in the cause split into factions with different goals and vastly different methods. The "moral rationalists," led by Millicent Fawcett, who had faith that sweet reason would ultimately prevail had little in common with the "militants," led by Emmeline Pankhurst, who especially after 1903 concluded that argument must be fortified by violence. Since there were concurrent feminist movement in Europe and in America, some of the English suffragettes favored international coordination, while others were patriotically committed to nationalism. The outbreak of World War I brought this issue to its climax. Some of the feminists believed that the national crisis offered a particularly promising opportunity to attain equality. Others felt strongly that no crusade should disrupt the national unity needed to win the war. [10]

Such is the general outline of the movement. At the heart of the campaign were the three Pankhursts, mother and daughters. In their energetic personalities, in their choice of issues, in the arguments and appeals that they developed, in the resistance they encountered, and in their means of countering it, the role of public speaking is illuminated. By no means did they stand alone. But the role of the Pankhursts is not only illustrative but central in the long crusade.

"We Threw Away Notions of What Was 'Ladylike'"

"I suppose I had always been a suffragist," Emmeline Goulden Pankhurst wrote in her autobiography. "With my temperament and my surroundings I could scarcely have been otherwise." Her mother was active in the earliest stages of the movement and Emmeline was just fourteen when she accompanied her mother to her first suffragette meeting. Feminism was one of the many liberal causes fostered in Manchester. John Bright's brother Jacob was chief among the men who favored rights for women; and he was a friend of Emmeline's father. The girl grew up hearing much talk of the need for better treatment of women. But, as she gradually understood, it was talk that led no further than the occasional adoption of futile resolutions.

At the age of twenty Emmeline married Dr. Pankhurst, who was twice her age. Like her father, he was an advocate of liberal reforms. Up to a point he gave his young bride every encouragement and support in her feminist views. But he could not escape from his masculine-centric perspective. What Emmeline wrote about him shows the rhetorical problem the women had to deal with:

> He . . . was quite in sympathy with the militant campaign; but men are not as single-minded as women are; they are too much given to talking about their ideas, rather than working for them. Even as Socialists they seldom translate their faith into works, being still conservative at heart, especially where women are concerned. Most of us who were married found that "Votes for Women" were of less interest to our husbands than their own dinners. They simply could not understand why we made so much fuss about it.[11]

Even in her own home, despite her husband's sympathetic understanding and support in their relationship and in their circle of acquaintances "it was made quite clear that men considered themselves superior to women, and that women apparently acquiesced in that view."[12] It was a view that Emmeline Pankhurst utterly rejected and she took to the platform to renounce it.

From her mid-teens, the speeches she heard in the Manchester Suffrage Society "interested and excited me." Her parents listened to her pleas and let her go off to Paris for three years of schooling that she could not have had at home. On her return, she threw herself enthusiastically into the women's rights movement. It was through these activities that she met the man she married. Her home life was both happy and busy, as children came in quick succession. But even as her babies were in their cradles, she served as an officer and speaker in the feminist organizations. She also was enabled to leave home to travel around England to meet with and speak to groups in other cities.

"For several years," she wrote, describing the period leading up to 1882, the year in which married women were granted legal control over their own property, "we had been holding the most splendid meetings in cities all over the kingdom. The crowds, the enthusiasm, the generous response to appeals for support, all these seemed to justify us in our belief that women's suffrage was near."[13]

Instead, the victory they hoped for was snatched away and converted into an enforced retreat. Gladstone decisively rejected their plea for votes. He attempted to placate them by calling them "political partners" of the men and by organizing "Women's Liberal Associations," through which the women were to campaign for votes that were not for themselves but for male candidates of the Liberal Party. To Emmeline's disgust, "the avidity with which women swallowed this promise, and left off working for themselves, and threw themselves into the men's work, was amazing." It was also disheartening. For a time it appeared to mark the end of her leaderhsip or even her participation in the crusade.

Dr. Pankhurst's profession as a lawyer offered him a wider sphere in London and that is where they went. For the next eight years Emmeline busied herself with her growing children and with the social duties of a metropolitan barrister's wife. Following Gladstone's skillful diversion of the movement and in surroundings far removed from her lifelong friends, Emmeline joined in the general withdrawal of women from their crusading enthusiasm. After all, she was enjoying what women were supposed to want: a happy home presided over by a successful husband and the supervision of a growing family.

Then in 1893 with Dr. Pankhurst ready to retire, the family moved back to Manchester. Once again Emmeline was surrounded by her friends and she felt again the invigorating spirit of Manchester's liberalism. Quickly she sought and won election to the board of the Poor Law Guardians. In this position she vividly and daily encountered instances of laws that discriminated harshly against women—most particularly against mothers of illegitimate children. Her enthusiasm for activism revived. Once again she realized the urgency of the need to fight for reforms. As she analyzed the situation, she found "the Government all-powerful and consistently hostile; the rank and file of legislators impotent; the country apathetic; the women divided in their interests."[14]

What she did about it was to initiate a new campaign that took her often back to London. Both her goal and her methods were clearly defined. In order to win the vote she knew that public opinion must be aroused and that it must be brought to bear upon Parliament. Her renewed enthusiasm is evident in her description of what transpired. "We adopted Salvation Army methods and went into the highways and byways after converts. We threw away all our conventional notions of what was 'ladylike' and 'good form' and we applied to our methods the one test question, Will it help?" For their street corner meetings

> With a chair for a rostrum, one of us would ring a bell until people began to stop to see what was going to happen. What happened, of course, was a lively suffrage speech. . . . We covered London in this way; we never lacked an audience. . . . We were increasing our favourable public as well as waking it up. Besides these street corner meetings, we held many hall and drawing-room meetings, and we got a great deal of press publicity, which was something never accorded the older suffrage methods.[15]

Following Mrs. Pankhurst's leadership, the crusading women commenced to use more violent methods. One was to attend meetings addressed by government officials to heckle the speakers and to try to break up the meetings by marching down the aisles bearing signs, "Votes for Women." Another method was throwing rocks through the windows of the prime minister's residence at 10 Downing Street. Still another was holding mass demonstrations before and around Westminster Hall.

For Sunday 21 June 1908 the women planned a huge demonstration to be held in Hyde Park. The largest gathering ever held there was said to have numbered 72,000—and the women defiantly set a goal of assembling 250,000. The following day the London *Times*, no doubt with journalistic exaggeration, estimated the actual number to have been double or even triple that number.

Twenty platforms for speakers were erected at various points in the park and the speaking went on all day. Few could hear what the speakers said but the enthusiasm was contagious and the crowd remained until nightfall.

Emmeline Pankhurst was ecstatic. But the outcome was another rejection such as the one they had received from Gladstone in 1884. Prime Minister Herbert Asquith was indomitably opposed to their demands. When they presented a petition asking for the right to vote, his cool reply was that female suffrage *might* come about on some indeterminate future date. This time, however, instead of retreating into silence, the defeat spurred the feminists to even greater efforts.

Mrs. Pankhurst set about organizing another huge demonstration to be held in mid-October in Parliament Square. On the appointed day the square and the streets that radiated from it were completely filled. The police intervened to arrest Emmeline, her daughter Christabel, and their close associate, Flora Drummond—who was so effective that she was called "the General." Their request for a jury trial was refused and their case was heard immediately on 13 October by a magistrate. Christabel, who had earned an L1. B. degree but (as a woman) was not allowed to plead courtroom cases in general practice combined the roles of defendant and advocate by conducting the case for the three of them. Her cross-examination of government witnesses was skillful; and in her summation of the defense, "with passion and fervour," she concluded:

> Remember that we are demanding of Liberal statesmen that which is for us the greatest boon and the most essential right—and if the present Government cannot reconcile order with our demand for the vote without delay, it will mark the breakdown of their statesmanship. Yes, their statesmanship has broken down already. They are a disgrace. It is only in this court that they have the smallest hope of being supported.[16]

Emmeline Pankhurst then rose to speak on their behalf, "assuming an appearance of calmness," to endorse what her daughter had said and to review Mrs. Drummond's "worthy career as a wife, a mother, and a self-sustaining business woman." Then she went on to speak of her own long struggle for equal justice.

> I have seen that men are encouraged by law to take advantage of the helplessness of women. Many women have thought as I have, and for many, many years have tried, by that influence of which we have been so many times reminded, to alter these laws, but we find that influence counts for nothing. . . .
> We women have presented larger petitions in support of our enfranchisement than were ever presented for any other reform; we have succeeded in holding greater public meetings than men have ever held for any reform. . . . We have faced hostile mobs at street corners. . . . Because we have done this we have been misrepresented, we have been ridiculed, we have had contempt poured upon us. . . .

This is all I have to say to you, sir. We are here not because we are law-breakers; we are here in our efforts to become law-makers. [17]

"Persons Outside the Constituency"

Christabel Pankhurst described how the movement developed.

In those days Annie Kenney joined us. The Oldham Trades Counsel asked me to address a meeting, and as my subject was the vote, women were to be present. A small gathering it was—but Annie Kenney was there! . . . When I had spoken, three eager, vividly intelligent girls, with shining eyes, came up to me. They were Annie Kenney and her sisters. . . . Mother met her and she became one of our family. Evening after evening, after her day's work, and on Saturday afternoons, she would take train to Manchester, make for our house, and join in whatever work was doing for the cause. . . . She gained platform experience and the W. S. P. U. had one speaker more. [18]

Another adherent was the wealthy and aristocratic Mrs. Emmeline Pethwick-Lawrence, whose home was in South Africa. She came to London to meet Emmeline Pankhurst and to find what she could do to help. She accepted the demanding position of treasurer of the society with the responsibility for raising funds. In many ways, "with wisdom in counsel, eloquence on the platform, courage in the fight, and true friendship," as Mrs. Pankhurst described her, she helped to strengthen the campaign.

Problems multiplied following the adoption of militant tactics. Political speakers feared them and tried to avoid them. When in 1908 Lloyd George was invited to speak in Liverpool, he accepted only on condition that women would be barred from the hall. The women responded to this exclusion by projecting their "Votes for Women" slogan by megaphone from an adjoining building. Meanwhile, while Lloyd George was speaking inside the hall, "Crowds assembling in the street were addressed by our speakers and cheers were raised for the women imprisoned for the cause." [19]

Reasons why some women were imprisoned are indicated in Christabel's account of what happened in Birmingham in the following year when Prime Minister Asquith came to address a large audience.

Two suffragettes had climbed on the roof adjacent to Bingley Hall and were seen crouching behind a chimney stack about thirty feet from the ground. . . . The position was serious, seeing that Mr. Asquith was due to leave the hall to address an overflow meeting. . . . Just as the police reached the roof Mr. Asquith drove past the women's fort and a brick, hurled from the roof, passed over the premier's car. There were muffled cries as the police officers seized the two women on the very edge of the coping overlooking the street thirty feet below. . . .

Under strong police guard the Prime Minister got away from the hall. . . .
Women were at the train to question him, but with police aid he escaped the
hearing and the answering of their questions, and the train glided away . . .
leaving behind the women who, as their final word, broke a window in the
train's last retreating coach. [20]

A more relaxed phase in the movement commenced in 1910. Under the
influence of sympathy for Queen Alexandra after the death of her husband, King
Edward VII, the suffragettes set up a Conciliation Committee for Woman
Suffrage and agreed to postpone violence. Emmeline Pankhurst organized a
peaceable march by scores of thousands of women to Albert Hall, where she,
Annie Kenney, and Christabel Pankhurst addressed the gathering. The meeting
was climaxed with a speech by Mrs. Pankhurst that so impressed Henry Nevin-
son, a newspaper writer who had come to report the event, that he promptly
wrote a book, *Votes for Women*. What he said in it regarding that meeting was
quoted by Christabel Pankhurst in her *Unshackled*.

No word can express the sense of determination, of confident triumph and
unity in noble purpose that breathed from that vast assembly. I do not know
which was the more impressive—the shout of devotion which greeted each
leader as she came forward or the dead silence of the ten thousand listening to
every word. . . . Yet there was one moment that abides in my mind as
supreme. It was the moment when a slight and elegant figure in black,
endowed with all the influence of a noble career and an unflinching personality, rose from her chair, and after the wild storm of applause had subsided,
uttered in that calm but penetrating voice the simple sentence: "We have only
one word in our thoughts today, and that word is Victory."[21]

Following that meeting, a suffrage bill was introduced in the House of
Commons, but Prime Minister Asquith refused to allow it to come to a vote.
When Lloyd George, who was in the cabinet, was asked to explain why, his
retort was that to vote on such a bill would be "madness." Explaining why he
said, "We cannot allow our British Parliament to be dictated to by persons
outside the constituencies."[22] How the women were to get into the constituencies he did not say. Still the women maintained their truce, expecting favorable
action soon. There was reason to hope. Australia had adopted women's suffrage
and its Parliament had sent an official report to the British government asserting
that it "has had the most beneficial results." Instead of action, however, the
suffragettes received only more rejections. The next year in 1911 and again in
1912, the government refused to bring the measure to a vote, pleading the
pressure of more urgent business.

During this interval Emmeline Pankhurst went on an extended lecture tour of
the United States where both her courageous struggle and her current cessation
of violence were applauded. Upon her return home, with the Parliament still
refusing to vote on women's suffrage, she issued a call for another giant protest
meeting to be held in Parliament Square on 4 March 1912. When the meeting

was held and Prime Minister Asquith refused to receive a delegation of women, two days of rioting broke out.

As the *Daily Telegraph* described the scene: "The attack was begun practically simultaneously. It was one of the busiest periods of the day. Suddenly women, who a moment before had appeared to be on peaceful shopping expeditions, produced from bags or muffs, hammers, stones, and sticks and began an attack on the nearest windows."

When Mrs. Pankhurst was brought by the police before a magistrate, she told him "if you send me to prison, as soon as I come out I shall go further and show that women must have some voice in the laws which they must obey." On a charge of conspiracy all the leaders of the movement were arrested. A well-publicized conspiracy trial lasted for three weeks. The basis for the defense was stated by Mr. Pethwick-Lawrence: "The breaking of windows is repugnant to me, but the women who have taken this course have been driven by the logic of facts to do what they did." Another lawyer, Tim Healy, summed up the defense by saying: "I wish that all my learned friend's colleagues could examine their conscience . . . and say that their political actions have been as unselfish and self-sacrificing."[23]

The verdict was "guilty." The sentence was nine months of imprisonment. Even so, as it turned out, the result was at least partially a defeat for the government. The women went on a hunger strike and after a few days were released. How this struggle should be assessed depends on one's point of view. George Lansbury, a prominent member of the Labour Party, shook his fist in Prime Minister Asquith's face in the House of Commons, telling him that he would "go down in history as the man who tortured innocent women." From another perspective, "the actions of the Pankhurst group probably reinforced the prejudices of a male society."[24] The suffragettes had no doubt that their "extremism" had forced the issue into the public's attention. The immediate effect, at least, was to cause a negative reaction.

Two bills enacted in 1912 threw down the gauntlet to the feminists and induced them to resume rioting and other acts of violence. One was a franchise reform bill that explicitly broadened the vote to all adult "male persons." The other was a grant of home rule to Ireland, also restricting the voting right to men. On behalf of the government, Lord Haldane and Sir Edward Grey issued a statement warning the women that a "return to militancy" would end any possibility of including women in the franchise. As a signal that violence would not be tolerated, two English suffragettes who attacked Prime Minister Asquith when he visited Dublin were sentenced to five years of penal servitude. Again a hunger strike resulted in their release.

"We Who Are Militant Are Free!"

The resumption of violence led to a decisive split in the movement. Dame Fawcett, whose campaign had always been independent, firmly renounced the militants. The greatest blow to the Pankhursts was the resignation from their group of Mrs. Pethwick-Lawrence, who had been their effective fundraiser. To counter these losses, Emmeline Pankhurst and Annie Kenney called a mass meeting in Albert Hall to declare that the campaign of militancy would go on. Mrs. Pankhurst's speech was a virtual declaration of war against the government:

> I incite this meeting to rebellion! And my last word is for the Government. . . . Take me, if you will. But I tell you this: that so long as those who incite to armed rebellion and the destruction of human life are at liberty [meaning the Sinn Fieners in Ireland], you shall not keep me in prison. Women in this meeting, although the vote is not yet won, we who are militant are free. Remember only the freedom of the spirit and join this magnificent rebellion of the women of the twentieth century.[25]

Christabel's account of the meeting was admiring and proud, with a touch of pathos: "I can picture Mother on the Albert Hall platform that night, slender and fragile, rather tired, yet erect, head lifted, her eyes, large under their high-arched brows, looking upon the vast audience and through and beyond that place and hour—to what was coming upon her." It was why she entitled her account of the movement *Unshackled*.

The next two years were a bitter time. Emmeline Pankhurst, her daughter Sylvia, Mrs. Drummond, Annie Kenney, and many others were arrested and imprisoned repeatedly, each time to be released to prevent their death as martyrs when they refused to eat or to drink or even to sleep. Each time after their release they returned again to the platform to urge that militant violence be continued. Mrs. Pankhurst had become so weakened that she had to be carried to and from the platform in a wheel chair, but she refused to be silent. Christabel went to the safety of Paris from which she guided, directed, and supplied the organization. When war broke out in August 1914, Mrs. Pankhurst called upon her followers to end their campaign and instead to support the war effort. The government, she assured them, would not dare to withhold much longer the franchise for women. And so it proved to be.

With Lloyd George as prime minister, in 1916 the right to vote was extended to women over the age of thirty and such women were declared also to be eligible for election to public office. Mrs. Pankhurst died on 14 June 1928. In the very hour in which her body was lowered into its grave, the House of Lords voted its assent to the bill that finally extended to all British women all the voting rights held by men.

The biography written by her daughter Sylvia closes with the scene at the Brompton Cemetery in Westminister. During the burial service: "Friends, parted for years, there re-encountered, in the spell of the old comradeship, and the old glories. Again upon the waves of memory we saw the slender shape, gracefully proportioned, tense with energy, the pale, clear face, with those appealing eyes, and heard again the stirring, passionate, mournful music of her voice."[26]

What Emmeline Pankhurst stood for and the means by which she accomplished her goal are illuminated by a quotation from a single paragraph of the speech she gave in that Albert Hall meeting in 1912:

> It always seems to me that the anti-Suffrage Members of the Government who criticize militancy in women are like beasts of prey reproaching the gentler animals who turn in desperate resistance at the point of death. . . . The Suffragettes have been reckless of their own lives alone. It has never been, and never will be, the policy of the Women's Social and Political Union to endanger life. We leave that to the enemy. We leave that to men in their warfare. It is not the method of women! . . . We disregard your laws, gentlemen; we set the liberty, the dignity and the welfare of women above all such considerations. We shall continue this war, and what sacrifice of property or injury to property accrues will be the fault of the Government. . . . Be militant each in your own way. . . . Those of you who can break windows, break them. Those of you who can still further attack the secret idol of property . . . do so. I incite this meeting to rebellion![27]

Her statue, erected in 1930 in Victoria Towers Garden on the west side of the Houses of Parliament, was unveiled by Prime Minister Stanley Baldwin, who spoke appropriate words of eulogy. In her seventy years she had come a long way. In her own words, she had a "wonderful life."

"But What Good Came of It at Last?"

The poem by Robert Southey on the battle of Blenheim repeats as its refrain the plaintive question of little Peterkin: "But what good came of it at last?" It is a fair test to apply to any prolonged struggle.

What the feminist movement achieved is difficult to measure objectively. A fair judgment might be that it established the principle that women are people— not better, not worse, not exceptional: just people, like men.

There is ample evidence that this principle has yet to be brought into full effect. It is clear that women still do not have equality of opportunities, of recognition, and of rewards. Even so, the transformation to at least theoretical and legal egalitarianism is impressive. In the words of Winston Churchill, the nineteenth century had been "an age of proud and domineering men," until the feminists [he particularly named Florence Nightingale] won "a new status, which revolutionized the social life of the country."[28] Women have attained new rights to "speak their piece." They have entered into a new era even if as yet they stand only at its threshold.

Some sixty years after Lady Nancy Astor became the first woman to take her seat in Parliament, a woman, Margaret Thatcher on 4 May 1979 became Great Britain's prime minister. This was not owing to her public speaking. Eloquence is not her forté. Her speaking manner is sharp, sometimes even shrill, sounding somewhat like a school teacher scolding her class. Mrs. Thatcher herself believes, as she told the 1985 Conservative Party Conference at Bournemouth, that her greatest failure was to have been unable to communicate an appealing image to the public.

For whatever the reasons, women constitute 52 percent of the electorate in Great Britain but have only 25 of the 650 parliamentary seats.[29] Perhaps the nineteenth century view that the interests of women are "included" in those of their fathers and husbands is still held largely even by the women themselves. At least now they have the freedom to choose.

They also have the freedom to speak their minds. The public platform is available to them, as are the radio and television facilties for reaching large audiences. Remembering the many long centuries of the subjection of women and of their enforced silence, this is an enormous accomplishment. Its fruits are just beginning to appear: in attainment by women of at least some of the highest spots in government, business, religion, and the professions, along with a new sense of their own integrity and dignity; and in the concurrent losses of special privilege as sheltered dependents. Society is still trying to find a new balance, as family stability is undermined, adolescent delinquencies increase, and marital constancy has been weakened.

One major contribution the feminists and suffragettes made is their exemplification of the force of an organized rhetorical mass movement. They were not the inventors of the strategies for such movements, but they were in the pioneering forefront, along with such others as abolitionists, the labor movement, prohibitionism, pacifism, and such national rhetorical revolutions as Gandhi's campaign in India. Their movement in Great Britain illustrates the requirements for rhetorical mass movements: (1) the recognition of a problem or a wrong that afflicts great numbers sufficiently keenly to foment an upsurge of emotional resentment; (2) the advent of a charismatic leader (or leaders) to serve as incitive speakers, unifying spokespeople, and exemplars of courageous devotion; (3) a set of principles that can be simplified in speeches, slogans, and songs; and (4) a defined goal toward which to aim and by which to measure the progress of the movement. Finally, it may be said of the women's crusade in Great Britain as of other mass movements that as much is achieved, much more yet remains to be advocated and to be done. The "Victory!" Emmeline Pankhurst prophecied has been only partially attained. The goal of complete equality lies yet on ahead.

10
BRITAIN'S SOLEMN HOUR:
THE ROLE OF CHURCHILL'S ORATORY

In the old fashioned sense of the word, Winston Churchill during World War II was an orator, not, in the new fashion, a discussant.

His speeches were not spontaneous but they were carefully prepared, not conversational but formal even ornate in style. He did not identify himself with his listeners but deliberately spoke *to* not *with* them. His mode was that of a father figure. Too independent to be a party regular, he was also too solitary, too moody, too self-centered to engage in carefree comradeship with his political associates. He was like a majestic eagle soaring above its environment, demanding and receiving admiration and respect, yet to be viewed warily because of his ability to pounce. And like an eagle, he pounced with power and with style.

"An Outpouring of Words"

Churchill's whole life was engaged in an outpouring of words, written and spoken. He had too much respect for eloquence to phrase words carelessly. What he said was carefully worked out, the product of a search for the right ideas, the right words, the right rhythm. "It was largely to this gift of inspired and accurate prevision," a family member wrote of him, "that he owed his mastery of debate. For in spite of his command of words, unequalled in its power, originality and range, he never was a ready speaker. The artist in him forbade slipshod spontaneity. He was too verbally fastidious to leave his words to chance. To him a speech must be, in substance and in form, a work of art."[1]

This was the character of Churchill—solitary and remote, commanding rather than representing—as it was seen also by his personal physician, who probably knew him better than anyone except his wife Clementine. The tremendous effectiveness of his wartime speaking puzzled Lord Moran. Throughout the whole of his long life Churchill had been "living apart from people." Yet in these speeches, "for perhaps the first time in his life he seems to see things through the eyes of the average man." To the mass of the people he seemed to be like their own best selves, "saying what they would like to say for themselves if they knew how." Yet how could this be? "Does he know what is in people's minds? Though he may have learnt by long experience the feel of an audience, he knows nothing of their lives, their hopes and aspirations. When he speaks it is to express his ideas; he says a piece. In England, outside the House of Commons, all audiences are much the same to him; they differ only in size."[2]

As was true of his early career, discussed in chapter 8, Churchill persistently refused to play the political game of compromise and accommodation. He was a "loner," an aristocrat with a moody and stubborn temperament, knowing his own mind and valuing his self-guided integrity. His chosen activities were solitary: reading and writing, bricklaying, landscaping, and painting. He loved to dramatize himself by emphasizing habits that set him apart from the ordinary run of people, such as the constant smoking of huge cigars and the drinking of copious quantities of brandy (enough, he said, to float the Queen Mary). He delighted in such eccentricities as dictating speeches and memoranda while sitting late at night in his bath and parading before President Roosevelt draped only in a towel. His conversation typically consisted of monologues. When matters were going well, "his arrogance, intolerance, and cocksureness assume alarming proportions."[3] His wife recorded how she communicated with him: "I don't argue with Winston, he shouts me down. So whenever I have anything important to say I write a note to him."[4] Lord Moran compares him to Queen Victoria in his aloofness and dislike of social renovations. "What then is the ultimate secret of Winston Churchill's mastery over men? . . . It may seem incredible in years to come that anyone so aloof, so out of sympathy with the spirit of the times, could have won the hearts of a democracy."[5]

A review of Winston Churchill's persuasive and inspirational speaking demands a reconsideration of the standards ordinarily applied in determining the effectiveness of a public speaker. He was not, in Lord Bacon's term, a "ready" man, at least in his public speaking, for he studiously prepared his speeches in advance. He did not "identify" with his listeners, as Kenneth Burke insists must be done, either in the content or in the manner of his speaking. Neither his voice nor his physical appearance and bearing were impressive. He possessed in high degree the ethos that Aristotle believed to be the chief persuasive resource, but it derived from his standing aside from his listeners rather than sharing their attributes. While it is commonly understood that speeches are "timely" (in contrast to the "timelessness" of literature) Churchill typically discussed immediate issues in terms of their long-term historical significance. His rhetorical qualities were in sharp contrast with those of the only other orator-statesman of the time whose greatness in leadership matched his own, President Franklin D. Roosevelt, the master of "fireside chatting," with a "You and I know" air of familiarity.[6] Churchill resembled Lord Chatham and Edmund Burke in the grandeur of his pronouncements of his own superior vision of veritable truth, but he was also very unlike either of them. He was far too sophisticated a craftsman to indulge in Chatham's cascades of sometimes ungrammatical emotionalism.

And his was simpler, clearer, and more direct than the philosophical and qualification-bound reasoning of Burke.

His "go-it-alone" spirit of independence, so evident to his associates, was limited and disciplined by some of his most basic traits. For one example, he was insatiably eager to learn. His particular interest was history, especially English history, which he both read and wrote copiously. He was always grasping for facts and determined to understand and to spell out their meanings. He maintained a small circle of friends, chosen because they were intelligent, knowledgeable, and well able to argue persuasively for his acceptance of their views. Prominent among them in the period during which his mature views were taking form were Professor Frederick Lindemann of Oxford; a military intelligence expert and close neighbor, Desmond Morton; a foreign affairs expert of "profound comprehension," Ralph Wigram, who died young in 1936; and Ian Colvin, a Berlin-based reporter. With all of them he had "many talks into the small hours of the morning," and they helped him to "form and fortify" his views of the significance of Hitlerism.[7] His reading, the kind of interpretative thinking required for his writing, and his searching discussions with well-informed friends helped him to attain an historical perspective that was both capacious and clear.

Another trait that disciplined his self-centeredness was his depth of patriotism, a genuine love and admiration for English traditions and purposes that he felt were very personally exemplified in his own ancestry and his own career. He could speak for both himself and the nation with such complete harmony of feeling that he came to be viewed as "John Bull himself." Beyond this, his interest and his ability in painting developed habits of objective observation and of paying close attention to meaningful details. In consequence of all these various traits, his views concerning the international developments in the twenties and the thirties were generally though by no means always insightful and correct.

His significance was partly as a symbol—an indomitable figure who personified the English refusal to knuckle-under or to give up, no matter what resistance cost or how long the odds were against them. But this suggests a passivity of role that was far from the fact. On the contrary, Churchill was a dynamo of energy, a volcanic center of inspiration and of confident command. His emergence into successful leadership occurred late in his life, not until he was sixty-six. And finally, near the end of his life, he sadly confessed that, "I have achieved a great deal to achieve nothing in the end." Much that he valued had been lost—the Victorian manners, the superiority of the aristocracy, the stability of a settled social order, the integrity of the British Empire. His ideal was "the structured world of his Victorian youth headed by a powerful monarch, environed by a gleaming empire. Not all his successes as a war leader could salvage that world; indeed, his very successes speeded its transformation."[8] Despite his disappointments, his success was other than and greater than he knew.

"The Enormously Difficult Rhetorical Problem"

During the 1920s Churchill served as chancellor of the exchequer in Stanley Baldwin's cabinet, when his attention had to be devoted to the rebuilding of England's war-shattered economy. When Ramsay MacDonald's Labour government came into office in 1931, Churchill set off on a lecture tour of America and afterward settled down to write his lengthy *Life of Marlborough*, his history of World War I, the first draft of his *History of the English-Speaking Peoples*, and other books almost as ambitious. In his spare time, for recreation, he built rockeries and waterworks, brick walls, and two cottages on his estate. During this time he "never had a dull or idle moment . . . at peace within my habitation." In 1935 when Stanley Baldwin became Prime Minister, Churchill briefly expected to be brought into the cabinet, but when this prospect faded he consoled himself happily in his own solitary mode. "I set out with my paintbox for more genial climes without waiting for the meeting of Parliament."[9]

Neither his conduct nor his judgment was winning trust in his wisdom and dependability. During World War I his ill-judged, mismanaged, and tragically costly foray against Gallipoli branded him as weak in military strategy. As international tensions increased he proved to be less than prophetic. Like most of his fellow Englishmen he disdained Mahatma Gandhi as a "fakir." Along with many others, his first reaction to Hitler's advent in Germany was cautious approval for his energizing of the spirit of nationalism. For Mussolini he showed a much more durable admiration.[10] When Italy invaded Ethiopia, Churchill favored strong sanctions to resist the aggression, even to the possible use of British naval force. But he thought the League of Nations went too far in voting for economic sanctions when it had no authority to enforce them. Nevertheless, despite flaws in his interpretation of events, he was far more clearsighted than most.

The enormously difficult rhetorical problem with which Churchill had to deal was, first of all, to clarify and correct his own interpretation of global circumstances in the 1930s; and then to find means of countering the fundamentally false assumptions that distorted public sentiment and misdirected governmental policies. He well understood that the major powers were split into two groupings that were sharp contrasts. Russia, Japan, Italy, and Germany were totalitarian and militaristic; the United States, Great Britain, and France were weakened by internal disunity and by sentiments of isolationism and pacifism. In England in 1932 the Oxford Union resolved "That this House will in no circumstances fight for its King and Country," and according to public opinion polls, this sentiment was widespread among the nation's youth. Despite the belligerence of the Axis Powers, the English public felt safe behind its "great ditch." The antidemocratic dictatorships in Germany and Italy were perceived as at least having the beneficial effect of standing as barriers against Soviet communism. Besides, whatever the problems might be, modern warfare was too terrible to be contemplated. There was substantial agreement with what Stanley Baldwin said in a speech he made in 1926: "Who in Europe does not know that one more war in the West, and the civilization of the ages will fall with as great a shock as that of Rome?"[11] Among those who agreed was Churchill, as he wrote his 1929 book *The Aftermath* on the theme that war had become intolerable. But what could and should be done to avert it?

Revisionist historians were insisting that World War I had been precipitated by an arms race and by cynical balance-of-power diplomacy, rather than by German aggressiveness. These were mistakes, therefore, that must not be repeated. Churchill held the different view that preparedness was the surest bulwark of peace, and he was far more aware than most of the weakness of the British military. When in March 1933 Ramsay MacDonald proposed a military budget with only nominal increases, the Conservatives supported it. But Churchill split from his colleagues to denounce the budget as being wholly inadequate. Somberly he told the House that: "We are, it is admitted, the fifth Air Power only—if that. We are but half the strength of France, our nearest neighbor. Germany is arming fast and no one is going to stop her. That seems clear. . . . She is going to arm; she is doing it; she has been doing it."[12]

Few in any party felt as Churchill did. In the ensuing debate, Clement Attlee speaking for the Labour Party said that, "We deny the need for increased air armaments." Sir Herbert Samuel on behalf of the Liberals asserted that "Nothing we have seen or heard would suggest that our present air force is not adequate to meet any peril at the present time." Even the German affairs expert, J. Wheeler-Bennett (who was soon thereafter to support Churchill's views), told a London audience in April following the debate in the Commons that "Hitler, I am convinced, does not want war. He is susceptible to reason in matters of foreign policy. He is greatly anxious to make Germany once more self-respecting and is himself anxious to be respectable. He may be described as the most moderate member of his party."[13] Such was the audience to which Churchill had to address his arguments and appeals.

Although Churchill was more clearminded on foreign policies than were most of his associates, he too had difficulty in determining what needed to be done. In 1935, when Italy invaded Ethiopia and Germany reoccupied the Rhineland, Churchill agreed with the Baldwin Conservatives and the Labour opposition that these moves ought not to be opposed with force. It was not until the Nazi seizure of Austria and subsequent threats were made against Czechoslovakia that Churchill made up his mind that Hitler must be stopped. When Neville Chamberlain returned from Munich in 1938 with his assurances to cheering London crowds that his agreement to allow Hitler to occupy Czechoslovakia ensured "peace in our time," Churchill broke with his party to tell the Commons that "We have sustained an unmitigated defeat." Members expressed their disagreement so loudly and so rudely that for a time he was unable to continue.[14]

The English pledge of "all possible assistance" to Poland, made in 1939 in the event that it should be invaded, brought Churchill once again back into the Conservative ranks, animated by hope of appointment to the cabinet so that he might foster rearmament. The general view of both the ministry and the public, however, remained firm that war was improbable. For one thing, the Maginot Line was believed to be impregnable. For another, as Chamberlain assured the American ambassador to Great Britain, "Hitler is highly intelligent and therefore would not be prepared to wage world war."[15] Churchill was indeed appointed to the cabinet, and in such a position could make no more speeches demanding policy changes.

What he could and did do was to talk privately with various leaders to seek their support for rearmament. One of them, Sir Edward Spears, has described vividly how he went about it:

> Churchill, who can jump from one subject to another with the agility of a grasshopper, has nevertheless the same power of concentration that was so characteristic of Napoleon. He can pull out one drawer of his mind and then another with great rapidity, yet nothing can deflect him from the subject in the drawer he is dealing with at any particular moment. Every question appertaining to it is carefully sorted out and catalogued, nothing is forgotten or mislaid and everything flashes back to his memory in orderly array when required.
>   . . . What I do remember is Churchill's pursed mouth, his look centered on the fruit on the table as if he were crystal-gazing. His face had ceased smiling, and the shake of his head was ominous.[16]

When Germany invaded Poland on Sunday morning 1 September 1939 and the British government vacillated, Churchill was in a quandary. He could not denounce the ministry without resigning from his cabinet position which gave him some opportunity for strengthening the military. When the Commons met on the next day to hear speeches by Leo Amery, Arthur Greenwood, and Lloyd George, all demanding an immediate declaration of war, Churchill sat silent. Even so, he was the center of attention. As Spears comments:

> I had never seen the Commons so stirred, so profoundly moved, as it was that afternoon. It was dawning upon even the most uncritical of the Government's supporters that Great Britain's honour, of which we were the collective guardians, was in danger. And I noted something else. Churchill was obviously advancing from the wings on to the stage of the political scene. His name was on many lips. The more the Cabinet vacillated the more numerous were the eyes turned toward him.

Spears went on to say that "Everyone was aware that he saw clearly the path to follow while others were still groping," but he also added that "Churchill was not trusted by the public, which was convinced that he was erratic and dangerous."[17]

When war was declared Churchill was named first lord of the Admiralty; and he became the chief spokesman for the Chamberlain government in the House debates. There was little about which to disagree during the ensuing months of "phony peace," until the next spring Germany suddenly invaded Denmark, Norway, and Finland. Again the government came under heavy attack for not dispatching the navy to Norway's defense. Churchill rose to defend Chamberlain against a clamor for his resignation. Duff Cooper, a friend of Churchill's who was leading the attack of the opposition, warned the House that when Churchill spoke, "He will be defending with his eloquence those who have so long refused to listen to his counsel, who treated his warnings with contempt, and who refused to take him into their confidence." The debate lasted for two days, 7 and 8 May, during which Leo Amery, another of Churchill's friends made the necessary case: "We must get into the Government men who can match our enemies in fighting spirit, in daring, in resolution, and in thirst for victory."[18]

Churchill responded with a powerful speech on behalf of Chamberlain that required him both to denounce his own friends and to renounce his own deeply held beliefs. Again the audience he faced repeatedly interrupted him noisily. In his later recounting of the circumstances, Churchill wrote: "When they broke in upon me, I retorted upon them and defied them, and several times the clamour was such that I could not make myself heard."[19] The circumstance was less a discussion or debate than a swirl of outpouring emotions. As Spears interpreted the scene: "By the time Winston rose to wind up the debate the House was as uninviting as a choppy sea on which floated the debris of missed opportunities, the splinters of lost reputations. Gusts of feeling were lashing waves of irritation or anger in every quarter. . . . Churchill was completely master of himself and of his subject, but presently he warmed up and there were interruptions from the Socialist benches. . . . He swung around and glared ferociously at those who were most anxious to see him assume the leadership."[20]

The ambiguity of Churchill's position as the chief defender of the government of which he did not approve ended on 10 May 1940 when the Nazi *blitzkrieg* swept around the end of the Maginot Line and into Belgium. Chamberlain realized that the end had come for him. He first offered the premiership to Lord Halifax, who refused it. Then he tendered it to Churchill. At six o'clock that evening, King George VI called Churchill in and asked him to form a new government.

"The prospect neither excited nor alarmed me," Churchill recorded. "I thought it would be by far the best plan." Promptly he began the discussions that knit together a coalition cabinet. It was three o'clock the next morning before he got to bed, "conscious of a deep sense of relief. I felt as if I were walking with destiny, and that all my past life had been but a preparation for this hour and for this trial."[21] Relieved of the anomaly of having to support policies of which he did not approve, he now for the first time in his life had the power to govern in his own hands. He could speak his own sentiments in his own way. What he told the House was: "I have nothing to offer but blood, toil, tears and sweat." Stylistically, it was a descending order of climax. But it set the tone for what was to come.

"The Domain of Persuasive Leadership"

No other prime minister in the history of Great Britain came into office in such dismal circumstances. The defeat of the allied armies in the Lowlands was followed by evacuation of 338,000 soldiers from Dunkirk. Many thousands more were left behind and the armaments they abandoned were almost all the country had. When Parliament assembled on 4 June Churchill realized that "it was imperative to explain not only to our own people but to the world" that England would fight on. The significance of the occasion was highlighted by Lord Moran:

> The fact is that Winston's story before the war is the chronicle of a self-centered man making his plans in order to win personal renown. . . . No party wanted him. If he had died before the war he would have been accounted a brilliant failure. . . .
> Norman Brooks speaks with care, and this is what he said to me, "If it had not been for Winston, anything might have happened after Dunkirk."
> He was indeed made for the hour. In the extraordinary circumstances of 1940, with the hopeless inequality of Germany and Britain—or so it seemed—we needed an unreasonable man at the top. . . . A sage would have been out of his element in 1940; we got instead another Joan of Arc.[22]

Churchill well knew that the prospects were bleak: "The British Government were prepared to wage war from the New World, if through some disaster England herself were laid waste."[23] He well knew that a speech was required that would convert the fear of defeat into an expectation of victory. The grievous and urgent need to speed production of armaments demanded his full attention; so did talks with the French leaders to try to keep France in the war. Even so, he realized that what was needed even more was the preservation and enhancement of the nation's and the free world's morale. Consequently, "June 4 was much occupied for me by the need to prepare and deliver the long and serious speech."[24]

The speech began with a disclaimer: "Wars are not won by evacuations." He paused and his voice dropped in pitch to the undertone of throaty resonance that suggested his bulldog determination: "But there is a victory inside this deliverance. . . . It was gained by the Air Force." He described the effort made by the numerically greatly superior German air power. "They tried hard, and they were beaten back; they were frustrated in their task. We got the Army away." He turned toward the future: "We are told that Herr Hitler has a plan for invading the British Isles." Then came his exalted conclusion:

Even though large tracts of Europe and many old and famous States have fallen or may fall into the grip of the Gestapo and all the odious apparatus of Nazi rule, we shall not flag or fail. We shall go on to the end. We shall fight in France, we shall fight in the seas and oceans, we shall fight with growing confidence and growing strength in the air; we shall defend our island, whatever the cost may be. We shall fight on the beaches, we shall fight on the landing grounds, we shall fight in the fields and in the streets, we shall fight in the hills; we shall never surrender; and even if, which I do not for a moment believe, this island or a large part of it were subjugated and starving, then our Empire beyond the seas, armed and guarded by the British fleet, would carry on the struggle, until, in God's good time, the New World, with all its power and might, steps forth to the rescue and the liberation of the Old.[25]

Churchill well understood that England's greatest need was to arouse the support of the United States. He knew too that the majority of Americans were both isolationist and pacifist. Roosevelt was seeking to win his unprecedented third term by promising to keep America out of war. Senator Gerald Nye, a leader of the isolationists, responded to Churchill's Dunkirk speech by warning against "a campaign of fear that is pushing the country into Europe's war." Charles A. Lindbergh a few months later made a speech asking for an accord with Germany: "In the future," he said, "we may have to deal with a Europe dominated by Germany. . . . An agreement between us could maintain peace and civilization throughout the world as far into the future as we can see."[26] Obviously the United States was not inclined to stand by England's side. There were no military victories to encourage the English to resist and to prevail. What served the need of the time was eloquence—that of Churchill in this and in subsequent speeches; and, across the water, the persuasive speeches of President Franklin D. Roosevelt.

The speech that Roosevelt gave to the Congress on 16 May 1940 launching his "Lend-Lease" plan to assist Great Britain and France offers sharp contrasts with Churchill's speaking in several respects. Whereas Churchill had to prepare his speech on the day of its delivery under the stress of other urgent duties, Roosevelt set about the preparation of his speech with ample time to devote to it. Churchill, as was his custom, wrote his speech himself; he could not possibly have even contemplated having the text written for him. Roosevelt, according to his custom, used a team of ghost writers. Both speeches had great merit as persuasion and as inspiration; but their tone and style were greatly different. Churchill spoke as though from a pinnacle, spreading a light that was peculiarly his own. Roosevelt, even when addressing the Congress, struck a folksy tone with the conversational directness of his "fireside chats." Then, with a follow-up speech similarly prepared, he did speak to the public from his study on 26 May with the opening invitation: "Let us sit down together again, you and I, to consider our own pressing problems that confront us." He stated his appeal as though he were conversing, one-to-one, with his fellow citizens: "Let us not be calamity-howlers, and discount our strength. Let us have done with both fears and illusions. On this Sabbath evening, in our homes in the midst of our American families, let us calmly consider what we have done and what we must do."[27] Both Churchill and Roosevelt were masterful speakers, both governed events largely through their skill in guiding minds and stirring spirits with their words; and the differences between them help to reveal the breadth and the diversity of the domain of persuasive leadership.

What Churchill said of the greatly outnumbered British aviators who were defending the British skies—"Never before in the field of human conflict was so much owed by so many to so few"—might also be said of these two eloquent leaders. The challenges that Churchill had to overcome were the more evident and the more immediate. The Nazi armies were everywhere successful. With unsparing candor Churchill depicted the circumstances in a speech in the Commons on 20 August 1940:

> We have seen great countries with powerful armies dashed out of coherent existence in a few weeks. We have seen the French Republic and the renowned French Army beaten into complete and total submission. . . .
>
> The whole of the warring nations are engaged, not only soldiers but the entire population—men, women, and children. The fronts are everywhere. The trenches are dug in the towns and streets. Every village is fortified. Every road is barred. The front line runs through the factories.

The British were enduring a bombardment of their homes and cities that brought them a heavier weight of suffering than in the earlier world war. No problem of leadership was more insistently demanding than that of maintaining the will to persist. In a voice that rumbled in a throaty growl, Churchill responded to the need:

> Hitler is now sprawled over Europe. Our offensive springs are being slowly compressed, and we must resolutely and methodically prepare ourselves for the campaigns of 1941 and 1942. Two or three years are not a long time even in our short, precarious lives. They are nothing in the history of the nation, and when we are doing the finest thing in the world and have the honour to be the sole champion of the liberties of all Europe. . . .
>
> Meanwhile, we have not only fortified our hearts but our island. We have rearmed and rebuilt our armies. . . . Our Navy is far stronger. . . .
>
> Why do I say all this? Not assuredly to boast. . . . I recount them because the people have a right to know that there are solid grounds for the confidence which we feel. . . . I say it also because the fact that the British Empire stands invincible and that Nazidom is still being resisted will kindle again the spark of hope in the breasts of hundreds of millions of downtrodden or despairing men and women throughout Europe and far beyond its bounds, and that from these sparks there will presently come a cleansing and devouring flame.

The language and the rhythm were deliberately not folksily conversational; they reflected rather more of the Old Testament tone of the prophets in the King James version, more also of the oracular style of Macaulay and of Bourke Cockran, which Churchill had studied while developing his own. But he was also capable, when he deemed the time right for it, of being colloquial—as when he responded to Hitler's threat to ring the neck of Great Britain as though it were the neck of a chicken by exclaiming, "Some chicken! Some neck!" Neither was he averse to using rhetorical tricks that might warm the hearts of listeners, as in his persistence in the deliberately contemptuous mispronunciation of Nazis as "Nahzies." With his short neck hunched down between his shoulders, his glasses slid down low on his nose, his eyes raised only causally from his manuscript, and his minimal use of gestures, he seemed deliberately to avoid being an orator. Somehow—and it must have come from his spirit and his style—both what he said and how he said it proved to be effectively inspirational, not only to the British but around the world.

"A Shadow Has Fallen Upon the Scene"

After the entrance of the Soviet Union and later, of the United States into the war, with Great Britain no longer standing alone, Churchill's role declined for much the reason that Joan of Arc lost her status in the French court: other leaders with more power to exert shouldered him from center stage. American equipment and American troops crowded the countryside; British forces were placed under Eisenhower's command; and the political course of the war was largely determined by Roosevelt, by Stalin, and only in lesser degree by Churchill. The need to sustain the spirits of the British people was less urgent; what they came to need most was reassurance that British interests would not be subordinated to plans advocated by the United States and by Russia—and this is what Churchill could not tell them without attacking and thereby weakening the essential alliance. His speeches thereafter were less eloquent and less effective.

What he needed to do was to render explanations to England's old Greek ally as to why allied naval forces did not come to rescue Greece. He had to justify to his people the failure to win agreement with his plan to push up from the Mediterranean into the "weak underbelly" of occupied Europe. He had to accept American insistence on yielding to Soviet demands for dominance of eastern Europe. He had to contemplate the final dismemberment of the British Empire. His spirits became depressed and in recollecting the apex of his leadership in 1940, his interpretation was that what prevailed was English pluck: "I was only privileged to give the roar."[28] Indeed, the English electorate recognized, too, that his role had been served; when victory was achieved, they turned him out.

The nature of his position in the later years of the war is well stated in General Eisenhower's account:

> He was a man of extraordinarily strong convictions, and a master in argument and debate . . . he was difficult indeed to combat when conviction compelled disagreement with his views. . . . He could become intensely oratorical, even in discussion with a single person, but at the same time his intensity of purpose made his delivery seem natural and appropriate. . . . Some of the questions in which I found myself, at various periods of the war, opposed to the Prime Minister were among the most critical I faced. . . . I shall always owe him an immeasurable debt of gratitude for his unfailing courtesy and zealous support, regardless of his dislike of some important decisions. He was a great war leader and he is a great man.[29]

Despite Churchill's fundamental disagreement with critical decisions about both the conduct of the war and the plans for the peace settlement, he attained some of his prior eloquence in a worldwide broadcast on 26 March 1944 in which he announced that "The hour of our greatest effort is approaching." His tone was somber as he commenced by confessing to "my many shortcomings."

> It is a year almost to the day since I spoke to you on the broadcast here at home. This has been a time of disappointments as well as successes. But there is no doubt that the good news has far outweighed the bad. . . .
> The long and terrible march which the rescuing Powers are making is being accomplished stage by stage, and . . . the tragedy which threatened the whole world and might have put out all its lights and left our children and descendents in darkness and bondage—perhaps for centuries—that tragedy will not come to pass.

He appeared to forget his "world audience" and devoted the major part of his speech to discussing domestic issues on which he wanted to assure the electorate that his party was in the right. Then, reverting again to form, he concluded: "And when the signal is given, the whole circle of avenging nations will hurl themselves upon the foe and batter out the life of the cruellest tyranny which has ever sought to bar the progress of mankind."[30]

The greatest speech of his later years, after his forced retirement from office, was presented to a small audience in an inconspicuous college in midwest America, at a time when many of his apprehensions concerning the peace settlement were proving to be well founded. Once again, as during the years before the war, he sought to be "an alarm bell in the night," warning of dangers that were not much noted and not well understood. His situation was not now that of an ambitious politician, striving for a top place among his peers, but of a retired statesman, respected as a relic of a great past.

Churchill was spending the winter months of 1945–46 in the United States when he received and accepted an invitation to speak on 5 March to a convocation at Westminster College in Fulton, Missouri. President Truman offered to preside and to introduce him. It was an honorific occasion that might well have been dealt with in a few politely congratulatory paragraphs. Churchill determined to present a speech that would be historically significant. He prepared it with great care:

> This was several months ahead, and I kept myself as fully informed as was possible. I made inquiries both at the White House and at the State Department. . . . One always has to be very careful about speeches which you make in other people's countries.[31]

He commenced casually, even whimsically, referring to "Westminster" as a name that "somehow or other . . . I feel as if I had heard of it before." Whatever "private ambitions" he had had were already satisfied "beyond my wildest dreams." From the personal and casual mode, he shifted quickly to a solemn tone. In this "morrow of our absolute victory," it was time to consider "what has been gained with so much sacrifice and suffering."

Inevitably there was an aura of sadness in the role he had to play—that of a statesman no longer with hope for power, and of a sensitively patriotic Briton who was forced to realize that his country had fallen into a secondary role. What he undertook was to arouse Americans to an awareness of unfelt dangers, much the same mission he had undertaken for his own countrymen a decade earlier. The difference was that now he was speaking not to his own people and not as a potential leader but as a private guest in a country that with reason thought of itself as the most successful and most powerful in the world. He had never prepared a speech with so much care and had never presented one that was better adjusted to the peculiar character of its circumstances. "It is a solemn moment," he said, "for the American democracy":

> For with this primacy in power is also joined an awe-inspiring accountability to the future. As you look around you, you must feel not only the sense of duty done, but also you must feel anxiety lest you fall below the level of achievement. Opportunity is here now, clear and shining, for both our countries. To reject it or ignore it or fritter it away will bring upon us all the long reproaches of the after-time.[32]

What was needed, he went on, was to shield the peoples of the world from "the two gaunt marauders—war and tyranny." In the wake of victory, "at this sad and breathless moment," many peoples around the world are suffering famine—"and there is no reason except human folly or subhuman crime which should deny to all nations the inauguration and enjoyment of an age of plenty." And along with want, the world was also threatened by another war. "Beware, I say," because "the gleaming wings of science" that "might now shower immeasurable material blessings upon mankind may even bring about its total destruction."

He spoke wistfully of a possible time to come when the United States and Great Britain might join together in "the principle of common citizenship"; but this "we may be content to leave to destiny." He spoke next of Russia, concerning whom "We aim at nothing but mutual assistance and collaboration." He came, then, to the point for which he had so carefully prepared his speech:

> A shadow has fallen upon the scenes so lately lighted by the Allied victory. . . . From Stettin in the Baltic to Trieste in the Adriatic, an iron curtain has descended across the Continent. Behind that line . . . police governments are pervading from Moscow. . . . In front of the iron curtain which lies across Europe are other causes for anxiety. . . . Communist fifth columns are established and work in complete unity and absolute obedience to directions they receive from the Communist centre.

His conclusion was serious but upbeat. "I repulse the idea that a new war is inevitable." To prevent it, "the western democracies [must] stand together." He likened his appeal now to what he had attempted before World War II. "There never was a war in history easier to prevent . . . without the firing of a single shot . . . but no one would listen." Hopefully, he stated his conclusion:

> If we adhere faithfully to the Charter of the United Nations and walk forward in sedate and sober strength, seeking no one's land or treasure, seeking to lay no arbitrary control upon the thoughts of men—if all British moral and material forces and convictions are joined with your own in fraternal association—the high roads of the future will be clear, not only for us but for all, not only for our time, but for a century to come.[33]

With the utmost thoughtfulness and care, he had said what he most deeply felt. He lived on for another nine years. But thereafter, his voice was stilled. He had done what he could. In Great Britain's and in the world's time of greatest need, he was granted the strongest trust, was supported with the utmost of loyalty, and was granted within his country the greatest authority that his people could bestow. No prior leader in British history had had more. And there was none who more justly deserved both the trust and the gratitude that he received.

"An Orator in Spite of Himself"

Both admirers and critics of Churchill generally agree that for a brief period in his mid-sixties during World War II with a few speeches or portions of speeches, he elevated himself into the first rank of the world's most eloquent orators. Throughout the whole of his long career, his mastery of words, written and spoken, was his principal resource—the basis of his prominence and of his leadership. His writing won for him a large and admiring audience, but it never attained to literary greatness. His speaking from the start of his public career was effective and impressive, in a forum where speaking well mattered and where he was tested by comparison with exceptionally able associates and adversaries. But, like Abraham Lincoln, his truly memorable passages surpass his general discourse much as mountain peaks surmount their surrounding slopes.

It is tempting to conclude that he did not fit the pattern of great oratory. But as the catalogue of the world's most eloquent speakers is considered—including Demosthenes and Cicero; Danton, Robespierre and Napoleon; Mazzini and Bismark; Patrick Henry, Webster, Calhoun, and Clay; Lord Chatham, Fox, Sheridan, and Burke—it is evident that there is no such pattern. It is a characteristic of genius, whether in music or in words or in other forms of creative expression that its productions are highly individualized if not actually unique.

In a genuine sense, Churchill was an orator in spite of himself. His personality transcended his speech. He neither had nor sought to have platform arts. His delivery, vocal and physical, does not serve as a model for aspiring public speakers. As his son Randolph wrote of him, he forced his way into the front rank as a writer, speaker, and political leader, through sheer unstinting determination. Throughout much of his life he was a "loner" and seemed to prefer to be. Like Lord Chatham and Edmund Burke, he radiated an enormous self-confidence that amounted to an assurance of superiority. Like them too he both overawed his associates and at the same time aroused resentment and distrust. Yet it was he to whom the nation turned in trust and dependence in its time of greatest danger and distress; and it was he whose inspiration elevated their spirits and fortified their will to prevail.

An excellent portrayal of Churchill as a public speaker has been given in bits and pieces by Harold Nicolson, a subordinate associate who knew him well and watched him with the anxiety of an ambitious follower. Nicolson was appointed by Churchill as Britain's chief propagandist in charge of the overseas broadcasts by the BBC during the war; and Nicolson was bitterly disappointed and resentful at not being named to one of the major cabinet positions. He was fully aware of Churchill's greatness while being also sharply critical of his foibles and flaws. In seeking himself to understand the source of Churchill's persuasive power, Nicolson again and again came back to personality as the crucial factor.

Commenting on Churchill's speech in the Commons on 4 June 1940 in which he rallied the spirits of the nation after the Dunkirk evacuation, Nicolson wrote in his diary: "I think that one of the reasons why one is stirred by his Elizabethan phrases is that one feels the whole massive backing of power and resolve behind them, like a great fortress: they are never words for word's sake."[34] A few months later on 5 November Nicolson judged that: "By putting the grim side forward he impresses us with his ability to face the worst. He rubs the palms of his hands with five fingers extended up and down the front of his coat, searching for the right phrase, indicating cautious selection, conveying almost medicinal poise." A few days later on 20 November he recorded his further effort to comprehend what it was in Churchill's manner that won the trust of the nation in his leadership:

> there is something odd about his eyes. The lids are not in the least weary, nor are there any pouches or black lines. But the eyes themselves are glaucous, vigilant, angry, combative, visionary and tragic. In a way they are the eyes of a man who is much preoccupied and unable to rivet his attention on minor things (such as me). But in another sense they are the eyes of a man faced by an ordeal or tragedy, and combining vision, truculence, resolution and great unhappiness.

Churchill's delivery was indeed unusual. As Nicolson noted on 9 September 1941: "He stands there very stout and black, smoothing his palms down across his frame—beginning by patting his chest, then smoothing his stomach and ending down at the groin." All of this added up he noted on 23 April 1942 to "his stolid, obstinate, ploughman manner." But this was far from all. On 27 January 1942, Nicolson jotted down a different kind of impression: "When he feels he has the whole House with him, he finds it difficult to conceal his enjoyment of his speeches, and that, in fact, is part of his amazing charm."

When he did not enjoy speaking, Churchill, seemingly deliberately, did it badly. After his "finest hour" speech had inspired the Commons, Nicolson insisted against Churchill's wry objections that he give it again over the BBC, to reach a worldwide audience. This proved to be a mistake. As Nicolson reports: "He hates the microphone and when we bullied him into speaking last night [over the BBC] he just sulked and read his House of Commons speech again. Now, as delivered in the House of Commons, the speech was magnificent, especially in the concluding sentences. But it sounded ghastly on the wireless. All the great vigour he put into it seemed to evaporate."[35]

Unlike other greatest orators, Churchill's characteristic manner of speaking need never be a mystery to students of history or of public speaking. Ample examples remain in radio and film recordings. It is easy to picture him, with his lower lip pouting defiance, with his spectacles slid far down on his nose, with his shoulders stooped, and with his whole stolid appearance seeming to convey far more interest in expressing himself than in communicating with listeners. No doubt this was part of his power: he would not go to the mountain, it must come to him. But transcending his mannerisms was the quality of his mind and his spirit as revealed in his carefully crafted sentences and precisely definitive words. Not since his time have we seen his like, nor is it credible that we shall again.

EPILOGUE
THE ROLE OF RHETORIC IN RESHAPING HISTORY:
CHANGING AND EXPANDING

The reshaping of British democracy is a continuing process. Its history, like all historical accounts, may be rounded off but cannot be concluded. The antithesis between liberty and equality requires constant adjustments in the effort to maintain an acceptable balance. Events continue to unfold and to be discussed and debated. Problems concerning the Welfare State and problems between government and private enterprise continue to vex British politics and society. The process demands continual reconsideration.

World Wars I and II, coming close together, not only seriously altered the internal sociopolitical structure of Great Britain but also basically affected its relations with the dissolving empire, the dominions, and the rest of the world. No longer is the island nation the most powerful or the wealthiest or perhaps the most admired of the world's sovereignties. The proud sense of superiority that for centuries fortified the British spirit has been assailed by a miasma of self-doubt. An inrush of immigration from former colonies is modifying the nature of the population. Whatever Great Britain has been it is not now and cannot be again.

A major consequence is that its public speeches now derive from different assumptions and premises. "Greatness" as a crowd-pleasing theme has yielded to "practicality." The time when Great Britain could "do anything" has melded into a feeling that "something must be done." How to retain or to regain the best under rule by the most is the moot question. Leadership is further challenged to present suitable solutions for problems that are at best only partially understood. The perplexities of the mid-nineteenth century are fully matched by those of the latter years of the twentieth.

"Duty . . . with Sufficient Persuasive Skill"

It is this theme of the search of public leaders for viable answers and for means of making them effective to which this book is devoted. The general pattern of British history has often been retold. Yet there has been a curious neglect of historical consideration of the duty of leaders, in dealing with social problems, in religion, and in politics, to search for tenable programs, to make necessary adjustments, and to present their preferred solutions with sufficient persuasive skill to win their acceptance. Tracing this process is the function that this book has sought to serve. It is this that distinguishes it from other histories.

Perhaps Terence was right when he said that "Nullum est jam dictum, quod non dictum sit prius." There is little point in reviewing what is already well known. But there is value in reexamining history from a new perspective, in a search for new understanding. One conclusion that ought to emerge from this history of British public speaking is a heightened respect for leadership—for the function of discerning the nature of problems, of devising new ways of dealing with them, and of winning support to bring new policies and programs into effect.

During recent years public speaking, whether political, religious, or general, has tended to be less grand, less impressive, less oracular. Whether it has also lost the high consequence Macaulay attributed to it in his observation that government is 75 percent talk merits serious consideration. Either an affirmative or a negative answer can be respectably supported. Significant evidence points in contrary directions.

The independence of mind and of personal judgment by members of both the ministerial and opposition parties has been greatly curbed since Asquith developed the modes of party discipline. This obviously reduces the effects of persuasive discourse. On the other hand, the broadening of education and the development of radio and television have tremendously increased the available audience. If contemporary speeches are less splendid than those of earlier times, they are at least far more widely heard and read. It is beyond question that a new era, governed by new conditions, has emerged. Direct communication has become worldwide and the problems with which leaders must deal intermesh peoples and nations in every part of the globe. One result is that the history of public speaking no longer can be merely national.

To borrow words with which I concluded my *History of Public Speaking in America,*

> In the new age that was dawning there ceased to be an American oratory, or a British or French or Russian or German or Chinese arena of closed controversy. There opened instead a forum of the world, where the voices came to speak in accents of the Orient and Africa as well as of Europe and America, and where no leader could any longer speak of the problems of his own people without considering how they fit into the fabric of the Great Society that spreads across all continents and all seas.

The time remains distant but may wistfully be envisioned for consummation of the prayer with which Benjamin Franklin, in a letter to David Hartley dated 4 December 1789 concluded his life:

> God grant, that not only the Love of Liberty, but a thorough Knowledge of the Rights of Man, may pervade all the Nations of the Earth, so that a Phi-

losopher may set his foot anywhere on the Surface and say, "This is my country."

"What the Postwar Society Should Be Like"

The climax of the history of British public speaking became an anticlimax with the parliamentary elections held in June 1945. As the war in Europe ended, the National Coalition of the war years dissolved amid differences of opinion concerning what the postwar society should be like. Winston Churchill had one answer. His major opponent, Clement Attlee, who had been his chief lieutenant in the National Coalition, had another.

It was evident that the goals asserted in the Atlantic Charter as the guide for a peace settlement would not be achieved. It was also clear that the Soviet Union, second only to the United States as Great Britain's major wartime ally, was to be a formidable opponent. The empire was breaking quickly into independent parts. Surprisingly soon the Germans and the Japanese were converting from enemies to friends. The United States was inheriting the position of power and prestige that had been beyond challenge the foundation of British pride. These were but a few of the changes that signified a new role for Great Britain in the oncoming new era.

For the 1945 parliamentary elections the central issue was the nature of the domestic programs that should be brought into effect. After years of severe destruction and of personal deprivation—with continued rationing, high prices, and scarcities causing hardships that were yet further aggravated by increasing unemployment—the British public wondered anxiously what would be the reward for their wartime sacrifices and courageous efforts. This was the question the candidates had to answer.

Churchill was defeated because his was perceived as a nineteenth-century mentality that yearned more for a retreat into the past than for an advance into a different kind of future. This was a liability that he brought upon himself. In his major campaign address, over the BBC on 4 June he made the cardinal mistake of clarifying the unpopular course that he proposed to follow. In a tiresomely long and generally uninspired speech, he rejected the policy of redistributing income in order to enhance the welfare of the poorer part of the population. In a brief conclusion he sought to rise again to the elevated tone and the emotion-stirring rhythms of his wartime eloquence. But even there his appeal was to a past that had vanished and could not be reclaimed. After clumsily likening the socialists to the Nazi Gestapo, he declaimed once more his favorite theme of nationalistic pride:

Here in old England, in Great Britain, of which old England forms no inconspicuous part, here in this glorious island, the cradle and citadel of free democracy throughout the world, we do not like to be regimented and ordered about and have every action of our lives prescribed for us.

It was time for a transitional pause. Then, as though to emphasize how out of touch he was with the conditions, the mood, and the needs of the time, he ended with the assumption that the populace still lived on farms or in small villages—a kind of life such as their grandparents had known:

> Leave these Socialist dreamers to their Utopias or their nightmares, let us be constant to the heavy job that is right on top of us, and make sure that the cottage home to which the warrior will return is blessed with modest but solid prosperity, well-fenced and guarded against misfortune, and that Britons remain free to plan their lives for themselves and for those they love.

Clement Attlee's reply was made the following evening, also over the BBC. Attlee surprised the listening audience with his quiet but moving eloquence, for during the war years he had remained in the background. As deputy prime minister his duty had been not to rally public opinion but to administer programs. Such speeches as he gave were merely routine reports.[1] This BBC campaign speech was different. He emerged before the British public as a new man, with a new vision. In his introduction he stated his theme: "We do not want our beautiful island spoilt by haphazard development, dictated only by the hope of gain." He went on to explain his proposed program of justice and welfare for those in need. Then he concluded, less with the grandeur of oratory than with the simplicity and directness of elevated conversation:

> We call you to another great adventure which will demand the same high qualities as those shown during the war—the adventure of civilization. We have seen a great and powerful nation return to barbarism. We have seen European civilization almost destroyed and attempt made to set aside the moral principles on which it has been built. It is for us to reknit the fabric of civilized life woven through the centuries and with other nations to seek to create and share in an increasing material prosperity free from the fear of want. We have to preserve and enhance the beauty of our country, to make it a place where men and women may live finely and happily, free to worship in their own way, free to speak their minds, free citizens of a great country.

Of course Attlee's implication that the Conservative candidates were against civilization and free worship was unreal. But whether or not his own program was the best available and whether or not the vision of better times that he suggested would be brought closer by his political recipe, at least, in contrast to Churchill, Attlee was directing attention toward a hopeful future. When the votes were counted, his party won—and by a large margin. In consequence, the goal of expanding and fortifying the Welfare State was pursued by the Labour Government. Afterward, in due course, a Conservative ministry (the first in the nation's history to be headed by a woman) was given the task of curbing and limiting it. The debates and discussions go on, and will go on, for the problems are severe and difficult choices always have to be made.

In the course of these decades Aneurin Bevan was heard, and Anthony Eden, and Jo Grimond; Ernest Bevin and Herbert Morrison; Harold Wilson and Edward Heath; George Brown and Lord Hailsham; Michael Foot and Shirley Williams; Enos Powell and Arthur Cargill; Hugh Gaitskill and Neil Kinnock; Harold Macmillan and then Margaret Thatcher.

Mrs. Thatcher, not only the first woman prime minister, but the daughter of a middleclass grocer, was elevated to that position in 1979, and her tenure was extended further in the elections of 1983. She had practiced law for a time but, as she says, "I loved the law, but always, always, always, I returned to this fascinating thing of contemporary history, of today's problems, of trying to solve them." She described her own feelings about her success:

> I think I had a flair for it, but natural feelings are never enough. You have got to marry these feelings with really hard work. . . . When I walk into the House of Commons to answer questions or to do a speech, I say to myself two things: keep calm, concentrate. . . . Basically, the good Lord gave me certain talents, and it is up to me to use them. I am fantastically lucky to be using them in the job that I want to do best. There is also a great feeling that you can make a contribution to the present and to the future. There is some magnetism about being absolutely at the center. . . . What drives one and motivates one is that if only you could get your policies so that they draw more of the best out of people than the worst, then you are going the right way. In a free society life is a matter of choice, and we set the framework and rules by which people can make their own choices. Because that is the essence of freedom and the law.[2]

To this self-analysis, Prince Michael of Greece, concluding his interview of Mrs. Thatcher, added his own estimate: "She is not one of the flamboyant meteors that cross history. Rather, she is an inexorable will whose steadfastness ignores the bumps on the road. Perfectly 'transparent,' as one observer described her, she is not an original and does not try to be one. Yet her determination, tenacity, disdain of compromise, and guts have made her, in spite of herself, an original in our time."

More than most of the leading post-Churchillian public speakers in Great Britain, Mrs. Thatcher has clarified the questions that must be dealt with, however much disagreement remains about the answers. What is to be England's role in the world is a conundrum for which available answers are both unclear and unsatisfactory. But overmatching this question in urgency has been the overriding issue of how to restore competitive productivity and consequent material prosperity without endangering the assurance of at least minimal well-being for all. Democracy, slowly developing through several generations, has largely and basically been achieved. But in these times it is being put to the test. Does it work? In some respects Great Britain has slipped from its once un-challengeable pinnacle of grandeur. Even so it retains a special aura that is beyond challenge of being a major citadel of free speech.

"Issues Faced Honestly and Debated Openly"

What, finally should be concluded as we look back over the history of public speaking in these centuries of modernizing change?

It is evident that democracy developed slowly, painfully, and under conditions of stress in Great Britain. It was not brought into being by violent revolution, but in a process of trial-and-error experimentation. Its coming was welcomed, in fact demanded, by a too rapidly urbanized population whose traditional rural and cottage-industry independence was undermined by the new industrialization. The examples of the American and French revolutions inspired insistence upon equality, and the intellectual revolution shook loose old ideas to make way for new.

The shaping of democracy was guided, supported, and hastened by public speakers of great persuasive ability. It was also retarded, circumscribed, and qualified by others, whose devotion to traditional ideals was maintained with equal eloquence. There was no simple straightline development from aristo-cratic to democratic government and to egalitarian social practices and patterns. The problems that had to be dealt with were too complex and too unprecedented for solutions to be obvious. Not all concerns about the limitations of populism are chimerical. Nevertheless, the dread that "power to the people" meant debasement of intellectual and moral standards was overcome. On the whole the issues have been faced honestly and debated openly, including the diminishing of the advantages of the privileged classes. Free speech has proved its worth. So has the broadened electoral system whereby the nation's leadership is chosen by the whole adult population. However reluctantly, hesitantly, and imperfectly, the structure of democracy has been erected by the vital processes of discussion and debate.

It is significant that this transmogrification of British political, social and religious life was accomplished without the violent revolutionism that swept through Europe in the 1840s and again in the 1870s. Despite a damaging heightening of ill-will in Northern Ireland and in British industrial regions, the people as a whole has adhered to leadership that staked its claims on argument and on popular appeals. This is the central thread in the history of rhetorical influence in the shaping of British democracy.

As for the subject matter that has been discussed, the concern with domestic welfare has extended also to a steadily broadening of interest by the whole society as sharpened ethnic antagonisms bring world problems into focus in the streets of English cities. The nineteenth and twentieth centuries present sharp contrasts concerning the nature of the problems that are of central interest. This has brought a change, too, in the nature and in the role of public speaking as the decades advanced. Successively developing issues were vital and the tone of their discussion was often acrimonious. But as one world war followed another, the severity of the suffering and the sacrifices they demanded had a sobering effect.

Something of the disillusionment that followed the Napoleonic Wars is evident. Idealism and even patriotism has yielded something to self-interest. This is partly because the problems of basic welfare, of employment, and of just distribution of wealth and benefits remain acute.

The comprehensive and the essential meanings of democracy are not yet wholly clear. The ancient gradations of the society were reshaped under the influence of egalitarianism into a new social consciousness that often exhibits not so much a community of interest as a competition of interests. Nevertheless, the verbal contests for power are far more constrained and reasoned than is the "class warfare" that is preached and practiced in other parts of the world. The difference in great part derives from the distinction between a closed society that restrains or denies freedom of discussion and an open society that permits and encourages it.

The history of public speaking is basically a history of the shaping growth of national ideas, ideals, and institutions. These are the products of the public forum, in which the speakers, one after another, rise in their places to present their views and to make their appeals.

"Incredible That Democracy Could Have Been Shaped"

What effects, really, did the speeches and the speakers have? There is no system of measurement that could justify a confident answer. History is by far more complicated than a baseball game; and even for baseball, it is not by one play or one player that the outcome is determined but the work of the entire team, and of the opposing team, and even the nature of the playing field, the weather, and the attitude of the watching crowd. A significant body of historians, following in their differing ways the mode set by Marx, and Spengler, and Toynbee, have insisted that individuals and their special efforts make little or no difference in major historical trends. Recent prestigious advocates of this depersonalized historiography include William McNeill, with his *Rise of the West: A History of the Human Community,* and Fernand Braudel, author of the massive three-volume *Civilization and Capitalism.* Their general view is capsulized by Braudel in his introduction to his chapter on "The Spread of Technology," where he declares that the flow of history is "slow, mute, and complicated." He adds that progress is impeded by "memory that obstinately repeats known solutions, to avoid the difficulty and danger of imagining something else."

Such historians as these would not have become prestigious if there were not considerable truth supporting their depersonalizations of history. Singly and together they make an impressive case for the view that crucial changes "just happen" because of interrelations between human nature and the environment. In the preceding chapters of this book it has been recurrently evident that old patterns (or "memories") do stubbornly persist; and also that intellectual and social changes have swept through society like vast tidal waves that no individual and no social structure could either divert or control.

Nevertheless, what also emerges is the fact that leadership does not always "obstinately repeat known solutions"; and that some individuals with superior insight, great courage, and persuasive eloquence have in fact confronted "the difficulty and the danger of imagining something else." The transformation of the society of Great Britain during these past two centuries has been guided at critical junctures in crucial ways by persuasive leaders who were able to see the significance of new facts, to work out new ways for dealing with them, and to win the following required to make necessary readjustments. It is true that none of them was omniscient, omnipotent, or entirely free from selfish motives. Such understanding as they have had developed slowly and partially, and their prevision was limited and incomplete when not just simply wrong. But since they also were generally well in advance of their time, and since often they sought to serve the public weal at serious cost to their own status and advancement, they merit, as a group, far more admiration than censure. Without them it seems incredible that democracy would have been shaped as it has been. Probably, as Gladstone posited, the results attained did not flow from single speeches, but rather from the cumulative effects of the societal agreement that problems should be identified, interpreted, examined, and threshed out in processes of talk—with the listening playing its own part, along with the speaking.[3] It is worthy of pointing out again and of emphasizing that in Great Britain the public forum has been kept secure.

"Decisions . . . through Discussion and Debate"

The current rhetorical circumstances in Great Britain are different in important respects than they have been during the preceding centuries. A vastly larger audience is available to well-known public figures than could have been dreamed of in earlier years. The million persons who attended (but of course could not hear) Daniel O'Connell's speech at Tara are dwarfed by the multiple millions who now as a matter of course listen to radio and television commentators, news analysts, interview programs, and on occasion public addresses. What this finally means in terms of the influence exerted by public speaking remains uncertain. But some of the questions that need to be considered have become clear. The answers are both obvious and significant.

• Would any individual be able to rise to prominent leadership in British public life without the ability to speak acceptably well?

• Is the ability to explain, to justify, and to persuade an important, perhaps even an essential, requirement for membership in key positions in the cabinet?

• Would English society as we know it be conceivable without the direct, free, and frequent exchange of views in oral discourse?

• If the basic factors that distinguish democracy were listed would not freedom of speech be high on the list?

• Among all the attributes or skills that distinguish humanity is not the power to communicate essential if not actually primary among them?

How important the ability to communicate can be to an individual was illuminated poignantly by Thomas DeQuincey in his autobiographical *Confessions of an English Opium Eater*. As a young child, he relates, he was sent by his parents to a public school where he was so miserable and homesick that he ran away. When he appeared at his home, his shocked mother asked why he had been so disobedient, and in his shame he was unable to explain. Then he says: "If a new Sphinx should arise and should ask what alone of all the burdens mankind bears is the one burden that is insupportable, I should reply, *it is the burden of the incommunicable.*" Even more unbearable would be such a burden for society. For, as has often been said, it is communication and most especially oral communication that makes civilized society possible.

Even so, under the dire threat of atomic war and other international complications, the question has been raised whether critical national decisions should be made through processes of discussion and debate, with the electorate enabled to listen and to judge, or whether national security requires that such questions be considered secretly, behind closed doors. The discernible trend appears to be in the direction of secretive deliberations. Even when national electoral campaigns are waged, presumably to give voters their ultimate choices between parties and policies, the tendency is for presumptive and prospective leaders to seek the lowest common denominator of generalizations or to substitute ambiguity for clarity. Practical politicians appear to believe that what they don't say can't hurt them, and that to take a stand on crucial issues risks losing more votes than would be gained by it.

The effects of the greatly enlarged audience are diverse. Since factual detail seems too uninteresting to hold the brief attention span of uninformed listeners, demagoguery is encouraged to heighten excitement. Serious argumentation may bring forth ridicule as being highbrow pretentiousness. In any event microphones and cameras create a situation very different from the club-like familiarity of the old sequestered parliamentary chambers. On the other hand, government no longer is controlled by a few power brokers, as it was in the days of "pocket boroughs," but is dependent upon the free votes of the national majority.

One question as yet unsettled is whether the participatory nature of democracy demands that parliamentary sessions should be open to public scrutiny through radio and television coverage? In the eighteenth century, the great fear of the legislators was that even the admission of reporters to the galleries or the publication of the texts of speeches would induce members to seek popularity rather than to strive to be statesmanlike. This same kind of fear has impeded the televizing of sessions of the Commons; and the Lords indulge in it only infrequently.

As Professor Vernon Jensen reports in his survey of plans that have been suggested to open parliamentary sessions to television cameras, interpretations of what would happen have been various. Some argue that "this would draw people and Parliament closer together, would stimulate interest in Parliament, would better serve front and back benchers in all parties, would restore to Parliament the power which has been usurped by the executive branch of government, would encourage procedural reform in Parliament, and would reduce the current monopoly of the printed media of parliamentary debates."[4] Another view that he cites stresses the danger of rendering the debates theatrical. "One soon felt that any *Hansard in extenso* would need speakers to change their style to address the outside audience, rather than their audience in the Chamber, much as speakers nowadays do at party Conferences. Is that what Parliament wants?" Professor Jensen sums up the contrary views:

Many fear that television will give exposure and prestige to abnormal behavior, to flamboyant speaking, to photogenic qualities, to moments of conflict, and to extreme points of view, so that the unemotional, intelligent, nonaggressive, middle-of-the-road person will go unnoticed and unsung. Advocates, on the other hand, feel that the camera will expose and reduce superficial theatrics, ungentlemanly behavior, unreasonableness, incompetence, arrogance, and insincerity; and that the statements will be on a higher plane and will be more carefully prepared.

"Citizens of the Whole Community"

The arguments pro-and-con concerning the potential effects of television on parliamentary discussions might with equal cogency be applied to the effects of television upon speeches addressed to the general public. As speakers are viewed on television screens in homes, they inevitably have to compete in some degree with the general array of entertainment—motion pictures, soap operas, comedies, adventure sequences, music, sporting events—that viewers are accustomed to watching on these same screens. It is far easier now for Britons to hear public speeches than in former times when they had to dress and go out to some hall, nearby or distant. Speakers are brought into their homes by a mere flick of the dial; and with equal ease they can be tuned out. Obviously, standards of judgment concerning the merit of speeches have undergone considerable change.[5] A prime criterion has to be interestingness. Another is personalization: "How does what he is talking about affect me?" The length of speeches has had to be drastically curtailed; instead of the four- and five-hour speeches sometimes delivered by orators of prior times, speeches utilizing television must generally be limited to twenty or thirty minutes. All of these factors together affect the subjects that may be discussed and the complexity of the discussion. Brevity, simplicity, dramatic intensity, and appeal to the self-interest of viewers have become virtual requirements dictated by television and radio. Public speaking today is not and cannot be what it has been in the past.

Still another factor affecting the potency of public address in the shaping of society is the tremendous growth of the influence of labor and trade organizations—which, however, seems in decline under the Thatcher ministry. The effects of strikes, monopolies, shut-outs, and corporate decisions concerning employment are all means of "fighting out solutions" rather than "talking them out." In such struggles negotiation is a vital process, but in the negotiations the appeal is commonly as much to force of one kind or another as to facts and reason. Even so, in all these confrontations public opinion remains as the major monitor and a considerable influence. And public speaking has a significant role in shaping how the public interprets the pattern of events.

We must always question Macaulay's estimate that government (and other social and personal relations) consists actually "seventy-five percent of talk." Even in earlier times such a percentage would naturally vary considerably with circumstances—of peace or war, for example—and also varied relative to the kinds of personalities of speakers and listeners that were involved.

What may confidently be concluded is that throughout the whole of British history public speaking has been among the shaping forces and that to a high degree it still is. By no means is it true as Braudel and similar historians have implied that history has been "mute." Quite to the contrary, man is essentially a symbolizer. Our world is largely made for us by the words we see and hear. There is substantial evidence to support the claim that Joseph Conrad recorded in his journal: "Give me the right words, and the right accent for speaking them, as a fulcrum on which to rest, and I will move the world."

The Gutenberg revolution of print vastly changed the nature of society and the course of history. The electronic extension of personality and of voice, whether by telephone, radio, television, or film, is having and will have an even more momentous effect. Enormous influence has been exerted in our own century by the public speaking of such leaders as Sun Yat-Sen, Ali Jinnah, Sukarno, Gandhi, and Nehru in Asia, and of Lenin and Trotsky, Mussolini and Hitler, and Roosevelt and Churchill in the West. It would be paradoxical not to think that in our time the role of public speaking is not only still vital but is intensifying and expanding.

Changes of course have been made and will continue to be made in the mode and the mood, the style and the manner of public discourse. In the British Parliament the changes during these past two centuries have been dramatic. Throughout most of the nineteenth century as had been true in all the preceding parliamentary history, the two Houses had been much like clubs in which members of similar backgrounds and education and even of similar tastes and interests spoke to one another as self-conscious aristocrats, safely insulated from immediate contacts with the public. They exchanged views as gentlemen must—sometimes it is true with acrimony, sarcasm, and ridicule, but with the distinct consciousness that they all together constituted a special class, a class educated and selected to rule. The successive franchise extensions in 1832, 1867, and 1884 capped once again by the extension of the vote to women in 1916 and 1928 gradually brought about an epochal change.

Members more and more came to be and to think of themselves as citizens of the whole community, speaking as representatives rather than as mentors or guides. In part this has meant speaking for special interests within the community, which has acerbated feelings of us-against-them. But concurrently the increasing strictness of party discipline has tended to diminish individual assertiveness. *Hansard,* like the newspapers of the past hundred and fifty years—and like the novels and the poetry—reads differently than it used to. So far as the public speaking is concerned, it is less grand, less oracular, less architectonic, less imagistic. It is less interesting to read, as the speeches are less interesting to hear. But the impact of public discussion and debate, rather than being diminished, has probably increased. Government in free societies continues to be government by talk.

Quod erat demonstrandum. The rhetorical interpretation of history is that affairs are guided by leaders who define, interpret, and induce support for their views of issues, of conditions, and of events.

NOTES

Introduction

1. See Karl R. Popper, *The Logic of Scientific Discovery* (New York: Harper, 1957); Michael Polonyi, *Personal Knowledge* (Chicago: University of Chicago Press, 1957; and Herbert W. Simons, "The Rhetoric of Science and the Science of Rhetoric," *Western Journal of Speech Communication* 42 (1978): 37–43, for cogent discussions of the rhetorical methods of scientific reasoning.

2. Alexis de Tocqueville, *Democracy in America*, 2 vols. (New York: Alfred A. Knopf, 1945) 1: 254 and 259, and 2: 392.

3. William R. Burch, Jr., "Nature and Society—Seeking the Ghost in the Sociological Machine," *Communication Quarterly* (Winter 1984), 9.

4. Cited by Eric Wm. Scopec, "Ethical Implications of Thomas Reid's Philosophy of Rhetoric," *Pennsylvania Speech Association Annual* (1983): 8.

5. Kenneth Burke, *A Rhetoric of Motives* (New York: George Brazilier, 1955), 43.

6. Ralph Waldo Emerson, *Works*, 12 vols., edited by Edward Waldo Emerson (New York: Wise, 1929), 7:66–67.

7. Emerson, *Works*, 8:115–30. For a fuller discussion of Emersonian rhetoric see my *History of Public Speaking in America* (Boston: Allyn and Bacon, 1965, reprinted by Westport, Conn.: Greenwood Press, 1978), 119–29.

8. Lincoln Steffens, *The Letters of Lincoln Steffens*, 2 vols. edited by E. Winters and G. Hicks (New York: Harcourt, Brace & World, 1938), 2:574.

9. Alfred Korzybski, *Science and Society: An Introduction to Non-Aristotelian Systems and General Semantics* (Lancaster, Pa.: Science Press Printing Co., 1933).

10. Chaim Perelman and I. Obrechts-Tyteca, *The New Rhetoric: A Treatise on Argumentation*, trans. by John Wilkinson and Purcell Weaver (Notre Dame, Ind.: University of Notre Dame Press,1960).

11. Thomas Mann, *The Magic Mountain*, trans. H. T. Lowe-Porter (New York: Alfred A. Knopf, 1949), 518. For a cogent argument that words are far from being the only significant forms of symbolism, see J. Vernon Jensen, "Communicative Functions of Silence," *Etc.: A Review of General Semantics* 30 (September 1974): 249–57.

12. Hugh Dalziel Duncan, *Communication and the Social Order* (New York: Bedminster Press, 1962), xxvii.

13. Ernst Cassirer, *An Essay on Man* (New Haven: Yale University Press, 1944), 25.

Chapter 1. A Challenge to Rhetoric

1. George Macaulay Trevelyan, *Lord Grey of the Reform Bill* (London: Longmans, Green, 1920), 98.

2. David Cecil, *Melbourne* (Indianapolis, Ind.: Bobbs-Merrill, 1939), 178.

3. For a detailed examination of this problem, see Robert T. Oliver, *The Psychology of Persuasive Speech* (New York: Longmans, Green, 1942; David McKay, 1960).

4. Esmé Wingfield-Stratford, *The History of British Civilization* (London: Routledge & Kegan Paul, 1928), 973–74.

5. Cited by Cecil Driver, *Tory Radical: The Life of Richard Oastler* (New York: Oxford University Press, 1946), 269, and all of his chapter 4.

6. Cited by O. F. Christie, *The Transition from Aristocracy, 1832–1867* (New York: G. P. Putnam's, 1928).

7. John Prest, *Lord John Russell* (Columbia: University of South Carolina Press, 1972), 9.

8. See Sir Samuel Romilly, *Memoirs* (London: John Murray, 1842); and C. G. Oakes, *Sir Samuel Romilly* (London: George Allen and Unwin, 1935).

9. The speech is included in David B. Strother, *Modern English Eloquence* (New York: Funk and Wagnalls, 1969), 143–48.

10. E. J. Hobsbawn, *The Age of Revolution in Europe, 1789–1848* (London: Weidenfeld and Nicolson, 1962), 198.

11. Wellington's speech is included in Strother, *Modern British Eloquence*, 171–85.

12. An excellent summation of the historic trends of this period of emerging democracy is provided by Wingfield-Stratford, *The History of British Civilization*, 968–1086.

13. D. C. Somervell, *English Thought in the Nineteenth Century* (London: Methuen, 1929), 30. Cf. the confirmatory biography by Daniel Green, *Great Cobbett: The Noblest Agitator* (London: Hodder and Stoughton, 1984).

14. Wingfield-Stratford, *History of British Civilization*, 913–15.

15. Somervell, *English Thought in the Nineteenth Century*, 30–36.

16. Driver, *Tory Radical*, 42–43.

17. Ibid, 127.

18. Ibid., 131. Driver devotes his chapter 11 to an excellent rhetorical overview of Oastler's speaking.

19. Ibid., 170–77.

Chapter 2. The Old versus the New

1. Walter Bagehot, *Biographical Studies* (London: Longmans, Green, 1881), 25.

2. Wingfield-Stratford, *History of British Civilization*, 790–91.

3. This is the theme of Bagehot's chapter on Peel in his *Biographical Studies.*

4. Chauncey A. Goodrich, *Select British Eloquence* (1854; rpt. Indianapolis, Ind.: Bobbs-Merrill, 1963), 853.

5. Harold Temperley, *The Foreign Policy of Canning, 1822–1827* (New York: Archon Books, 1966), chapter 2.

6. Cited by Goodrich, *Select British Eloquence*, 857.

7. This, and other speeches by Canning that will be cited were collected by Goodrich, *Select British Eloquence*, 859–85.

8. Temperley, *The Foreign Policy of Canning*, 5, 7.

9. Ibid., 444.

10. Cited by Prest, *Lord John Russell*, 9.

11. Ibid., 18.

12. Ibid., 72.

13. Ibid., p. 30.

14. Driver, *Tory Radical*, 19–20.

15. Trevelyan, *Lord Grey of the Reform Bill*, 98.

16. For Grey's perplexity, see Wingfield-Stratford, *History of British Civilization*, 938–39.

17. Trevelyan, *Lord Grey of the Reform Bill*, 126.

18. Ibid., 163.

19. George Macaulay Trevelyan, *The Life of John Bright* (London: Longmans, Green, 1913), 365.

20. Trevelyan, *Lord Grey of the Reform Bill,* 273.

21. Ibid., 275.

22. Ibid., 279.

23. Ibid., 107.

24. Ibid., 110, 112, 342.

25. Ibid., 368–69.

26. Ibid., 368.

27. Chester W. New, *The Life of Henry Brougham to 1830* (Oxford: Clarendon Press, 1961), 265.

28. Donald C. Bryant et al., eds., *An Historical Anthology of Select British Speeches* (New York: Ronald Press, 1967), 322–23.

29. G. T. Garratt, *Lord Brougham* (London: Macmillan, 1935), 2.

30. Arthur Aspinall, *Lord Brougham and the Whig Party* (Manchester: University Press, 1927), 294.

31. Lloyd I. Watkins, "Lord Brougham's Authorship of Rhetorical Articles in the *Edinburgh Review,*" *Quarterly Journal of Speech* 42 (1956): 55–63.

32. Goodrich, *Select British Eloquence,* 888.

33. Ibid., 889.

34. In picturing this established and accepted form of military discipline, Brougham wrote an excruciating description of what it meant: ". . . his back torn to the bone by the merciless cutting whipcord, applied by persons who relieve each other at short intervals that they may bring the full unexhausted strength of a man to the work of scourging." Cited by New, *Brougham,* 53.

35. Aspinall, *Brougham and the Whig Party,* 245.

36. Henry Lord Brougham, *Historical Sketches of Statesmen . . . in the Time of George III,* (Philadelphia: Lea and Blanchard, 1842), 1:9.

37. Goodrich, *Select British Eloquence,* 889.

38. New, *Brougham,* 392.

39. Strother, *Modern British Eloquence,* presents the introductory portion of this speech, 153–65.

40. The abridged text of this speech is taken from Bryant et al, *Select British Speeches,* 325–58.

41. Ibid., p. 358.

Chapter 3. The Focus of Argument

1. Sir Ivor Jennings, *The Queen's Government* (Hammondsworth: Penguin Books, 1954), 28.

2. For descriptions of speaking in the Parliament after it became representational, see Charles D. Smith, "Debate in the House of Commons," *Today's Speech* 5 (April 1957): 21–23; Waldo W. Braden, "Speaking in the House of Commons," *Southern States Journal of Communication,* 24 (Winter 1958): 67–74; and works on the modern British Parliament in Selected Readings on pp. 232–41 of this book.

3. Donald Southgate, *The Passing of the Whigs, 1832–1886* (London: Macmillan, 1962), 420 and passim. Cf. also David Cecil, *Melbourne,* particularly in his "Prologue," 15–25.

4. Christopher Dawson, "The Humanitarians," in a collection of BBC Broadcasts, *Ideas and Beliefs of the Victorians* (London: Sylvan Press, 1949), 248 and 249.

5. Ibid., 250. For a detailed study of these ideas, see Gertrude Himmelfarb, *The Idea of Poverty: England in the Early Industrial Age* (London: Faber and Faber, 1984).

6. The Chartist Movement has been analyzed in such studies as Mark Hovell's *the Chartist Movement* (Manchester: Victoria University, Historical Series No. 31, 1918); Asa Briggs, ed., *Chartist Struggles,* (London: Macmillan, 1959); and J. F. C. Harrison, *Robert Owen and the Owenites in Britain and America* (London: Routledge and Kegan Paul, 1969).

7. Walter L. Arnstein, *Britain Yesterday and Today, 1830 to the Present* (Lexington, Mass.: D. C. Heath, 1976), 34.

8. This cogent summation is from Wingfield-Stratford, *History of British Civilization,* 902–5.

9. J. A. Hobson, *Richard Cobden: International Man* (New York: Holt, 1919), 24.

10. Ibid., 391.

11. Ibid., 38.

12. John Morley, *The Life of Richard Cobden* (London: T. Fisher Unwin, 1896), 196.

13. Hobson, *Cobden*, 402.

14. Ibid., 197.

15. Ibid., 228.

16. Ibid., 161.

17. The text of this speech is included by Strother, *Modern British Eloquence*, 246–66.

18. George Macaulay Trevelyan, *The Life of John Bright* (London: Constable, 1913), 3.

19. Herman Ausubel, *John Bright: Victorian Reformer* (New York: John Wiley and Sons, 1966), vii.

20. Trevelyan, *John Bright* 3.

21. Ausubel, *John Bright*, viii.

22. Ibid., 69.

23. Trevelyan, *John Bright*, 1.

24. Ausubel, *John Bright*, 9.

25. Trevelyan, *John Bright*, 102–3.

26. Ibid., 100.

27. Mrs. Boyce, in *Records of a Quaker Family*, cited by Trevelyan, ibid., 104.

28. Ibid., 117.

29. The text of this speech is included in Strother, *Modern British Eloquence*, 271–95.

30. The text of this speech is included in Bryant et al., *Select British Speeches*, 401–12.

31. Strother, *Modern British Eloquence*, 289.

32. James E. Thorold Rogers, ed., *Speeches on Questions of Public Policy by . . . John Bright, M. P.* (London: Macmillan, 1883), 281.

33. Ibid., 546.

34. Trevelyan, *John Bright*, 11.

35. Kenneth Young, *Macaulay* (London: Longmans Group, Ltd., 1976), p. 11.

36. This speech is included in A *Historical Anthology of British Political Speeches* (London: Everyman Series #715).

37. Young, *Macaulay*, p. 22.

Chapter 4. Uncertain Rhetoric

1. June Callwood, *Portrait of Canada* (New York: Doubleday, 1981), 172.

2. Winston Churchill, A *History of the English Speaking Peoples*, 4 vols. (New York: Dodd, Mead, 1958), 4:36.

3. These two and the following quotation are from W. E. H. Lecky, *Leaders of Public Opinion in Ireland*, 2 vols. rev. ed. (London: Longmans, Green, 1891), 2: 2 et seq.

4. Claude G. Bowers, *The Irish Orators* (Indianapolis, Ind.: Bobbs-Merrill, 1916), 320–22.

5. Cf. Walter Lippmann, *Public Opinion*, reprinted, (London: Penguin Books, 1946), 61: "for the most part we do not first see and then define, we define first and then see."

6. Seàn O'Faolàin, *King of Beggars* (New York: Viking Press, 1938), 330.

7. Lecky, *Leaders of Public Opinion in Ireland* 2:7.

8. Philip Ziegler, *Melbourne* (New York: Alfred A. Knopf, 1976), 92–93.

9. Philip Whitwell Wilson, *The Greville Diary*, ed., 2 vols. (Garden City, N.Y.: Doubleday, Page, 1927), 1:351.

10. William E. White, "Daniel O'Connell's Oratory on Repeal," Ph.D. diss., University of Wisconsin, 1954, 345.

11. T. W. Woody and F. X. Martin, eds., *The Course of Irish History* (Cork: Merceir Press, 1967), 251.

12. It is this speech that was selected by Bryant et al., *Select British Speeches*, 361–70; and by Strother, *Modern British Eloquence*, 198–208.

13. Greville's diary entries are for 31 March and 25 February 1844.

14. Herbert C. F. Bell, *Lord Palmerston*, 2 vols. (London: Longmans, Green, 1936), 1:344.

15. Moody and Martin, *The Course of Irish History*, 261.

16. Wingfield-Stratford, *The History of British Civilization*, 1055.

17. Bell, *Palmerston*, 1:55.

18. Ibid., 2:26–28.

19. Ibid., 2:32.

20. Ibid., 2:404.

21. Ibid., 2:406.

22. Ibid.

23. Ibid., 2:426.

24. Donald Southgate, *"The Most English Minister . . ."*: *The Policies and Politics of Palmerston* (London: Macmillan, 1966), 279.

25. Cecil, *Melbourne*, 237–38.

26. Philip Ziegler, *Melbourne: A Biography of William Lamb, 2nd Viscount Melbourne* (New York: Alfred A. Knopf, 1976), 188–89.

27. *Greville Diary*, 2:6.

28. Arnstein, *Britain Yesterday and Today*, 105.

29. Callwood, *Portrait of Canada*, 135.

30. Ibid., 136.

31. John, Viscount Morley, *Recollections*, 2 vols. (New York: Macmillan, 1917), 1:236–49.

32. R. Barry O'Brien, *The Life of Charles Stewart Parnell, 1846–1891*, 2 vols. (London: Smith, Elder and Co., 1898; rpt., New York: Greenwood Press, 1969), 1:86.

33. Ibid., 98.

34. The citations in order are from ibid., 1:37, 40, 38, 43–44; 2:332; 1:74, 86, and 102.

35. Ibid., 86.

36. Ibid., 2:114.

37. Ibid., 355.

38. James Bryce, *Studies in Contemporary Biography* (New York: Macmillan, 1911), 248–49.

39. The text of the speech is included in Strother, *Modern British Eloquence*, 346–50.

40. O'Brien, *Parnell*, 2:367.

41. A fully detailed account of the post-Parnell history of Ireland and its spokesmen is Dorothy Macardle, *The Irish Republic* (New York: Farrar, Straus and Giroux, 1965).

Chapter 5. Challenge to the Church

1. Beginnings are hard to specify. Some constraints upon nonconformity were removed in 1778, others in 1791. But not until 1837 were Catholics allowed to marry without the services of a Church of England clergyman; not before 1880 could they be buried with services conducted solely by their own priests. Religious constraints tend to persist.

2. The quotations are from W. W. Dale, *The Life of W. R. Dale of Birmingham* (London: Hodder and Stroughton, 1902), 250; L. E. Elliott-Binns, *Religion in the Victorian Era* (London: Lutterworth Press, 1936), 71; and William Hanna, *Memoirs of the Life and Writings of Thomas Chalmers*, 2 vols. (Edinburgh: Thomas Constable and Company, 1852), 2:484.

3. Esme Wingfield-Stratford, *History of British Civilization*, 861, speaking particularly of Methodism.

4. Lord John Morley, *Recollections* (London: Macmillan, 1917), chapter 2.

5. Wingfield-Stratford, *History of British Civilization*, 860.

6. Elliott-Binns provides a descriptive listing in *Religion in the Victorian Era*, 331–37.

7. Dale, *Dale*, 104.
8. Ibid., 149.
9. Ibid., 230.
10. Ibid., 254.
11. Ibid., 255–56.
12. Ibid., 259.
13. Ibid., 262.
14. Elliott-Binns, *Religion in the Victorian Era*, 374.
15. Ibid., 461.
16. Ibid., 469.
17. Dale, *Dale*, 396.
18. Ibid., 600.
19. W. J. Townson, H. B. Workman, and George Eayrs, eds., *A New History of Methodism*, 2 vols. (London: Hodder and Stoughton, 1859), 1:437.
20. W. Y. Fullerton, *Charles Haddon Spurgeon* (Chicago: Moody Press, 1966), 41.
21. George Adam Smith, *The Life of Henry Drummond* (New York: Doubleday & McClure, 1898), 67ff.
22. Fullerton, *Spurgeon*, 173.
23. Ibid., 174.
24. Ibid., 79.
25. Ibid., 267.
26. Ibid., 79.
27. Ibid., 30–31.
28. *British Weekly*, 4 February 1892.
29. Fullerton, 207 and 208.
30. Ibid., 181. *Spurgeon*, 207 and 208.
31. George Adam Smith, *The Life of Henry Drummond*, 18.
32. Ibid., chapter 2.
33. Ibid., 7.
34. Ibid.,54.
35. Ibid., 114–15.
36. Ibid., 244–56.
37. Wilfrid Ward, *The Life of John Henry Cardinal Newman*, 2 vols. (London: Longmans, Green, 1921), 1:64–65 and 77, quoting from Principal Shairp.
38. Ibid., 73–74.
39. Ibid., 23.
40. Ibid., 36.
41. Ibid., 37.
42. Ibid., 61–63.
43. Ibid., 8.
44. Ibid., 44–45.
45. Ibid., 2:475.
46. Ibid., 1: 234.
47. Ibid., 247.
48. H. H. Hutton, *Cardinal Newman* (London: Methuen, 1890).
49. Ward, *Newman*, 2:355.
50. Ibid., 356.
51. Ibid., 393–94.
52. Ibid., 395.
53. Ibid., 577.
54. A. R. Widler, ed., *Soundings: Essays Concerning Christian Understanding* (Cambridge: Cambridge University Press, 1964), 394–95.

55. H. E. Root, "Beginning All Over Again," in Vidler, *Soundings*, 4.

56. J. S. Habgood, "The Uneasy Truce between Science and Theology," in Vidler, *Soundings*, 31.

57. G. F. Woods, "The Idea of the Transcendent," in Vidler, *Soundings*, 57.

58. H. A. Williams, "Theology and Self-Awareness," in Vidler, *Soundings*, 76.

59. Ninian Smart, "The Relations between Christianity and the Other Great Religions," in Vidler, *Soundings*, 106, 107, and 109.

60. For a detailed consideration of these two modes, see Desmond Bowen, *The Idea of the Victorian Church: A Study of the Church of England, 1833–1889* (Montreal: McGill University Press, 1968); and Herbert Leslie Stewart, *A Century of Anglo-Catholicism* (New York: Oxford University Press, 1929).

Chapter 6. The Central Triad

1. Jim Bishop, *The Birth of the United States* (New York: William Morrow and Co., 1976), 12.

2. Gertrude Himmelfarb, *The Idea of Poverty: England in the Early Industrial Age* (London: Faber & Faber, 1984).

3. Cf. B. W. Hill, *British Parliamentary Parties, 1742–1832* (London: George Allen and Unwin, 1985); and T. W. Heyck, *The Transformation of Intellectual Life in Victorian England*, (London and Canberra: Croom Helm, 1982.)

4. Arnstein, *Britain Yesterday and Today*, 134.

5. Wingfield-Stratford, *History of British Civilization*, 1105.

6. John Morley, *The Life of William Ewart Gladstone* 3 vols. (New York: Macmillan, 1911) 1:204.

7. Cecil Woodham-Smith, *Queen Victoria . . . to the Death of the Prince Consort* (New York: Alfred A. Knopf, 1972), 149.

8. Ibid., 214–35.

9. Robert Blake, *Disraeli* (New York: St. Martin's Press, 1967), 433.

10. Ibid., 490–94.

11. Hesketh Pearson, *Dizzy: The Life and Personality of Benjamin Disraeli, Earl of Beaconsfield* (New York: Harper, 1951), 248.

12. Morley, *Gladstone*, 3:348.

13. Pearson, *Dizzy*, 249.

14. A. G. Gardiner, *The Life of Sir William Harcourt*, 2 vols. (London: Constable and Co., 1923), 2:445–46.

15. Ibid.

16. Asa Briggs, "Benjamin Disraeli and the Leap in the Dark," in *Victorian People, A Reassessment of Persons and Themes, 1851–1867*, rev. ed. (London: Penguin Books, 1965), 272–303.

17. Bryant et al., *Select British Speeches*, 372.

18. F. J. C. Henshaw, ed., *Prime Ministers of the Nineteenth Century* (London: Macmillan, 1936), 210.

19. Pearson, *Dizzy*, 47.

20. Briggs, *Victorian People*, 273.

21. Pearson, *Dizzy*, 47.

22. Blake, *Disraeli*, 217.

23. William Flavelle Monypenny and George Earle Buckle, *The Life of Benjamin Disraeli*, 2 vols. (New York: Macmillan, rev. 1929), 1:275.

24. Pearson, *Dizzy*, 57–59.

25. Greville, *Memoirs*, 3:404.

26. Blake, *Disraeli*, 149.

27. Ibid., 117–18.

28. Monypenny and Buckle, *Disraeli*, 1:720.

29. Ibid., 2:117–18.

30. Ibid., 1:720.

31. Ibid., 1:752.

32. Pearson, Dizzy, 187.

33. Moneypenny and Buckle, Disraeli, 1:1350.

34. Ibid., 2:144.

35. Ibid., 2:261.

36. Ibid., 2:526–29.

37. Monypenny and Buckle, Disraeli, 2:1504.

38. Blake, Disraeli, 764–65.

39. Gardiner, Life of Harcourt, 1:208.

40. Bryant et al., Select British Speeches, avers that "he steadily and successfully supplied ideas, strategies, and language to speed the evolution of a socially conscious conservatism" 372.

41. Pearson, Dizzy, 191–92.

42. Morley, Gladstone, 1:17–18.

43. Ibid., 2:587–94.

44. Ibid., 594. "The campaign had a soul in it," Morley concluded. "Men were recalled to moral forces they had forgotten." Ibid., 595–96.

45. Blake, Disraeli, 650.

46. Morley, Gladstone, 2:589.

47. Ibid., 594.

48. Wingfield-Stratford, History of British Civilization, 1024–31 and 1105.

49. Francis Birrell, Gladstone (New York: Macmillan, 1933), 30.

50. Erich Eyck, Gladstone (London: George Allen and Unwin, 1938), 272.

51. Bryant et al., Select British Speeches, 414.

52. Morley, Gladstone, 1:194–95.

53. Ibid., 2:596.

54. Ibid., 3:173.

55. Ibid., 520.

Chapter 7. After the Watershed

1. Hippolyte Taine, Notes on England, trans. and ed. Edward Hyams (Fairlawn. N.J.: Essential Books, 1958), 155 and 242.

2. R. C. K. Esnor, England, 1870–94 (Oxford: The Clarendon Press, 1936), 136, where he identified 1870 as "the watershed year."

3. Leonard Huxley, Life and Letters of Thomas Henry Huxley, 2 vols. (New York: D. Appleton and Co., 1916), 1:172. For a study of how Huxley set about deliberately to make himself an effective speaker, see J. Vernon Jensen, "Thomas Henry Huxley's 'Baptism into Oratory'," Notes and Records of the Royal Society of London 30 (Jan. 1976): 181–207.

4. Quoted by Winston Churchill, History of the English-Speaking Peoples, 4:355.

5. Huxley, Life, 1: 219.

6. Ibid., 2:162, for both assertions.

7. Ibid., 1:239.

8. David Daiches, A Critical History of English Literature, 2 vols. (New York: Ronald Press, 1970), 2:983.

9. Raymond Chapman, The Victorian Debate (New York: Basic Books, 1968).

10. Frances Kingsley, ed., Charles Kingsley, His Letters and Memories of His Life (London: K. Paul Trench and Co., 1882).

11. Donald Read, England, 1868–1914 (London: Longmans, 1979, 147.

12. Arnstein, England Yesterday and Today, 146.

13. Peter Fraser, *Joseph Chamberlain, Radicalism and Empire, 1868–1914* (New York: A. S. Barnes, 1966), xii–xiii.

14. Strother, *Modern British Eloquence,* presents the complete text of the speech, 355–70.

15. Lady Gwendolyn Cecil, *Life of Robert, Marquis of Salisbury,* 3 vols. (London: Hodder and Stoughton, 1931), 3:64.

16. Winston S. Churchill, *History of the English-Speaking Peoples,* 4:355.

17. Sir Charles Petrie, *Joseph Chamberlain* (London: Duckworth, 1940, 137.

18. Justin McCarthy, *British Political Portraits* (New York: Outlook, 1903), 81.

19. Read, *England,* 147.

20. Ibid.

21. The text of this speech, printed in the London *Times,* 8 May 1902 is conveniently found in Strother, *Select British Eloquence,* 375–82.

22. J. A. S. Grenville, *Lord Salisbury and Foreign Policy* (London: Athlone Press, 1970), 439–40.

23. Quoted from Churchill by Wingfield-Stratford, *History of British Civilization,* 1176.

24. Lord Rosebery, *Lord Randolph Churchill* (London: Harper, 1906), 181.

25. Winston Spencer Churchill, *Lord Randolph Churchill,* 2 vols. (London: Macmillan, 1906), 2:274.

26. Robert Rhodes James, *Lord Randolph Churchill* (London: Weidenfeld and Nicolson, 1959).

27. *Speeches of the Right Honourable Lord Randolph Churchill, 1880–1888,* 2 vols. (London: Longmans, Green, 1889), 1:97–117. See Strothers, *Modern British Eloquence,* 355–70.

28. James L. Garvin, *Life of Joseph Chamberlain* 3 vols. with vol. 4 added by Julian Amery (London: Macmillan, 1933), 2:191.

29. Peter Fraser, *Joseph Chamberlain: Radicalism and Empire, 1868–1914* (New York: A. S. Barnes, 1966), 261, quoting his third wife, Beatrice Webb.

30. Donald Read, *England,* 57.

31. Fraser, *Chamberlain: Radicalism and Empire,* xii–xiii.

32. Ibid., 129.

33. For the text of this and Chamberlain's other major addresses, see C. W. Boyd, ed., *Mr. Chamberlain's Speeches* 2 vols. (London: Longmans, 1914).

34. This is the summation offered by Garvin in his life of Chamberlain.

35. Fraser, *Chamberlain,* 261.

36. Ibid., 268.

37. H. C. G. Matthew et al., "The Franchise Factor in the Rise of the Labour Party," *English Historical Review* 91 (1976): 733. For a review of Balfour's career, see K. Young, *Arthur James Balfour* (London: G. Bell, 1963).

38. Alexander Mackintosh, *Joseph Chamberlain* (London: Hodder and Stoughton, 1906), 393.

39. Wingfield-Stratford, *History of British Civilization,* 1173.

40. Ibid., 1184.

41. The text of this speech is conveniently available in Strother, *Modern British Eloquence,* 387–402.

42. Arnstein, *Britain Yesterday and Today,* 202.

Chapter 8. Torchbearers of a New Revolution

1. Samuel Hynes, *The Edwardian Turn of Mind* (Princeton: Princeton University Press, 1968), 6.

2. Lucy Masterman, *C. F. G. Masterman* (London: Nicolson and Watson, 1939), 266.

3. Arnstein, *Britain Yesterday and Today,* 209.

4. John Grigg, *The Young Lloyd George* (Berkeley and Los Angeles: University of California Press, 1973), 121.

5. Wingfield-Stratford, *History of British Civilization,* 1263.

6. C. F. G. Masterman, *In Peril of Change* (London: Fisher and Unwin, 1905), xii.

7. John Maynard Keynes, *Essays in Biography* (New York: W. W. Norton, 1951).

8. E. T. Raymond, *Mr. Lloyd George* (New York: George H. Doran Co., 1922), 351.

9. Grigg, *The Young Lloyd George*, 42.

10. Ibid., 43.

11. Ibid., 85.

12. Ibid., 99.

13. Ibid., 209.

14. John Grigg, *Lloyd George: The People's Champion, 1902–1911* (London: Eyre Methuen, 1978), 21.

15. Ibid., 156.

16. Ibid., 153.

17. Herbert DuParq, *Life of David Lloyd George* (London: Caxton, 1912), 539.

18. The text for this speech is conveniently available in Strother, *Modern British Eloquence*, 407–17. See also Robert W. Smith, "David Lloyd George's Limehouse Address," *Central States Speech Journal* (August 1967): 169–76.

19. His secretary, long-time mistress, and second wife, Frances Stevenson, helped in the writing of them. See A. J. P. Taylor, ed., *Lloyd George, A Diary by Frances Stevenson* (New York: Harper and Row, 1971), x and passim.

20. These judgments are all from Grigg, *Lloyd George: The People's Champion*, 64–67.

21. Ted Morgan, *Churchill, Young Man in a Hurry, 1874–1915* (New York: Simon and Schuster, 1982), 45, 48.

22. William Manchester, *The Last Lion: Winston Spencer Churchill, Visions of Glory, 1874–1932* (Boston: Little, Brown, 1983), 376 and 346.

23. Ibid., 30.

24. Randolph S. Churchill, *Winston S. Churchill: Youth, 1874–1900* (Boston: Houghton, Mifflin, 1966), 176.

25. Ibid., 382.

26. Manchester, *The Last Lion*, 21.

27. Quoted by Kay Halle, *Irrepressible Churchill* (Cleveland, Ohio: World Publishing Co., 1966), 51.

28. Morgan, *Young Man in a Hurry*, 91.

29. Randolph S. Churchill, *Winston S. Churchill: Young Statesman, 1901–1914* (Boston: Houghton, Mifflin, 1967), 1.

30. Manchester, *The Last Lion*, 812.

31. These citations are from Halle, *Irrepressible Churchill*, 29, 50, 52.

32. R. Churchill, *Young Statesman*, 483.

33. Manchester, *The Last Lion*, 27.

34. Ibid., 31.

35. Manchester, ibid., 331–33 describes the tour, from which descriptions these citations have been taken.

36. Morgan, *Young Man in a Hurry*, 145–49 is the source for these citations.

37. Manchester, *The Last Lion*, 404.

38. Ibid., 405.

39. Martin Gilbert, *Winston S. Churchill*, 3 vols. (Boston: Houghton, Mifflin, 1973), 3:104.

40. Morgan, *Young Man in a Hurry*, 227–28, 562.

41. Manchester, *The Last Lion*, 423.

42. Roy Jenkins, *Asquith: Portrait of a Man and an Era* (New York: Chilmark Press, 1964), chapter 14: "A Trial of Statesmanship," 194–211.

43. Ibid., 334–45.

44. Ibid., 61.

45. Ibid., 338–39.

46. Ibid., 17, 24, 139.

47. Ibid., 462–63.
48. Stephen Koss, *Asquith* (London: Allen Lane, 1976), 89. Although Koss described his biography as "revisionist," he does little to revise Jenkin's portrait of Asquith.
49. Andre Maurois, *The Edwardian Era* (New York: Appleton-Century, 1933), 284.
50. Samuel Hynes, *The Edwardian Turn of Mind*, 77.
51. Ibid., 63.
52. The text is included as an appendix in Hynes, *The Edwardisn Turn of Mind*, 390–409.
53. Included in Bryant et al, *Select British Speeches*, 476–90.
54. Anthony West, *H. G. Wells: Aspects of a Life* (New York: Random House, 1984), 286.
55. Ibid., 11, 112, 147.
56. Hynes, *The Edwardian Turn of Mind*, 390–409.
57. Ibid, 121.
58. For studies of Shaw as a public speaker, see Dan H. Lawrence, ed., *Platform and Pulpit* (London: Robert Hart-Davis, 1962); and Warren S. Smith, ed., *The Religious Speeches of Bernard Shaw* (University Park, Pa.: Pennsylvania State University Press, 1963).
59. Bryant, *Select British Speeches*, 476–90.
60. J. Vernon Jensen, "London's Outdoor Oratory," *Today's Speech* 15 (February 1967): 3–6.

Chapter 9. Speaking Up for Women

1. Churchill, *A History of the English Speaking Peoples*, 4:79.
2. Oliver, *History of Public Speaking in America*, 438–50.
3. Bryant et al., *Select British Speeches*, 275.
4. See Emmeline Goulden Pankhurst, *My Own Story* (London: Evelyn Nash, 1914, reprinted, New York: Source Book Press, n.d.); and E. Sylvia Pankhurst, *The Life of Emmeline Pankhurst* (Boston: Houghton Mifflin, 1935).
5. Christabel Pankhurst, *Unshackled: The Story of How We Won the Vote* (London: Hutchinson, 1959), 11.
6. Cited by Elise Boulding, *The Underside of History: A View of Women through Time* (Boulder, Colo.: Westview Press, 1976), 675–78.
7. Morgan, *Churchill*, 86–87.
8. Algar Labouchere Thorold, *The Life of Henry Labouchere* (New York: Putnam's 1913), 244–45.
9. Boulding, *The Underside of History*, 621.
10. These various divergent trends are analyzed by T. C. Lloyd, *Empire to Welfare State: English History, 1906–1976* (Oxford University Press, 1979), 42–45; and by Anthony Wood, *Great Britain 1900–1965* (Burnt Mill, Harlow, Essex: Longman House, 1978), 74–75.
11. Sheila Rowbotham, *Hidden from History: Rediscovering Women in History from the 17th Century to the Present* (New York: Pantheon Books, 1974), 77.
12. Pankhurst, *My Own Story*, 6–11.
13. Ibid., 13–15.
14. Ibid., 58.
15. Ibid., 62.
16. Ibid., 127.
17. Ibid., 127–29.
18. Christabel Pankhurst, *Unshackled*, 44–45.
19. Ibid., 117.
20. Ibid., 138–39.
21. Ibid., p. 157.
22. Ibid., p. 162.
23. Ibid., 211–15.

24. Anthony Wood, *Great Britain 1900–1965*, 75 for both quotations.

25. E. Pankhurst, *My Own Story*, 231.

26. E. Sylvia Pankhurst, *The Life of Emmeline Pankhurst*, 175.

27. Ibid., 116–17.

28. Winston Churchill, *History of the English Speaking Peoples*, 4:79.

29. London *Sunday Times*, 8 October 1985, 3.

Chapter 10. Britain's Solemn Hour

1. Violet Bonham Carter, *Winston Churchill: An Intimate Portrait* (New York: Harcourt, Brace and World, 1965), 61.

2. Sir Charles Wilson, Lord Moran, *Churchill: The Struggle for Survival, 1940–1965* (Boston: Houghton Mifflin, 1966), 13–14.

3. Ibid., 321.

4. Ibid., 110.

5. Ibid., 822–23.

6. See Robert T. Oliver, "The Speech that Established Roosevelt's Reputation," *Quarterly Journal of Speech* 21 (October 1945): 274–82.

7. Winston S. Churchill, *Memoirs of the Second World War*, one-volume edition, (Boston, Houghton Mifflin, 1959), 39–40.

8. Joseph P. Lash, *Roosevelt and Churchill, 1939–1941: The Partnership that Saved the West* (New York: W. W. Norton, 1976), 9, for both quotations.

9. Churchill, *Memoirs*, 39, 82.

10. On 20 January 1927 Churchill assured Mussolini that, "Your movement has rendered a service to the whole world . . . [it has] provided the necessary antidote to Russian poison." In 1938 he wrote an enthusiastic appraisal of Mussolini for *Collier's* magazine. See Gaetano Salvemini, *Prelude to War II* (Garden City, N.Y.: Doubleday, 1954), 108 and passim.

11. Cited by Raymond J. Sontag, *A Broken World: 1919–1939* (New York: Harper and Row, 1971), 178. The book is an excellent interpretation of the period between the two world wars.

12. Churchill, *Memoirs*, 139.

13. These citations are from Martin Gilbert and Richard Gott, *The Appeasers* (Boston: Houghton Mifflin, 1963), 13.

14. Churchill, *Memoirs*, 139.

15. Sontag, *A Broken World*, 360.

16. Sir Edward Spears, *Assignment to Catastrophe*, 2 vols. (New York: A. A. Wyn, 1954), 1:6–7.

17. Ibid., 18–19.

18. Gilbert and Gott, *The Appeasers*, 349.

19. Churchill, *Memoirs*, 221–22.

20. Spears, *Assignment to Catastrophe*, 1:126–27.

21. Churchill, *Memoirs*, 222–27.

22. Moran, *Churchill*, 823.

23. Churchill, *Memoirs*, 281.

24. Ibid., 308.

25. The texts of all Churchill's wartime speeches are provided in four volumes: *The Unrelenting Struggle* (1942), *The End of the Beginning* (1943), *Onwards to Victory* (1944), and *The Dawn of Liberation* (1945), published by Little, Brown and Co.

26. Walter Johnson, *The Fight against Isolation* (Chicago: University of Chicago Press, 1944), 2 and passim.

27. Samuel I. Rosenman, *Working with Roosevelt* (New York: Harper, 1952), 193–96.

28. Churchill, in a speech to the Commons on 1 December 1954.

29. Dwight D. Eisenhower, *Crusade in Europe* (New York: Doubleday, 1948), 61–62.

30. Winston S. Churchill, *The Dawn of Liberation* (Boston: Little, Brown, 1945), 50–64.

31. Churchill, *Memoirs*, 996.

32. The text of this speech is conveniently available in James H. McBath and Walter R. Fisher, *British Public Addresses: 1828–1960* (Boston: Houghton Mifflin, 1971), 541–51.

33. Ibid.

34. Harold Nicolson, *The War Years, 1939–1945*, 2 vols., ed. Nigel Nicolson (New York: Atheneum, 1967), 93. Subsequent quotations from his diaries, from this same volume, are identified by his dates of entry.

35. Ibid., 97.

Epilogue

1. Nicolson, in his journal, *The War Years*, noted on 19 May 1942 the nature of Attlee's wartime speaking: "Attlee opens with a long and rambling statement which is so dull and so badly delivered that the House can scarcely refrain from yawning" (226).

2. Prince Michael of Greece, "I Am Fantastically Lucky," an interview with Margaret Thatcher for the newspaper supplement, *Parade*, 13 July 1986.

3. See Carroll C. Arnold, in "Oral Rhetoric, Rhetoric, and Literature," *Philosophy and Rhetoric* (Fall 1968) 1:97: "speaker and listener revise their views of self; experience becomes markedly other-directed; personality is recognized as an inevitable, legitimate, energizing element among affective forces; special communicative resources are seen to exist and to require use and control; special hazards are recognized, requiring to be mastered sufficiently to meet conventional standards of the oral mode."

4. J. Vernon Jensen, "Attempts to Televise Parliament," *Journal of Broadcasting* 16 (Fall 1972): 461–73.

5. Joshua Meyrowitz, *No Sense of Place: The Impact of Electronic Media on Social Behavior* (New York: Oxford University Press, 1985). The changing role of opposition in parliament is analyzed by Rodney Barker, ed., *Studies in Opposition* (London: Macmillan Press, 1971); and by Robert A. Dahl, *Political Opposition in Western Democracies* (New Haven: Yale University Press, 1966).

SELECTED READINGS

Anthologies

Adams, Charles K. *Representative British Orations*. 4 vols. New York: Putnam, 1900. Vol. 5 added by John Alden, 1907.

British Orations from Ethelbert to Churchill. Everyman's Library rev. ed. New York: E. P. Dutton, 1960.

Bryan, William Jennings, and Frances W. Halsey. *The World's Famous Orations*. 10 vols. New York: Funk and Wagnalls, 1906.

Bryant, Donald C., et al. *An Historical Anthology of Select British Speeches*. New York: Ronald Press, 1967.

George-Brown, Lord. *The Voices of History: Moments from the Great Speeches of the English Language*. New York: Stein and Day, 1980.

Goodrich, Chauncey A. *Select British Eloquence*. Reprint. Indianapolis, Ind.: Bobbs-Merrill, 1963.

Hazeltine, Mayo W., et al. *Masterpieces of Eloquence*. 25 vols. New York: P. F. Collier and Sons, 1905.

Jamieson, K. H. *Critical Anthology of Public Speeches*. Chicago: Science Research Associates, 1978.

McBath, James, and Walter Fisher. *British Public Address, 1828–1960*. Boston: Houghton Mifflin, 1971.

Peterson, Houston. *A Treasury of the World's Great Speeches*. Rev. ed. New York: Simon and Schuster, 1965.

Strother, David M. *Modern British Eloquence*. New York: Funk and Wagnalls, 1969.

General Sources

Aitken, Max, Lord Beaverbrook. *The Decline and Fall of Lloyd George*. London: Collins, 1963.

———. *Politicians and the War*. London: Hutchinson, 1968.

Alinsky, Saul D. *Rules for Radicals: A Practical Primer for Realistic Radicals*. New York: Vintage, 1972.

Amery, J. *Joseph Chamberlain*. 6 vols. London: Macmillan, 1969.

Asquith, Cynthia. *Diary 1915–1918.* London: Hutchinson, 1968.

Baker, Arthur. *The House Is Sitting.* London: Blandford, 1958.

Benson, Thomas W., ed. *Speech Communication in the Twentieth Century.* Carbondale, Ill.: Southern Illinois University Press, 1985.

Boardman, Harry. *The Glory of Parliament.* New York: Taplinger, 1959.

Bosmajian, Haig A., ed. *Dissent: Symbolic Behavior and Rhetorical Strategies.* Boston: Allyn and Bacon, 1972.

Bowers, John W., and Donovan J. Ochs. *The Rhetoric of Agitation and Control.* Reading, Mass.: Addison-Wesley, 1971.

Brandes, Paul D. *The Rhetoric of Revolt.* Englewood Cliffs, N.J.: Prentice-Hall, 1971.

Bulmer-Thomas, Ivor. *The Party System in Great Britain.* London: Phoenix House, 1984.

Burks, Don M., ed. *Rhetoric, Philosophy and Literature: An Explanation.* West Lafayette, Ind.: Purdue University Press, 1978.

Carr, E. H. *What Is History?* New York and London: Macmillan, 1961.

Chapman, Raymond. *The Victorian Debate.* New York: Basic Books, 1968.

Clarke, I. F. *Voices Prophesying War.* London: Oxford University Press, 1966.

Cole, G. D. H. *History of the Labour Party since 1914.* London: Routledge, 1948.

Cox, J. Robert, and Charles Arthur Willard. *Advances in Argumentation Theory and Research.* Carbondale, Ill.: Southern Illinois University Press, 1982.

Crick, Bernard. *The Reform of Parliament.* London: Weidenfeld and Nicolson, 1964.

Daiches, David. *A Critical History of English Literature.* 2 vols. New York: Ronald Press, 1970.

Dangerfield, George. *The Strange Death of Liberal England.* London: McGibbon and Key, 1966.

Edelman, Murray. *Political Language: Words That Succeed and Policies That Fail.* New York: Academic Press, 1977.

———. *The Symbolic Uses of Politics.* Urbana: University of Illinois Press, 1964.

Ensor, R. C. K. *England 1870–1914.* London: Oxford University Press, 1936.

Fulford, Roger. *Votes for Women.* London: Faber and Faber, 1957.

Gadamer, Hans-George. *Truth and Method.* New York: Crossroads Pub., 1975.

Gamson, William A. *Power and Discontent.* Homewood, Ill.: Dorsey, 1969.

———. *The Strategy of Social Protest.* Homewood, Ill.: Dorsey, 1975.

Geyl, Pieter. *Debates with Historians.* New York: Meridian Books, 1958.

Gregg, Richard B. *Symbolic Inducement and Knowing: A Study in the Foundations of Rhetoric.* Columbia: University of South Carolina Press, 1984.

Haiman, Franklyn S. *Speech and Law in a Free Society.* Chicago: University of Chicago Press, 1981.

Halevy, E. *History of the English People in the Nineteenth Century.* 6 vols. London: Benn, 1932.

Hanham, H. J. *The Nineteenth-Century Constitution.* Cambridge: University of Cambridge Press, 1969.

Heberle, Rudolf. *Social Movements: An Introduction to Political Sociology.* New York: Appleton-Century-Crofts, 1951.

James, R. R. *Churchill: A Study in Failure.* New York: Penguin Books, 1973.

Jennings, Sir Ivor. *Cabinet Government.* 3d ed. Cambridge: Cambridge University Press, 1969.

———. *Parliament.* 2d ed. Cambridge: Cambridge University Press, 1969.

———. *The Queen's Government.* Harmondsworth, Eng.: Penguin Books, 1954.

Kaplan, E. Ann, ed. *Regarding Television: Critical Approaches—An Anthology.* Frederick, Md.: University Publications of America, 1983.

Lentricchia, Frank. *Criticism and Social Change.* Chicago: University of Chicago Press, 1983.

McKenzie, R. T. *British Political Parties.* London: Heinemann, 1963.

McKeon, Zahava Karl. *Novels and Arguments: Inventing Rhetorical Criticism.* Chicago: University of Chicago Press, 1982.

Miller, Gerald R., and Herbert W. Simons, eds. *Perspectives on Communication in Social Conflict.* Englewood Cliffs, N.J.: Prentice-Hall, 1974.

Oliver, Robert T. *Persuasive Speaking: Principles and Methods.* New York: Longmans, Green, 1950.

———. *The Psychology of Persuasive Speech.* New York: Longmans, Green, 1942; reprinted David McKay, 1968.

Oliver, Robert T., and Dominick A. Barbara. *The Healthy Mind in Communion and Communication.* Springfield, Ill.: Charles C. Thomas, 1962.

Pankhurst, Sylvia. *The Suffragette Movement.* London: Longmans, Green, 1931; reprinted, London: Virago, 1977.

Pelling, H. *The Origins of the Labour Party.* London: Oxford University Press, 1965.

Ricoeur, Paul. *The Rule of Metaphor: Multi-disciplinary Studies of the Creation of Meaning in Language.* Translated by R. Czerny, with K. Mclaughlin and J. Costello. London: Routledge & Kegan Paul, 1978.

Roberts, Ron E., and Robert M. Kloss. *Social Movements: Between the Balcony and the Barricade.* St. Louis, Mo.: Mosby, 1974.

Russell, R. *The Ragged Philanthropists.* London: Lawrence and Wishart, 1955.

Shrapnel, Norman. *The Performers: Politics as Theatre.* London: Constable, 1978.

Simons, H. W., and A. A. Aghazarian, eds. *Politically Speaking: Forms and Genres of Political Discourse.* Colombia: University of South Carolina Press, 1984.

Slack, Jennifer Daryl. *Communication Technologies & Society: Conception of Causality & the Politics of Technological Intervention.* Norwood, N.J.: Pub. Corp., 1984.

Stewart, Charles, Craig Smith, and Robert E. Denton. *Persuasion and Social Movements.* Prospect Heights, Ill.: Waveland Press, 1984.

Taylor, Eric. *The House of Commons at Work.* London: Penguin Books, 1981.

Thompson, F. *A History of British Trade Unionism.* London: Oxford University Press, 1964.

Tosh, Hans. *The Social Psychology of Social Movements.* New York: Bobbs-Merrill, 1965.

Touraine, Alain. *The Voice and the Eye: An Analysis of Social Movements.* Translated by Alan Duff. Cambridge: Cambridge University Press, 1981.

Toynbee, Arnold. *A Study of History.* Abridged ed. by D. C. Somervell. New York: Oxford University Press, 1947.

Vallance, Elizabeth M. *Women in the House: A Study of Women Members of Parliament.* London: Athlone Press, 1979.

Webb, Beatrice. *Diaries, 1912–24.* London: Longman, 1952.

Willey, B. *Nineteenth-Century Studies: Coleridge to Matthew Arnold.* London: Chatto and Windus, 1949.

Wood, Anthony. *Great Britain 1900–1965.* London Longman, 1978.

Wood, James L., and Maurice Jackson. *Social Movements: Development, Participation and Dynamics.* Belmont, Calif.: Wadsworth, 1982.

Young, Kenneth. *Balfour.* London: Bell, 1963.

Articles

Addison, Paul. "Churchill." *History Today* 30 (August 1980): 7–13.

Anderson, Floyd D., and Andrew A. King. "William Hazlitt as a Critic of Parliamentary Address." *Quarterly Journal of Speech* 67 (February 1981): 47–56.

Anderson, Wayne C. " 'Perpetual Affirmation Unexplained': The Rhetoric of Reiteration in Coleridge, Carlyle and Emerson." *Quarterly Journal of Speech* 71 (February 1985): 37–51.

Andrews, James R. "The Ethos of Pacifism: The Problem of Image in the Early British Peace Movement." *Quarterly Journal of Speech* 53 (February 1967): 28–33.

———. "The Great Fear: The Restoration of the Catholic Hierarchy in England, 1850." *Quarterly Journal of Speech* 19 (Fall 1968); 163–68.

———. "The Passionate Negation: The Chartist Movement in Rhetorical Perspective." *Quarterly Journal of Speech* 59 (April 1973): 196–208.

———. "Piety and Pragmatism: Rhetorical Aspects of the Early British Peace Movement." *Communication Monographs* 34 (November 1967): 423–36.

———. "The Practical Strategy: Richard Cobden's Arbitration Speech of 1849." *Western Journal of Speech Communication* 32 (Winter 1968): 27–35.

————. "The Rhetoric of Coercion and Persuasion: The Reform Bill of 1832." *Quarterly Journal of Speech* 56 (April 1970): 187–95.

————. "Spindles versus Acres: Rhetorical Perceptions of the British Free Trade Movement." *Western Journal of Speech Communication* 38 (Winter 1974): 41–52.

Arnold, Carroll C. "Invention in the Parliamentary Speaking of Benjamin Disraeli." *Speech Monographs* 14 (1947): 66–80.

————. "The Speech Styles of Benjamin Disraeli." *Quarterly Journal of Speech* 33 (December 1947): 427–36.

Auer, J. Jeffrey. "The Image of the Right Honourable Margaret Thatcher." *Central States Speech Journal* 30 (Winter 1979): 289–310.

Backes, James G. "J. S. Mill and His Preposterous Motion." *Western Journal of Speech Communication* 34 (Spring 1970): 90–99.

Baskerville, Barnet. "Principal Themes of Nineteenth-Century Critics of Oratory." *Speech Monographs* 19 (March 1952): 11–26.

Becker, Samuel L. "Broadcasting and Politics in Great Britain." *Quarterly Journal of Speech* 53 (February 1967): 34–43.

Bennett, W. Lance. "Communication and Social Responsibility." *Quarterly Journal of Speech* 71 (August 1985): 259–88.

Bormann, Dennis R. "The Willing Suspension of Disbelief—Kames as a Forerunner of Coleridge." *Central States Speech Journal* 23 (Spring 1972): 56–60.

Bormann, Ernest G. "Fantasy and Rhetorical Vision: The Rhetorical Criticism of Social Reality." *Quarterly Journal of Speech* 58 (December 1972): 396–407.

Boyd, Newell D. "The Emergence of the Welsh Bounder: David Lloyd George's Oratorical Attacks during the Anglo-Boer War." *Communication Monographs* 52 (March 1985); 78–91.

————. "Gladstone, Midlothian, and Stump Oratory." *Central States Speech Journal* 30 (Summer 1979): 144–55.

Braden, Waldo W. "Contemporary Debating in the House of Commons." *Southern Speech Communication Journal* 27 (Summer 1962): 261–72.

————. "Speaking in the House of Commons." *Southern Speech Communication Journal* 24 (Winter 1958); 67–74.

Brockreide, Wayne E. "Bentham's Philosophy of Rhetoric." *Speech Monographs* 23 (November 1956): 235–46.

————. "Constructs, Experience, and Argument." *Quarterly Journal of Speech* 71 (May 1985): 151–63.

Brown, William E. "Sir Edward Grey's Rhetoric." *Southern Speech Communication Journal* 34 (Summer 1969): 276–87.

Brownlow, Paul C. "Winston Churchill and Fraternal Association: The History of a Phrase." *Central States Speech Journal* 21 (Winter 1970): 242–47.

Bryant, Donald C. "Of Style." *Western Journal of Speech Communication* 21 (Spring 1957): 103–10.

Burch, W. R., Jr. "Nature and Society—Seeking the Ghost in the Sociological Machine." *Communication Monographs* 32 (Winter 1984): 9–19.

Carleton, Walter M. "On Rhetorical Knowing." *Quarterly Journal of Speech* 71 (May 1985): 227–36.

———. "What Is Rhetorical Knowledge: A Response to Farrell—and More." *Quarterly Journal of Speech* 64 (October 1978): 313–28.

Cherwitz, Richard A., and James W. Hikins. "John Stuart Mills' *On Liberty:* Implications for the Epistemology of the New Rhetoric." *Quarterly Journal of Speech* 65 (February 1979): 12–24.

———. "Rhetoric as a 'Way of Knowledge.'" *Southern Speech Communication Journal* 42 (Spring 1977): 207–19.

Cheseboro, J. W. "The Symbolic Construction of Social Realities: A Case Study in the Rhetorical Criticism of Paradox." *Communication Monographs* 32 (Spring 1984): 164–71.

Clark, Thomas D. "Rhetoric, Reality, and Rationalization: A Study of the Masking Function of Rhetoric in the London Theosophical Movement." *Communication Quarterly* 26 (Fall 1978): 24–30.

Clarke, Peter. "Peers versus People." *History Today* 31 (November 1981): 26–29.

Condit, Celest Michelle. "The Function of Epideictic: The Boston Massacre Orations as Exemplar." *Communication Quarterly* 33 (Fall 1985): 284–98.

Corts, Paul R. "I. A. Richards on Rhetoric and Criticism." *Southern Speech Communication Journal* 36 (Winter 1970): 115–19.

Crawford, Paul. "John Redmond: Ireland's Voice of Moderation." *Central States Speech Journal* 19 (Summer 1968): 113–19.

Durham, Weldon B. "The Elements of Thomas DeQuincey's Rhetoric." *Speech Monographs* 37 (November 1970): 240–48.

Farrell, Thomas B. "Knowledge, Consensus, and Rhetorical Theory." *Quarterly Journal of Speech* 62 (February 1976): 1–14.

Feezel, Jerry D. "A Qualified Certainty: Verbal Probability in Arguments." *Speech Monographs* 41 (November 1974): 348–56.

Fernandez, Thomas L. "Sir Robert Peel: Nineteenth Century Parliamentary Orator." *Quarterly Journal of Speech* 53 (October 1966): 34–43.

Fisher, B. Aubrey. "I. A. Richard's Context of Language: An Overlooked Contribution to Rhetoric-Communication Theory." *Western Journal of Speech Communication* 35 (Spring 1971): 104–11.

Fisher, Walter R. "Gladstone's Speech at Newcastle-on-Tyne." *Speech Monographs* 26 (November 1959): 255–62.

———. "The Importance of Style in Systems of Rhetoric." *Southern Speech Communication Journal* 27 (Spring 1962): 173–82.

———. "Narration as a Human Communication Paradigm: The Case of Public Moral Argument." *Communication Monographs* 51 (March 1984): 1–22.

———. "Toward a Rhetoric of Good Reasons." *Quarterly Journal of Speech* 64 (December 1978): 376–84.

Gilbert, R. A. "John Bright's Contribution to the Anti-Corn Law League." *Western Journal of Speech Communication* 34 (Winter 1970): 16–20.

Giles, Edward, and Richard Y. Bourhis. "Voices and Racial Characterization in Britain." *Speech Monographs* 43 (June 1976): 108–14.

Gilley, Sheridan, and Ann Loades. "Thomas Henry Huxley: The War Between Science and Religion." *Journal of Religion* 61 (July 1981): 285–308.

Given, Stanford P. "Slavery and English Polarity: The Persuasive Campaign of John Bright against English Recognition of the Confederate States of America." *Southern Speech Communication Journal* 49 (Summer 1984): 406–19.

Goulding, Daniel J. "Macaulay as a Critic of Parliamentary Speaking." *Central States Speech Journal* 18 (November 1967): 299–307.

———. "The Role of Debate in Parliament: A Nineteenth-Century View." *Western Journal of Speech Communication* 33 (Summer 1969): 192–98.

Gravlee, G. Jack. "Reporting Proceedings and Debates in the British Commons." *Central Speech Journal* 32 (Summer 1981): 85–99.

Gronbeck, Bruce R. "John Morley and the Irish Question: Chart-Prayer-Dream." *Communication Monographs* 40 (November 1973): 287–95.

Hart, Roderick P. "The Rhetoric of the True Believer." *Speech Monographs* 38 (November 1971): 249–61.

Hesseltine, William B. "Speech and History." *Central States Speech Journal* 12 (Spring 1961): 76–81.

Hill, L. Brooks. "David Lloyd George as Minister of Munitions: A Study of His Speaking Tour of Industrial Centers." *Southern Speech Communication Journal* 36 (Summer 1971): 312–23.

Hillbruner, Anthony. "A Stop on Attlee's Farewell Tour." *Western Journal of Speech Communication* 25 (Summer 1961): 184–86.

Howard, Michael. "Empire, Race and War in Pre-1914 Britain." *History Today* 31 (December 1981): 4–11.

Howe, Roger J. "The Rhetoric of the Death of God Theology." *Southern Speech Communication Journal* 37 (Winter 1917): 150–62.

Hunt, James D. "Suffragettes and Satyagraha: Gandhi and the British Women's Suffrage Movement." 9, no. 1 *Indo-British Review* (1981).

Hyde, Michael, and Craig Smith. "Hermeneutics and Rhetoric: A Seen but Unobserved Relationship." *Quarterly Journal of Speech* 65 (December 1979): 347–63.

Hymes, Dell H. "The Functions of Speech: An Evolutionary Approach." In *Anthropology and Education,* edited by Frederick C. Gruber, 55–83. Philadelphia: University of Pennsylvania Press, 1961.

Jensen, J. Vernon. "Attempts to Televize Parliament." *Journal of Broadcasting* 16 (Fall 1972): 461–73.

———. "Clement R. Attlee and Twentieth-Century Parliamentary Speaking." *Parliamentary Affairs* 23 (Summer 1970): 277–85.

————. "The Rhetorical Strategies of Thomas Henry Huxley and Robert Green Ingersoll: Agnostics and Roadblock Removers." *Speech Monographs* 32 (March 1965): 59–68.

————. "Thomas Henry Huxley's 'Baptism into Oratory.'" *Notes and Records of the Royal Society of London* 30 (January 1976): 181–207.

Jensen, Keith I. Y. "I. A. Richards and His Models." *Southern Speech Communication Journal* 37 (Spring 1972): 304–14.

Kaplan-Tuckel, Barbara. "Disraeli on Jewish Disabilities: Another Look." *Central States Speech Journal* 30 (Summer 1979): 156–63.

King, Andrew A. "Thomas DeQuincey on Rhetoric and National Character." *Central States Speech Journal* 25 (Summer 1974): 128–34.

King, Andrew A., and Floyd D. Anderson. "William Hazlitt and the Decline of British Political Speaking." *Central States Speech Journal* 32 (Spring 1981): 54–59.

Kline, John A. "Dogmatism of the Speaker and Selection of Evidence." *Speech Monographs* 28 (November 1971): 354–56.

Knutson, Thomas J., and William E. Holdridge. "Orientation Behavior, Leadership and Consensus: A Possible Functional Relationship." *Speech Monographs* 62 (June 1975): 107–14.

Lomas, Charles W. "Churchill's Concept of His Audience." *Western Journal of Speech Communication* 22 (Spring 1958): 75–81.

————. "The Rhetoric of Demaguogery." *Western Journal of Speech Communication* 25 (Summer 1961): 160–68.

————. "Television in British Political Debate." *Central States Speech Journal* 17 (May 1962): 97–105.

Lyne, John. "Rhetoric of Inquiry." *Quarterly Journal of Speech* 71 (February 1985): 65–73.

McBath, James H. "Parliamentary Reporting in the Nineteenth Century." *Communication Monographs* 37 (March 1970): 12–20.

McCleary H. N. "Audience Effects of Apologia." *Communication Monographs* 32 (Winter 1983): 25–35.

McGee, Michael C. "The Fall of Wellington: A Case Study of the Relationship between Theory, Practice, and Rhetoric in History." *Quarterly Journal of Speech* 63 (February 1977): 28–42.

McGlon, Charles A. "Preparing Men to Speak for God—Foreword to a Study in Educational Research." *Southern Speech Communication Journal* 19 (May 1954): 261–76.

McLeod, Alan Lindsey. "Commonwealth Public Address and the Voice of Dissent." *Communication Quarterly* 19 (Fall 1971): 59–64.

Miller, Melvin H. "Charles Dickens and His Audience." *Central States Speech Journal* 13 (Autumn 1962): 283–88.

Minnick, Wayne C. "The Froude-Burke Controversy." *Speech Monographs* 18 (March 1951): 31–36.

————. "Parnell in America." *Speech Monographs* 20 (March 1953): 39–48.

————. "Thomas Henry Huxley's American Lectures on Evolution." *Southern Speech Communication Journal* 17 (May 1952): 225–33.

Moore, Dwain E. "Morley's Concept of the Nature and Function of Rhetoric." *Western Journal of Speech Communication* 32 (Fall 1968): 252–65.

Morgan, Kenneth C. "The Rise of Socialism." *History Today* 31 (November 1981): 30–34.

Newman, H. N. "The Sounds of Silence in Communicative Encounters." *Communication Monographs* 31 (Spring 1982): 142–49.

Nibley, Hugh. "Victoriosa Loquitas: The Rise of Rhetoric and the Decline of Everything Else." *Western Journal of Speech Communication* 20 (Spring 1956): 57–82.

Oliver, Robert T. "Asian Public Address and Comparative Public Address." *Speech Teacher* 23 (March 1971): 101–8.

————. "Culture and Communication." *Vital Speeches of the Day* 29 (September 1963): 721–24.

————. "Speech and the Community." *Vital Speeches of the Day* 29 (May 1963): 459–62.

Peterson, Owen M. "A London Guide for the Student of British Public Address." *Communication Education* 18 (September 1969): 230–33.

Phelps, Lynn A., and Edwin Cohen. "The Wilberforce-Huxley Debate." *Western Journal of Speech Communication* 37 (Winter 1973): 56–64.

Pitt, Carl Allen. "Contemporary Speaking in the House of Commons." *Central States Speech Journal* 15 (May 1964): 117–25.

Post, Robert M. "Charles Stewart Parnell before Congress." *Quarterly Journal of Speech* 51 (December 1956): 419–25.

Powell, Larry. "Satirical Persuasion and Topic Salience." *Southern Speech Communication Journal* 42 (Winter 1977): 151–62.

Quimby, Rollin W. "The Changing Image of the Ministry and Its Influence on Sermons." *Southern Speech Communication Journal* 33 (Summer 1970): 303–14.

Reid, Christopher. "Brougham and the Trial of Queen Caroline." *Southern Speech Communication Journal* 26 (Spring 1961); 190–200.

Reid, Loren. "Gladstone's Essay on Public Speaking." *Quarterly Journal of Speech* 39 (October 1953): 265–72.

————. "John Bright: Spokesman for America." *Western Journal of Speech Communication* 38 (Fall 1974): 233–43.

————. "John Bright: The Orator as Teacher." *Southern Speech Communication Journal* 41 (Fall 1975): 45–58.

Schenck-Hamlin, William J., Richard L. Wiseman, and G. N. Georgacarakos, "A Model of Properties of Compliance-Gaining Strategies." *Communication Quarterly* 30 (Spring 1982): 92–100.

Schmidt, Patricia L. "The Role of Moral Idealism in Social Change: Lord Ashley and the Ten Hours Factory Act." *Quarterly Journal of Speech* 63 (February 1977): 14–27.

Scott, Eugene P. "The Political Preaching Tradition in Ulster: Prelude to Paisley." *Western Journal of Speech Communication* 40 (Fall 1976): 249–59.

Scrag, Calvin O. "Rhetoric Resituated at the End of Philosophy." *Quarterly Journal of Speech* 71 (May 1985): 164–74.

Simons, H. W. "Genres, Rules, and Collective Rhetorics: Requirements-Problems-Strategies Approach." *Communication Monographs* 31 (Summer 1982): 181–89.

Skorkowsky, George R. "British University Debating." *Quarterly Journal of Speech* 57 (October 1971): 335–43.

Smith, Charles D. "Debate in the House of Commons." *Today's Speech* 5 (April 1957): 21–23.

Smith, Robert W. "David Lloyd George's Limehouse Address." *Central States Speech Journal* 18 (August 1967): 169–76.

Strother, David B. "John Bright: The Devil's Advocate." *Southern Speech Communication Journal* 24 (Summer 1959): 201–9.

Talley, Paul M. "DeQuincey on Persuasion, Invention and Style." *Central States Speech Journal* 16 (November 1965): 243–54.

Vincent, John. "Was Disraeli a Failure?" *History Today* 31 (October 1981): 5–8.

Wallace, Karl R. "Rhetoric and Politics." *Southern Speech Communication Journal* 20 (Spring 1955): 195–203.

Wander, Philip, and Steven Jenkins. "Rhetoric, Society, and the Critical Response." *Quarterly Journal of Speech* 58 (December 1972): 441–50.

Watkins, Lloyd I. "Lord Brougham's Comments on the Education of an Orator." *Western Journal of Speech Communication* 29 (Spring 1965): 102–7.

Weidhorn, Manfred. "Churchill as an Orator: Wish and Fulfillment." *Southern Speech Communication Journal* 40 (Spring 1975): 217–27.

Williams, Donald E. "Speech Criticism on the British Campus." *Southern Speech Communication Journal* 31 (Winter 1963): 83–94.

Woodward, Gary C. "Prime Ministers and Presidents: A Survey of the Differing Rhetorical Possibilities of High Office." *Communication Monographs* 27 (Summer 1979): 41–49.

Zacharias, John C. "Emmeline Pankhurst: An English Suffragette Influences America." *Communication Monographs* 38 (August 1971): 198–206.

Zelinsky, Steven. "William Gladstone's Speech at West Calder: A Rhetorical Analysis: *Speech Association of Minnesota Journal* 8 (1981): 26–29.

INDEX

In such indexes . . . there is seen
the baby figure of the giant mass.

—William Shakespeare
Troilus and Cressida, 1.3